Status Enhancement and Fertility

*Reproductive Responses to Social Mobility
and Educational Opportunity*

This is a volume in

STUDIES IN POPULATION

Under the Editorship of: H. H. WINSBOROUGH

Department of Sociology
University of Wisconsin
Madison, Wisconsin

A complete list of titles in this series is available from the publisher on request.

STATUS ENHANCEMENT AND FERTILITY

Reproductive Responses to Social Mobility and Educational Opportunity

John D. Kasarda

DEPARTMENT OF SOCIOLOGY
THE UNIVERSITY OF NORTH CAROLINA AT CHAPEL HILL
CHAPEL HILL, NORTH CAROLINA

John O. G. Billy

BATTELLE HUMAN AFFAIRS RESEARCH CENTER
SEATTLE, WASHINGTON

Kirsten West

DEPARTMENT OF SOCIOLOGY
UNIVERSITY OF MARYLAND, BALTIMORE COUNTY
CATONSVILLE, MARYLAND

 1986

ACADEMIC PRESS, INC.
Harcourt Brace Jovanovich, Publishers
Orlando   San Diego   New York   Austin
Boston   London   Sydney   Tokyo   Toronto

ACADEMIC PRESS, INC.
Orlando, Florida 32887

United Kingdom Edition published by
ACADEMIC PRESS INC. (LONDON) LTD.
24–28 Oval Road, London NW1 7DX

Library of Congress Cataloging in Publication Data

Kasarda, John D.
    Status enhancement and fertility.

    (Studies in population)
    Bibliography: p.
    Includes index.
    1. Birth control—Cross-cultural studies.
2. Family size—Cross-cultural studies.   3. Fertility,
Human—Cross-cultural studies.   4. Social status—Cross-
cultural studies.   5. Social mobility—Cross-cultural
studies.   I. Billy, John O. G.   II. West, Kirsten B.
III. Title.   IV. Series.
HQ766.K345   1986   304.6'32   86-3428
ISBN 0—12—400310—9 (alk. paper)

PRINTED IN THE UNITED STATES OF AMERICA

86 87 88 89   9 8 7 6 5 4 3 2 1

To Our Families

Contents

Chapter 10   Age at Marriage and First Birth

Chapter 11   Family Planning Knowledge and Practice

Chapter 12   General Conclusions and Policy Issues

Preface

Spurred by intractably high birth rates in many developing nations and concurrently below-replacement birth rates in some developed nations, interest in the socioeconomic determinants of fertility continues to grow. Demographic researchers, representing a range of disciplines, have applied various models seeking to explain these different patterns. Because of the diversity of models, methods, and units of analysis used, there have been increasingly frequent calls for synthesizing conceptual frameworks around which research on the determinants of fertility may be organized. This book answers that call.

We begin with the working assumption that the status of women is a critical factor shaping reproductive behavior in developing and in developed countries. Elaborating underlying causal dynamics, we specify how both traditional and more modern status attainment processes affect fertility. The former focuses on female status and social mobility as determined by birth and marriage; that is, the status of women as derived from their fathers and, after marriage, from their husbands. The latter approach examines the implications for fertility of status attained by women more independently of the men in their lives. In this agenda, emphasis is given to the potent role education plays in developing modern sex-role orientations among women and in providing them with the means to pursue rewarding alternatives to bearing large families. We will show how women's education, enlightenment, social options, and knowledge to control their reproductive destinies are intricately related.

Whereas a basic purpose is to provide a theoretical framework in which research findings on the socioeconomic determinants of fertility may be integrated, the book is structured so that it may be used as an upper division or graduate level text in population courses. Following an introductory chapter on the substantive scope of the book, Chapters 2 through 4 provide a detailed review, appraisal, and synthesis of the complex research literature on social mobility and fertility. In these chapters, we chronicle the evolution of social mobility–fertility research, discussing theoretical perspectives underlying the research, causal operators proposed to interpret observed associations, and analytical methods used. For those interested in extending empirical knowledge of the effects of social mobility on fertility, Chapter 5 examines various statistical methodologies and suggests some fruitful avenues future research might pursue.

A fundamental conclusion drawn from our assessment of social mobility–fertility research is that a shift is required from a predominantly male-dependent status orientation to a more female-oriented focus. Thus, the second half of the book examines mechanisms through which women achieve status by their own initiatives and how this achievement is reflected in reproductive behavior. Chapter 6 details the instrumental role education plays in enhancing the status of women and discusses the main intervening variables that link education to reproductive behavior. The chapters that follow elaborate the causal processes through which education affects these key intervening variables and how, in turn, each intervening variable influences fertility. Chapter 7 examines female labor force participation; Chapter 8, the value of children; Chapter 9, infant and child mortality; Chapter 10, age at marriage and first birth; and Chapter 11, family planning knowledge and practice. In each chapter we draw on cross-national data from the World Fertility Survey and other sources to document basic associations. We go beyond describing the relationships, however, to explicate the causal operators that we believe account for the associations reported. Chapter 12 concludes the volume by discussing policy issues derived from models and assessments presented in the preceding chapters.

Our work incorporated in this book was initiated through a grant to the senior author by the United States Agency for International Development Research Program on female status and fertility (AID/PHA 932-0606). Additional support was provided by the Carolina Population Center. For valuable comments on draft chapters of the manuscripts, we would like to thank Barbara Entwisle, William R. Grady, David T. Lewis, David McFarland, Ronald Rindfuss, Rachel Rosenfeld, Amy Tsui, and J. Richard Udry. Lynn Igoe, manuscript editor at the Carolina Population Center, University of North Carolina at Chapel Hill, was especially helpful in sharpening our prose and aiding in preparation of references, figures, and tables. Despite all the fine assistance we received, errors in theoretical specification, inference, and fact possibly remain, for which the authors accept full responsibility.

Chapter 1 | Introduction

Social scientists have become increasingly cognizant that investigators of fertility determinants contribute substantially more to basic and policy research if guided by clearly formulated theories. Lacking such guidance, empirical analyses of social and economic factors influencing fertility have often resulted in a long series of disconnected studies and, therefore, noncumulative research. Immense fiscal and human efforts have been expended with less than commensurate knowledge contributed to our understanding of the underlying forces shaping reproductive behavior.

In this book, top priority is assigned to theoretical specification of the causal operators that implement empirical associations between social and economic variables and reproductive behavior. We do this on the premise that theoretical development will not only provide a foundation for more fruitful empirical research but also aid other investigators in the often difficult task of interpreting observed statistical associations. From a population policy standpoint, specification and explication of the causal operators linking social and economic variables to fertility can provide valuable insights to program alternatives for those nations desiring to slow their population growth.

We present theories and specify models of reproductive behavior that, for the most part, will be as appropriate to nations with low fertility rates as to those exhibiting relatively high fertility. However, our recognition of cultural differences across nations and concern with population policy for those countries experiencing rapid population growth will skew attention to the latter context. Here, we believe reduced fertility levels are most likely to be obtained under the general rubric of enhancing women's status. We therefore organize the contents of the book around two general processes increasingly treated as synonymous with status enhancement: social mobility and educational attainment. Specification of variables linking these two factors to fertility leads us to branch out and

1

address virtually the full range of social and economic factors hypothesized to play causal roles in reproductive behavior.

The first half of the book assesses what we know about the relationship between social mobility and fertility and attempts to advance this knowledge through theoretical synthesis. We begin with an extensive review of what we quickly discovered is largely a hodge-podge of poorly formulated research and theories addressing the social mobility–fertility association. Not only have previous researchers approached the subject from divergent perspectives, but often it is difficult to ascertain exactly what they have tested and sometimes it is not even possible to tell whether a particular study supports or refutes the existence of a relationship.

The basic problem has been the paucity of cohesive theories guiding the research. Thus, specific hypotheses about the nature of the relationship, along with conceptualizations and operationalizations of indicators in the social mobility–fertility relationship, vary substantially from study to study without reference to the theoretical reasons for such variability. For example, some researchers emphasize the subjective dimension of mobility—aspirations and motivations to be socially mobile. Others examine the effect of an objective dimension of social mobility, such as intragenerational, intergenerational, or nuptial mobility. Too often the multidimensionality of the concept goes unrecognized, and investigators treat their particular measurement as evidence of the existence or nonexistence of an association between social mobility and fertility in general. Similarly, reproductive behavior is variously represented as completed family size, children ever born, birth spacing, early and later childbearing, and intended and unintended births.

Further contributing to the complexity and confusion, investigators cannot agree on the direction of causality; some examine the effect of mobility on fertility while others reverse the causal order. Nor can researchers agree on the expected nature of the relationship. At least four theoretical perspectives to account for an effect of mobility on reproductive behavior can be identified in the literature. There is even a debate as to whether a relationship should be expected.

Methods of analysis also diverge without contributing further insight. Of particular importance is what is to be accepted as an indication of a social mobility–fertility relationship. What constitutes a "true" mobility effect? Researchers differ according to whether or not they distinguish between the effect of the *process* of mobility and the *additive* effects of the social origin and destination variables used to define it.

These different approaches to measuring the concepts of mobility and fertility, theoretical development, and methodology often go undetected by investigators who then proceed to compare their findings with those of previous works. As a result, researchers are prone to state that the findings to date are inconclusive.

Our examination of the mobility–fertility relationship is designed to redress some of the deficiencies of past research. As might be suspected, one reason why investigators have approached the problem from so many different perspectives is that they have not been totally familiar with the research preceding their own. Lack of familiarity with previous studies, in turn, contributes to the probability of repeating errors in theory and methodology, and impedes the cumulation of knowledge about the relationship. This situation is the primary motive for our beginning with a thorough literature review that systematically details previous research and theory on the social mobility–fertility association. Our review illustrates what has been done in social mobility–fertility study and why it is often regarded as a quagmire of social research.

Following our literature review, we synthesize previous research findings and theory to develop a coherent body from which to derive testable propositions. We try to provide an accurate account of why one would expect a relationship between social mobility and reproductive behavior.

In a chapter devoted to the methodology needed to analyze the social mobility–fertility relationship, we discuss the shortcomings of previous analytical methods and describe a method that we feel appropriately assesses whether social mobility affects fertility. This methodology extends and refines the Blau and Duncan (1967) approach, but, unlike it, permits the *systematic* search for a mobility model that adequately fits the data. It also allows more of a causal-modeling approach to the study of social mobility and fertility. We illustrate the use of this technique with sample survey data. We conclude our methodology chapter with a discussion of other recently proposed techniques for analyzing the relationship.

A fundamental problem we find repeatedly emerging in analytical approaches to the social mobility–fertility question is the male-oriented focus on the research. Conceptualization and measurement of social mobility and its relationship to reproductive behavior remains largely geared to married women and their status measured by that of their fathers and husbands.

In many nations, the structure under which mobility and childbearing takes place has changed markedly during recent decades. Increasingly, women are attaining social status independently of their fathers or husbands, with important consequences for reproductive behavior (Bulatao and Lee, 1983; Cain, 1982; Caldwell, 1982; Dyson and Moore, 1983; Mason, 1984; Safilios-Rothschild, 1982).

Yet, despite increased attention to women's status attainment and its role in reproductive behavior, there is little consensus about operational definitions. Like social mobility, conceptualization of female status is multidimensional and measurement diverse, referring to a broad range of social standings, rather than *the* status of women (Chaudhury, 1982; Curtin, 1982; Mason, 1984; Niphuis-Nell, 1978; Oppong, 1983; Whyte, 1978). For example, women's status has been variously conceptualized and measured in terms of their political, economic, and social resource positions in society. In the political sphere, indicators include political participation and women's legal rights. Involvement in income-generating activities, control over production resources, and economic self-sufficiency are used to measure economic position. Social recognition, rights, duties, and expectations ascribed to women are used to indicate social position (Curtin, 1982).

Of course, not all researchers agree with such conceptualizations of status. When female status is construed broadly in terms of resource positions, the distinction between stratification by gender and by class is often obscured (Mason, 1984). A woman may lack resources because of gender, class, or both. Moreover, class effects may interact with gender effects in determining a woman's net level of resources.

Following this rationale, several researchers have focused on differential access by women to prestige and power and their control of material resources as indicators of women's overall status (Dixon, 1975b; Mason, 1984). Freedom to obtain knowledge, freedom from control of men, and, more generally, female autonomy have also been used as indicators of women's status (Dyson and Moore, 1983). In the words of one researcher, "autonomy is to the individual what independence is to the nation" (Niphuis-Nell, 1978, p. 16). Autonomy is self-government. Personal autonomy has been equated with status and status with power (Curtin, 1982). The question for our purpose is, how is such power derived and expressed in reproductive choices?

As Safilios-Rothschild (1982) pointed out, women can derive power from men *and* independently of men, the relative proportions predicated on cultural circumstances. The first type of power does allow women to have some say in domestic matters. Even so, their power is limited to control over others, most likely, younger women and children. Such women have scant control over their own lives. The second type of power, derived more on the basis of her own achievements rather than derived from her husband's or father's, results in far greater autonomy for women.

How power is derived has critical implications for reproductive behavior. In cultural settings where power comes exclusively or primarily from men, a woman might well maximize her power (and therefore status) by having a large family. Reproductive behavior would be an important means to such power. Where power is derived, in large part, independently of men, a woman's status would stem from a role behavior that might compete with bearing and rearing a large family.

Our interest in how women may achieve status and fulfillment through their own pursuits and its consequences for reproductive behavior orients the second part of the book to this important issue. In this section, special emphasis is given to education as the *sine qua non* for female status enhancement. We describe how education alters a woman's world view and increases her knowledge and competencies in virtually all sectors of life; how it makes her aware of alternatives to the roles of wife and mother, and, most importantly, how education enables a woman to pursue such alternatives to improve her standing within her household and community and gain greater control over her social and reproductive destinies.

Our treatment of female status enhancement and fertility will be more in the tradition of demographic research literature than that of recent gender inequality studies, which focus on such issues as sex segregation within occupational structures (Mason, 1984; Stycos, 1982). Rather than comparing the situation of women with that of men, we compare women with each other in terms of such factors as labor force participation and age at first birth. We bring together data and synthesize theories to gain a better understanding of how education serves as an independent status enhancement mechanism for women by influencing these factors and, ultimately, how this influence affects fertility.[1]

Female education is selected for special emphasis not only because of its potent role in enhancing so many aspects of the status of women but also because it has come to be viewed as the prime institutional variable amenable to policy manipulation in developing nations that can help lower fertility rates. Indeed, there appears to be substantial faith in the mass education of young women as the one sure hope for slowing rapid population growth (Caldwell, 1980; World Bank, 1984). This faith has been affirmed in the past two decades by a number of empirical studies that have shown education to exhibit a stronger and more consistent negative relationship to fertility than any other single variable [see Cochrane (1979) and Stout (1984) for literature reviews]. As one early, still useful illustration, Bogue (1969), analyzing the relative impact of nine modernization indexes on fertility, found that education alone accounted for 56% of the variance in the movement of nations from high to low fertility, whereas all other indexes of modernization combined accounted for only an additional 16% of the variance. On the basis of this analysis he concluded,

> Rising education levels, increased school attendance, and elimination of early marriage are much more powerful in promoting fertility reduction than simple urbanization and rising levels of living. A major driving force behind fertility reduction appears to be education. . . . If this is true, *it should be comparatively easy to discover what aspect of rising literacy and educational attainment is most intimately related to lower fertility and then to "mass produce" it on a large scale to hasten fertility decline* in advance of other aspects of education attainment (pp. 676–677, emphasis added).

Most researchers and population planners would likely agree that the underlined portion of Bogue's conclusion is a key to programs designed to reduce

---

[1]As the body of empirical data generated from studies of gender inequality grows, this knowledge must be incorporated into traditional demographic study frameworks as well, so that we may gain a more complete understanding of fertility determinants.

fertility in developing nations. However, whether there are only one or a few major intervening variables through which female education operates in affecting fertility—and which governments can "mass produce"—is an important policy question in need of an answer. Unfortunately, the research literature to date helps us little. Despite an abundance of studies documenting negative zero-order and partial correlations between education and fertility, none has specified adequately the causal operators linking greater female education to lower fertility (either at individual or aggregate levels) and submitted these operators to systematic empirical tests. What we have, instead, is a plethora of theoretically undeveloped studies that typically lack specification of the explicit processes or mechanisms through which female education influences fertility.

Female education, of course, affects or interacts with a wide variety of factors such as labor force participation, age at marriage, husband–wife communication, breast-feeding practices, religiosity, perceived value of children, infant mortality, contraceptive knowledge and practice, and the like, each of which, in turn, has been proposed to bear directly on fertility. Thus, discovering which aspects of increased female education account for reduced fertility requires considerable refinement in our conceptualization of the education–fertility relationship *and* identification of the range of causal variables and operators that mediate female education's effects.

To pursue this agenda, the second part of the book begins with an overview of basic propositions in the research literature on formal education, status enhancement, and fertility. Separate chapters elaborate the roles of key intervening factors in the female education–fertility causal chain (labor force participation, the value of children, infant and child mortality, age at marriage or first birth, and family planning knowledge and practice). These chapters present models specifying the causal operators proposed to explain reported empirical associations between female education and each intervening variable and, in turn, between the variable under study and reproductive behavior.

The reason for our concentrating on theoretical development of causal processes is straightforward. Our examination of the extensive literature on socioeconomic determinants of fertility made it clear that statistical methodologies are powerful and measurement is improving. Yet theory remains relatively undeveloped, especially systematically integrated theory. Where theories and models are undeveloped, empirical associations are often reported unambiguously without appreciation of the multifaceted and complex social processes that bring about observed associations. Insights to the underlying factors shaping reproductive behavior are limited and the empirical knowledge generated is rarely cumulative.

Thus, while each section of the book overviews empirical associations reported to date apropos status enhancement and fertility, our main thrust throughout is to specify and elaborate causal processes proposed to explain observed associations. We believe such specification and elaboration is necessary if we are to gain better understanding of the socioeconomic determinants of fertility and why various decisions affecting reproductive behavior are made. In so doing, we raise a number of conceptual and measurement issues that investigators must resolve if their research is to contribute more effectively to population policies, as well as to analytical progress.

Chapter 2 | The Evolution of Theory and Research on Social Mobility and Fertility

Research has examined the relationship between socioeconomic status and fertility from two points of view. One body has taken a static approach, analyzing fertility differentials according to an individual's or family's status at a given time. The effect of social mobility on fertility, or vice versa, goes undetected using this approach. A second approach has been dynamic, recognizing that persons may have been immobile, upwardly mobile, or downwardly mobile at any given time. Such research has focused on the relationship between *changing* statuses and reproductive behavior. This approach posits that observed fertility differentials by socioeconomic status may be totally or in large part because of the process of social mobility. Thus, more than three decades ago, Westoff (1953, p. 31) commented,

> It is just as plausible to hypothesize that these social–psychological variables in addition to fertility planning and planned fertility are as much dependent upon the presence or absence and type of social mobility as they are on the more static phenomenon of a given occupation, financial status, or educational level.

Blau and Duncan (1967, pp. 367–368) go farther to distinguish between a *strong form* and a *weak form* of the social mobility hypothesis. The strong form contends that social mobility totally explains differential fertility by socioeconomic status:

> Classes with low average fertility are those into which individuals or couples with low fertility have moved, whereas classes with high average fertility are those whose ranks have been thinned of low-fertility couples or individuals. Thus, if it were possible to examine only those persons or marriages not undergoing mobility, no class differences in average number of births should appear (Blau and Duncan, 1967, p. 367).

In contrast, the weak form of the hypothesis merely suggests that social mobility is related to reproductive behavior and leaves open the question of whether there

8

are fertility differentials by socioeconomic status other than those attributable to mobility.

Few are willing to support the strong form of the social mobility–fertility hypothesis. However, the hypothesis in its weak form has intrigued scholars for decades. In this and the following chapter we examine what we know about the relationship between social mobility and fertility. For organizational purposes, we chronologically divide the research literature into (1) early studies (1890 to the 1940s); (2) intermediate studies (1940s to the late 1960s); and (3) more recent studies (late 1960s to 1984). The epistemological rationale for these particular chronological breakdowns will become evident as we develop each part.

1 Early Studies (1890–1940s)

Interest in the mobility–fertility relationship began in 1890 when Arsene Dumont observed France's declining population during the late nineteenth century (Dumont, 1890). Dumont proposed that the development of numbers in a nation is in inverse ratio to the development of the individual[1] (Dumont, 1901, p. 33). According to his hypothesis, a person has a "natural" desire to climb the social ladder and in the process becomes less and less likely to have children. He is drawn out of his natural milieu which results in loss of interest in the family and the welfare of the race with corresponding adverse effects on fertility (Thompson and Lewis, 1965, pp. 46–47).

Even in this earliest formulation of the social mobility–fertility relationship a problem comes to light. In proposing his theory of *social capillarity,* Dumont says that just as a column of liquid has to be thin in order to rise under the force of gravity, so a family must be small in order to rise on the social ladder (Dumont, 1890, as cited in Westoff, 1953, p. 30). Here, Dumont sees fertility affecting mobility adversely and the question of direction of causality arises.

Early thoughts on the mobility–fertility relationship focus on the consequences of fertility (or infertility) for social mobility and emphasize the biological or eugenic aspects of the relationship. This view is commonly called "the social promotion of the relatively infertile." Galton (1900) argues that the greater upward mobility of the infertile caused the extinction of 30 British peerages, and Wagner-Manslau (1932) contends the same about members of the German

---

[1] Evidence that this notion was widely accepted during the first third of the twentieth century appears in the statement of the New South Wales Royal Commission (1904) that "the effect of the race towards its increase in numbers is in inverse ratio to the effort of the individual toward his personal development" and von Ungern-Sternberg's (1931) conclusion that the historical decline of fertility in Europe was attributable to the "striving spirit of capitalism," the determination of all social classes to improve their position.

nobility (Scott, 1958, p. 251). Fisher (1930) maintains that ancient civilizations declined because the ruling class failed to reproduce because of the promotion of people to it whose mobility was caused by infertility. He argues that infertility in all classes enhances social advancement and that selection of the naturally infertile is the major cause of an inverse relationship between social class and fertility. Fisher quotes Huntington and Whitney's (1927) figures from *Who's Who in America* and shows that *for a given socioeconomic category,* family size varies directly with education. Fisher assumed that those with less education had been the most mobile and the least fertile (Scott, 1958, pp. 251–252).

Later scholars criticised Fisher's work. Berent (1952, p. 252) found Fisher's study fraught with errors in measurement and methodology. Reanalyzing Fisher's data, Berent finds no clear pattern between educational experience and average family size. Berent's own data show an *inverse* relationship between education and family size within each occupational category. In a study of intergenerational occupational mobility, Berent found the upwardly mobile had fewer children than those in their class of origin but *more* than those in their class of destination—contradicting the infertility selection theory. Tien (1965a, pp. 77–79), too, criticizes Fisher because he failed to distinguish between *fecundity* and *fertility*.[2] In short, the thesis of the social promotion of the relatively infertile neither gained acceptance nor won empirical confirmation.

2 Intermediate Studies (1940s–1960s)

By 1940, emphasis on the biological and eugenic aspects of the mobility–fertility relationship had waned in favor of the effects of social mobility on fertility. Studies dating from the 1940s to the late 1960s illustrate this change of emphasis.

The central theme of the mid-century studies is that fertility is inversely related to social class, and childbearing and social mobility are inimical to one another. Westoff (1953, p. 30) maintains that the disposition to be mobile may lead to voluntary limitations of childbearing owing to a high degree of rationality on the part of mobile couples, "a pervasive success-orientation and all that is implied by it." A quotation from a United Nations publication succinctly expresses this view:

> The desire to improve one's position in the social scale has been stressed as an important motive for family limitation. . . . The effect of social mobility on fertility appears to be attributed in general to the fact that rearing children absorbs money, time, and effort which could otherwise be used to rise the social scale (United Nations, 1953, p. 79).

---

[2]For additional discussion of Fisher's thesis and critique of his model, see Vining (1982).

Assuming that having children and being socially mobile are incompatible, the following seemingly straightforward hypothesis guided most of the intermediate studies:

Social mobility is inversely related to family size within otherwise homogeneous groups.

Careful scrutiny reveals the hypothesis is ambiguous. If there is a relationship between mobility and fertility, the appropriate way to detect it is to compare the fertility of the mobile and the nonmobile. The mobile have gained status (upward mobility) or been demoted (downward mobility). The hypothesis does not specify direction and leads one to believe that both upwardly and downwardly mobile persons are predicted to have lower fertility than the nonmobile. However, most researchers were concerned only with differences in mean levels of fertility between the *upwardly* mobile and the nonmobile.

The nature of the sample limited a number of studies to examining only fertility differences between the upwardly mobile and nonmobile at destination. These empirical works focus on the mobility of members of elite groups. By definition, they could not have experienced downward mobility. Moreover, most of these are studies of intergenerational mobility, comparing father's status with the respondent's current status.

Baltzell (1953) conducted the earliest of these studies. Using 1940s data from *Who's Who in America* and the Philadelphia "Social Register," he reasoned that the 226 men listed in both books were more likely to be of high ascribed status and were therefore less mobile than the remaining 544 listed only in "Who's Who" and who presumably had achieved their status. Most of the men's wives had completed their childbearing. After calculating the average family sizes of both groups, Baltzell found those listed in both books (the nonmobile) had larger families and were less likely to have only a single child than those included only in "Who's Who" (the upwardly mobile). Baltzell attributed the inverse relationship between upward mobility and family size to the financial necessity for family limitation among the mobile and the prevalence of small family norms in the class of destination.[3]

Hollingsworth's (1957) historical study of mortality and fertility trends in British ducal families also supports an inverse relationship between fertility and upward *nuptial* mobility.[4] Using peerage records, he examined 1908 legitimate

---

[3]In another study using data from *Who's Who in America,* Kirk (1957) found that Princeton, Harvard, or Yale alumni had higher fertility than those who attended other universities. Kirk assumed that those educated in a private school or prestigious university had been less intergenerationally upwardly mobile than those educated in a public school or whose fathers could only afford to send their children to universities of lower quality.

[4]While Hollingsworth does not use the term, we define *nuptial* mobility as a comparison between wife's and husband's social origins. For example, a woman of low social status who marries a man of high status is considered upwardly mobile.

sons of British kings, queens, dukes, or duchesses born between 1330 and 1954. After dividing the sample into seven roughly equal birth cohorts and classifying the son's wives as those from peerage families, commoners, or of foreign descent, Hollingsworth found that wives from the peerage had on average more children than the others for all cohorts. Most noteworthy is that Hollingsworth found an intervening variable, age at marriage, that may operate in the mobility–fertility relationship. He discovered wives from peerage families married younger which might account for some of the differential completed family size by nuptial mobility. Hollingsworth does not, unfortunately, offer any theory as to why women's upward nuptial mobility would be expected to affect their age at marriage and consequent family size. We suggest that women of common birth found it difficult to be accepted into the ranks of the nobility and they married later than women of noble families who had less difficulty in being accepted by their male peers.[5]

While other studies during this period investigated the association between family size and upward mobility into an elite group (see, e.g., Tomasson, 1966), Tien's work stands out as research that further explicated the theoretical nature of this relationship. Tien (1961, 1965a) studied permanent full-time male faculty members at the University of Sidney and University of Melbourne in 1957 who were native born, once and currently married for 10 or more years. He argued that these couples had for all practical purposes completed childbearing. To investigate whether intergenerational mobility was significantly related to fertility under favorable and unfavorable socioeconomic conditions, Tien divided his sample into two cohorts—those wed between 1920 and 1939, and between 1940 and 1947. He measured mobility by placing the respondent's father's occupation at death or retirement into a seven-point occupational prestige scale. If the respondent's father was engaged in a professional or semiprofessional occupation, or a high official or managerial occupation, the respondent was considered nonmobile; if the father's occupation fell in any of the other five occupational categories, the respondent was considered upwardly mobile. Tien used number of children ever born as the measure of fertility.

For the 1920–1939 cohort, Tien found average family size for each mobility group was approximately 2.0; for the 1940–1947 cohort, both groups had an average family size of 2.4. Tien suggests that the lack of a relationship might be because the mobile experienced their mobility early in life, making it independent of their subsequent fertility. The mobile improved their status at the expense

---

[5]Many persons (see, e.g., Boyd, 1971; Scott, 1958) have regarded Hollingsworth as a eugenicist who subscribed to the thesis of the social promotion of the relatively infertile. We find no such evidence. Indeed, that he offered age at marriage as a mechanism by which differential fertility by mobility status obtains is a fairly sophisticated observation at this time, and one that clearly places him in the camp of those stressing the social aspects of the mobility–fertility relationship rather than those of the eugenicists.

of their parents, who provided their education, rather than at the expense of their having children. Moreover, the mobile and the nonmobile had the same formal education, eliminating whatever social distinctions there were among the university teachers.

Whereas completed family sizes of the mobile and nonmobile were the same, Tien argued that intergenerational mobility might affect another aspect of reproductive behavior: the family-building pattern. He was the first to test the hypothesis that upward mobility is associated with a longer interval between marriage and first birth. Tien's analysis reveals that, holding age at marriage constant, upward intergenerational mobility is associated, albeit weakly, with a longer interval between marriage and first birth. This relationship held for both marriage cohorts, except for those in the 1940–1947 cohort married before age 25. Tien states,

> Although the general acceptance of contraceptive practice has tremendously minimized the variability in the number of children ever born to the couples investigated, social mobility may still be regarded as a significant factor in relation to fertility behavior; that is, the regulation of reproduction at chosen intervals or postponement of the first birth. Presumably, postponement of parenthood is of a greater immediate significance as it allows the budgetry of time and financial resources to activities in keeping with the desire for occupational advancement if bachelorhood becomes unsatisfactory or marriage irresistable (Tien, 1965a, p. 155).

None of the wives of the nonmobile respondents in the 1920–1939 cohort was ever employed, but almost all of the wives of the mobile respondents were employed before and after marriage. While all of the wives of respondents in the 1940–1947 cohort were employed at the time of marriage, a greater proportion of wives of mobile respondents continued to work after marriage. Tien concluded that female labor force participation might be an important intervening variable in the relationship between mobility and timing of fertility. Couples who improved their status could do so only by making such sacrifices as the wives' working after marriage, which delayed childbearing. Nonmobile respondents did not need to make such sacrifices (perhaps because of their fathers' greater ability to provide financial assistance), and their wives did not need to delay childbearing.

Tien's sample size (66 for the early cohort, 60 for the later cohort) is far too small to permit any valid inferences. He also was apparently unaware that his research by definition was limited to a study of upward mobility into an elite group. Nevertheless, Tien's work stands out from prior research in his challenge of the thesis that having children and being socially mobile are incompatible throughout an individual's married life. By considering the timing of births within marriage, he showed that upward mobility and fertility may be incompatible during early married life but not throughout the entire duration of marriage. Tien's evidence that the upwardly mobile couples delay childbearing but eventually catch up to the family size of the nonmobile couples at destination supports this.

Two other studies of elite groups support Tien's hypothesis. Based on a national probability sample of United States Baptist ministers, Natsis (1966) found longer intervals between marriage and the birth of the first three children for mobile couples compared with nonmobile couples in two of three marital duration cohorts, except for ministers married fewer than 10 years.

Similarly, Perrucci (1967) focused on intergenerational mobility and reproductive behavior in a sample of 1029 American engineers who received their B.S. degrees between 1947 and 1961 from two large West Coast universities. Perrucci argues that if an upwardly mobile person orders his life in a way that serves to enhance his mobility, then he is likely to defer marriage longer and have fewer children and at greater intervals than a nonmobile person. Her findings indicate that those in her sample from low origins married on average 14 months later than those from high origins. The former had a longer interval between college graduation and birth of the first child and waited on average 9 months longer to have their second child. No relationship was found between intergenerational mobility and length of the second to third birth interval or between mobility and completed family size. Like Tien, Perrucci argues that mobility has a greater effect on the timing of childbearing than on completed family size.[6]

The studies reviewed thus far have not been conclusive in comparing fertility of upwardly mobile couples to nonmobile couples at destination. Baltzell (1953), Hollingsworth (1957), and Kirk (1957) found support for an inverse relationship between upward mobility and family size. However, one could seriously question these three researchers' method of distinguishing between the upwardly mobile and nonmobile. Tien (1961, 1965a) and Perrucci (1967) found no evidence of a relationship, at least for completed family size.

What of studies that examine the mobility–fertility relationship by comparing fertility of the upwardly mobile to the nonmobile at destination and also at origin? Burks (1941) conducted one of the earliest of these studies. Using data from the archives of the Genetics Record Office, Burks divided couples into three groups and compared their average family sizes. Group 1 couples had superior attainment (professional and higher business groups and/or college educated) whose parents were of superior attainment; group 2 couples had superior attainment but their parents did not (less than a business occupation and/or less than college educated); and group 3 couples had nonsuperior attainment and parents of nonsuperior attainment. Group 1 was regarded as nonmobile at desti-

---

[6]Perrucci also examined the relationship between *intragenerational* mobility and reproductive behavior. She measured career mobility by the level of technical and supervisory responsibility respondents achieved in 1962 compared to the level achieved by others who had graduated in the same year. Engineers who had attained levels lower than the median for those of their graduation year were considered low mobiles; engineers above the median were considered high mobiles. The findings parallel those in the analysis of intergenerational mobility.

nation, group 2 as upwardly mobile, and group 3 as nonmobile at origin. Burks found fertility of group 2 lower than than of group 3, but higher than that of group 1. Hence, while Burks found support of the hypothesis suggesting an inverse relationship between fertility and social mobility for the nonmobile at origin,[7] her data suggest the socially mobile seem to carry with them the child-bearing pattern of the class of origin such that their fertility lies between that of the nonmobile at origin and at destination.

Boggs (1957) examined the relationship between intergenerational occupational mobility and completed family size of 123 male household heads in an elite California suburb. Boggs split the sample according to metropolitan or nonmetropolitan childhood residence. He found no statistically significant differences in family size between mobile and nonmobile men for either group and concludes that social mobility did not affect fertility.

Lack of statistical significance is hardly surprising considering the small sample sizes (56 of nonmetropolitan background, 67 of metropolitan), and the absolute differences in mean fertility levels nevertheless merit pointing out. The average family size of blue-collar respondents whose fathers were blue-collar (nonmobile at origin) was 2.10 for those of nonmetropolitan background and 1.76 for those of metropolitan origin. Average family size of white-collar respondents with blue collar fathers (upwardly mobile) was 1.65 for nonmetropolitan and 2.10 for metropolitan backgrounds. Average family size of those currently white collar whose father were white collar (nonmobile at destination) was 1.46 for nonmetropolitan and 1.70 for metropolitan backgrounds. Hence, nonmetropolitan origin, upwardly mobile respondents had smaller families than the nonmobile at origin but larger family size than the nonmobile at destination as Burks found. In contrast, upwardly mobile respondents of metropolitan origin had slightly higher fertility than either nonmobile group of metropolitan background.

While Boggs may have been hasty in concluding no relationship between fertility and mobility, his suggestion for the lack of association is of interest:

> Greater restriction of fertility may be seen as a consequence of individual social mobility under conditions which may appear to demand greater sacrifices in return for higher status. Prosperity, higher education, and successful experience in adapting to the social mobility required by the urban occupational system all minimize the impact of social mobility, with the result that younger white-collar men . . . no longer see children as inimical to advancement (Boggs, 1957, p. 213).

[7]Other early works found this relationship. Using data from a national sample of 3000 Frenchmen, both Bresard (1950) and Girard (1951) found that for intergenerational occupational and educational mobility, the proportion of small families was higher in cases of upward mobility than in immobility at origin. Similarly, by comparing the upwardly mobile with the nonmobile at origin, Lehner (1954) found in his 1954 investigation of 1673 Roman men that those with small families were in a more favorable situation in terms of intergenerational mobility than those with large families.

Thus, to the extent that social change has become accepted and expected in industrial societies, the process of social mobility may not elicit such responses as fertility behavior modifications.

Scott (1958) investigated the intra- and intergenerational mobility in 1955 of male teachers in England and Wales married before 1945. He found little association between average family size and position within the teaching profession; nor did he find any sizeable relationship between extent of movement along the professional hierarchy from a given class of origin and average family size. He reached the same conclusion measuring intergenerational mobility by comparing occupation of teachers' fathers-in-law with wives' current occupation as indicated by the husbands' occupation. Like Tien, Scott suggests there was no relationship because the teachers achieved their mobility early and quickly formed a homogenous group regardless of social origins. "The common standard of education presumably tends to iron out whatever social distinctions there were" (Scott, 1958, p. 261.).

As part of a larger study of fertility in West Bengal in which a random sample of Calcutta households and 24 rural villages was selected, Poti and Datta (1960) also looked at intergenerational mobility and fertility. They found in both rural and urban areas men remaining in their fathers' occupations had higher average family sizes than those who were upwardly mobile. Urban men moving into an occupational category had higher fertility than the nonmobile at destination; rural men moving into an occupation had higher or lower fertility than the nonmobile at destination depending on occupational category. Thus Poti and Datta's findings are similar to Burks's.

The findings of Burks (1941), Boggs (1957), Scott (1958), and Poti and Datta (1960) differ from those previously discussed. Except for Scott's study, which revealed no relationship between mobility and fertility, these researchers found the upwardly mobile had higher fertility than the nonmobile at destination. Excluding Scott, they found further that the upwardly mobile had lower fertility than the nonmobile at origin. In general, these studies found fertility of the upwardly mobile between that of the nonmobile at origin and destination.

Berent (1952) initiated one of the earliest studies of the fertility of the upwardly and *downwardly* mobile in relation to class of origin and destination. Berent's research is the most often cited, highly regarded early investigation of the mobility–fertility relationship. In a study of intergenerational mobility (comparing husband's current occupation with father's occupation) and intragenerational mobility (comparing husband's present occupation with his occupation at marriage), Berent used 1949 data from a random sample of 10,000 currently married English and Welsh couples, wed for 20 years or more. The fertility measure was live births per couple.

Apropos intergenerational mobility, Berent found that when class of origin was held constant, those who moved up had the smallest families, those who moved down the largest. Comparing persons in the same current class, those who moved up had the largest families, those who moved down the smallest. In all cases those who remained static had intermediate family size. Thus, Berent found fertility of the upwardly and downwardly mobile lying between that of class of origin and destination. He concluded that two forces were affecting family size: acquiring the fertility behavior of the class of destination and maintaining the family-building habits of the class of origin. As for intragenerational mobility, the same pattern of relationships generally held for the lower classes and all classes together. The pattern was not apparent among the higher classes in terms of downward mobility. Among those in the highest classes at marriage, those who went down had smaller average family sizes than the immobile.

In addition to his detailed analysis, Berent makes a number of interesting comments and observations. His findings contradict the thesis of the social promotion of the relatively infertile. He also questions whether the two forces affecting fertility (at origin and at destination) are equal in importance and suggests that the force at destination is probably the more significant. The findings of Tien (1965a) and Scott (1958) appear to support this assertion.

Finally, Berent addresses the problem of direction of causality. Is the fertility of the upwardly mobile or downwardly mobile intermediate between class of origin and destination because of persons' keeping the habits of origin and acquiring the habits of destination (mobility → fertility)? *Or* are persons enabled to move up because of the smallness of their families while others are constrained to move down under the burden of a large family (fertility → mobility)? Berent notes that it is impossible to determine direction of causality with his data; one must know the position of the family on the social scale at the birth of each child.

Two other studies, using data from the Indianapolis Study,[8] investigated differential fertility by upward and downward mobility in relation to status of origin and destination. Kantner and Kiser (1954) examined intergenerational mobility, while Riemer and Kiser (1954) examined intragenerational mobility. These studies differ from others, for in addition to considering total fertility they also investigated the relationship between mobility and *planned* families. Planned families included couples with all pregnancies deliberately planned by stopping contraception in order to conceive, and couples whose last pregnancy was so planned but who had one or more earlier pregnancies under other conditions. Both studies also examined the relationship between effectiveness in family planning and mobility.

Kantner and Kiser hypothesized that both the upwardly and downwardly mobile would have lower fertility than the nonmobile at origin or destination. In

---

[8]In general, the sample was confined to currently married couples in 1941, married 12 to 15 years, in which the wife was under 30 and the husband under 40 at the time of marriage. Only relatively fecund couples were used in the studies by Kantner and Kiser, and Riemer and Kiser.

most analyses mobility was measured in terms of the husbands' fathers' occupational class when the son was 6 and 16 years old compared to the husbands' longest occupation. They found that mobile couples, regardless of direction, had smaller families than nonmobile couples at origin; however, the difference in mean level of fertility between the downwardly mobile and nonmobile was not statistically significant. Except for clerical workers, family sizes of all mobile couples were lower than those of nonmobile couples of similar current occupations. Differences were small, but the same associations obtained when only couples who planned their families were considered. Kantner and Kiser also found the percentage of childlessness greater for mobile couples, regardless of direction of mobility, than for nonmobile couples at destination. Thus, the researchers generally found support for their first hypothesis.

Kantner and Kiser further hypothesized that both the upwardly and downwardly mobile would be more effective fertility planners than the nonmobile at origin and destination. However, they found upwardly mobile couples *less* effective in fertility planning than the nonmobile at destination, but more effective than nonmobile couples at origin. For downward mobility there was also a tendency for the fertility-planning effectiveness of mobile couples to fall between that of the origin and destination groups. Kantner and Kiser conclude by offering a rationale for the seemingly contradictory finding that the mobile have fewer children than the nonmobile at destination, but are nevertheless less effective family planners:

> At least in the case of upward mobility, the data are not inconsistent with the view that mobility partially overcomes resistances to contraception, giving upwardly mobile couples a position intermediate in fertility planning effectiveness of origin and destination groups. Consistent with this view also is the greater regularity of contraception among upwardly mobile couples. This is taken as an indication of the desire to regulate reproduction but a desire that is evidently handicapped by relatively ineffective practice (Kantner and Kiser, 1954, p. 102).

Riemer and Kiser's analysis of intragenerational mobility and fertility is one of the few studies offering theoretical insight into the relationship:

> Hypotheses about social mobility after marriage are based upon a familiar line of argument. The expense and responsibility of rearing children, especially if undertaken at an early age, are handicaps to social advancement since they divert time, energy, and money into family care which might otherwise be devoted to further education, apprenticeship, and other activities facilitating upward social mobility. In some cases they even force downward mobility. Couples successful in improving their social position subsequent to marriage would be selected, then, from those whose aspirations for advancement is implemented by restricted fertility. Downwardly mobile couples would include some whose lack of fertility control was either a causal factor in their demotion or concomitant with other disabilities, and some whose downward mobility motivated fertility restriction, i.e., who used fertility restriction as a means of resisting decline in their standard of living. This reasoning is presumably valid regardless of economic conditions, but seems particularly applicable to couples who experienced a depression early in marriage such that opportunities for advancement were restricted and threats to status were real. (That family responsibilities may stimulate the energy and ambition of some so that they achieve more than without the handicaps of a family; that the desired higher

position may be perceived as a way of life involving the presence of several children; that family building may take place as a means of validating a higher status once it has been achieved—these things are possible but are highly individualistic and therefore likely only to weaken the relationship but not override it.) And, in general, socially mobile persons are subject to some influence from their original status level and some acculturation to their new status level. However, for upwardly mobile persons, selections for low fertility and psychological orientation toward the higher status would minimize the influence of the background status level. Upwardly mobile couples thus would be likely to resemble the nonmobile couples at their destination much more than the nonmobile couples at their origin with respect to fertility control and fertility. For downwardly mobile persons, on the other hand, selection and psychological orientation pull in opposite directions and acculturation would be minimized. Selection is partly for inability to control fertility, but for some couples strenuous efforts at fertility control in order to maintain the old standard of living would keep their fertility low. Thus downwardly mobile couples may be quite heterogeneous, but taken as a group their fertility behavior is likely to be intermediate between that of the nonmobile couples at their origin and their destination (Riemer and Kiser, 1954, pp. 194–195).

In their analysis, the husband's first job after marriage was compared to his longest job as of 1940. Defining career mobility as a change in occupation between the manual and nonmanual sectors, Riemer and Kiser found the average number of living children for upwardly mobile couples well *below* the average for the nonmobile at the manual level but well *above* average for the nonmobile at the nonmanual level. Average family size for the downwardly mobile was also between that of the nonmobile at origin and destination. There was no evidence that upwardly mobile couples had smaller planned families than nonmobile couples at either origin or destination. The planned fertility of the downwardly mobile, however, lay between that of couples at origin and destination. Riemer and Kiser found the upwardly mobile better planners than the nonmobile at origin; their success approached that of the nonmobile at destination. The proportion of successful planners among the downwardly mobile was intermediate between that of the nonmobile at origin and destination.

Riemer and Kiser make several important points. They suggest that their failure to find that the upwardly mobile have lower fertility than those at destination might be because of the broad occupational categories used, such that those at destination had been mobile but, because of the broadness of categories, were classified as nonmobile. They note that their data did not let them investigate the stage of the respondent's career at which marriage took place, the period within marriage of the change in status, or the spacing of children in relation to status changes. Consideration of all of these is necessary to

. . . test the significance of fertility as a selective factor in upward and downward mobility, and conversely, to assess the degree to which fertility reflects socioeconomic status of childhood and youth, acculturation of a new status, or the severity of the struggle to improve or maintain status at various stages of marital life (Riemer and Kiser, 1954, p. 212).

That some of these suggestions have been incorporated into mobility and fertility studies, albeit minimally, is evidenced by our discussion of the works of Tien, Natsis, and Perrucci.

Finally, Riemer and Kiser stress the importance of investigating another dimension of social mobility—mobility aspirations—rather than actual movement. Their comments are similar to Westoff's who maintains that mobility aspiration is probably the more important factor influencing decisions on family size.

Westoff suggests aspirations for advancement and increasing success are important in making decisions about planned family size as well as the extent and effectiveness of contraceptive practice, while, conversely, the degree of subsequent mobility is at least partially because of the conditions resulting from these decisions (Westoff, 1953, p. 33). Moreover, the subjective dimension of mobility cannot be deduced entirely from the objective dimension since some aspire but are not mobile and some who are mobile have not had any great aspirations to be so.

As a test of the relationship between subjective mobility and fertility, Riemer and Kiser introduce the concept of *economic tension*—the difference between actual and desired standard of living. They hypothesize that the greater the economic tension, the higher the proportion of couples practicing contraception effectively and the smaller the planned families. To test the hypothesis, they used quantitative and qualitative measures of a couple's standard of living and what they would like to have.

Contrary to their prediction, Riemer and Kiser found that the greater the economic tension, the *lower* the proportion of couples practicing contraception effectively and the *larger* the planned family size. To explain the lack of support for their hypothesis, they note that the indexes of economic tension were inversely related to economic status itself and this association accounted for almost all of the inverse relationship between fertility planning success and economic tension. Moreover, they note the likelihood of reciprocal causation between economic tension and fertility and their inability to separate the effect of economic tension on fertility from the reverse effect. Desire for a higher standard of living may prompt family limitation; however, couples with large families, even large planned families, probably need higher incomes, larger houses, etc. Riemer and Kiser contend that this latter consideration produced a direct relationship between the two variables which overrode the effect of economic tension on fertility. They failed to find support for their hypothesis, but the effort itself was a major step in better explicating the relationship between the subjective dimension of social mobility and fertility.

The relationships between social mobility and fertility Kiser and colleagues found were not replicated in the successor to the Indianapolis Study—the Princeton Fertility Study—conducted by Westoff *et al.* (1961, 1963). The initial Princeton Fertility Study sample was 1100 white, urban, once-married couples who had their second child 5 to 7 months before the interview in 1957. The follow-up study reinterviewed these couples 3 years later.

The general hypothesis tested in these studies is similar to that which guided previous research: "the socioeconomic and psychological requirements for upward mobility are inconsistent with expenditures of time, energy, and money for children" (Westoff *et al.*, 1961, p. 237). The researchers immediately qualified the hypothesis and pointed out some of the complexities of the mobility–fertility relationship. For some persons the requirements for mobility may be heavier than for others. Costs of an additional child may not constitute a handicap for some status levels. The researchers also elaborate on the subjective dimension of mobility:

> Perhaps even more of a complication is . . . that social mobility as measured in objective categories of income or occupational change may not sufficiently reflect level of aspiration . . . Thus, couples who have moved up the scale rapidly may perceive their situation as not requiring so much devotion to the process of moving upward as other couples who may not have moved so rapidly. And, of course, many individuals may be extremely ambitious and yet be in a job situation where they have either already reached their ceiling of advancement or in which the rewards are assured over the long-term range. Thus, it seems clear that some measure of mobility aspirations had to be included to tap this more subjective and elusive dimension (Westoff *et al.*, 1961, pp. 237–238).

Westoff *et al.* (1961) studied intergenerational and intragenerational occupational mobility. Fertility differences by occupational mobility, whether inter- or intragenerational, were extremely small and mostly statistically nonsignificant. This was true whether fertility was measured as the number of children husband or wife desired, percentage of successful family planners, or interval between marriage and second birth. Measured by change in income since the first year of marriage, upward mobility was found to be weakly positively associated with a desire for smaller families, longer birth intervals, and more successful fertility planning. Attempts to measure the subjective dimension of social mobility were made by creating indexes that purportedly tapped the respondent's "drive to get ahead." The hypothesis tested was that "individuals who have a high desire to get ahead will want smaller families and will exhibit more successful levels of fertility control than couples whose aspirations are presumably lower" (Westoff *et al.*, 1961, p. 252). The findings were in the hypothesized direction but very low in magnitude.

Noting that "many persons conceive of social mobility in terms of the future status of their children and perceive their own role to be that of maximizing opportunities for their children," the researchers further tested that "mothers who reveal high levels of aspiration for their children's education will view additional children as incompatible with this goal and will thus desire fewer children" (Westoff *et al.*, 1961, pp. 254, 256). Testing this hypothesis, they found a significant negative relationship only for Jews. In summarizing their findings, Westoff *et al.* conclude there is little evidence of a relationship between any type of mobility and fertility.

In their follow-up study, Westoff *et al.* (1963) investigated whether changes in fertility or number of children desired in the 3 years between interviews were in any way associated with concomitant changes in socioeconomic status. They tested hypotheses comparable to those of the initial investigation, including relating fertility (number of additional pregnancies) to occupational mobility changes between 1957 and 1960, changes in income during this period, changes in drive to get ahead, and changes in aspirations to send children to college. The analyses in the follow-up study were no more successful in finding a relationship between social mobility and fertility than those in the initial study. The researchers conclude that social mobility at best had a trivial statistical association with reproductive behavior.

The failure to find significant relationships between social mobility and fertility in the Westoff *et al.* studies should not be regarded as too damaging evidence that a relationship between the two variables does not exist in any population. The sample was extremely selective. Westoff *et al.* noted that by restricting their study to a sample of two-child couples they automatically excluded the low-fertility couples (childless or with one child) who might most sharply exhibit an intense mobility drive. They suggest "it is reasonable to speculate that higher, and more consistently negative associations between mobility and fertility might be obtained if the study had included the possible effects of postponement of marriage, childlessness, and limiting fertility to only one child" (Westoff *et al.*, 1961, p. 261). The merit and relevance of these articles, however, lies in the Westoff groups', more than any others, developing and testing the relationship between *numerous* dimensions of fertility and social mobility.

Three remaining studies falling within the intermediate group of research dealing with the mobility–fertility relationship are worthy of brief comment.

Brooks and Henry (1958) examined the fertility and mobility of white, once-married, Catholic couples, with one or more children in the first grade of Catholic private or parochial schools in the Northeast. After investigating the relationship between intragenerational occupational mobility and mean number of children ever born, the researchers found the upwardly mobile had higher fertility than the class of origin and somewhat higher fertility than the class of destination. The downwardly mobile generally had lower fertility than the class of origin but higher than that of destination.

At first glance, these findings seem quite inconsistent from those previously discussed. However, Brooks and Henry note that in their sample there was a *direct* relationship between socioeconomic status and fertility. They reasoned that the mobile were likely to assimilate partially the fertility values of the status group into which they moved, and if higher rather than lower fertility was the norm, the mobile couples would conform to this value. Hence, Brooks and Henry's research supports Berent's contention that mobile couples are subject to influence from their status of origin and acculturation to their new status levels.

That the upwardly mobile had higher rather than lower fertility than the non-mobile at destination is explained as a tendency of the upwardly mobile to overconform to the fertility values of the status group at destination.

Goldberg (1959), using 1952–1958 data from the Detroit Area Study did not find support for Berent's thesis; nor did he find any relationship between mobility and fertility. Confining his study to married couples, husband present, with wife age 40 or older, Goldberg argues that the relationship between fertility and social mobility sometimes found for urban areas is a function of differential selectivity of status categories for farm migrants. That is, social mobility has been confused with geographical mobility. In examining the relationship between intergenerational occupational mobility and completed family size for two-generation urbanites, Goldberg found that in families with any history of white-collar employment, the stable white-collar workers and the up and down mobiles are indistinguishable from one another (Goldberg, 1959, p. 219).

Goldberg explains the lack of a relationship for two-generation urbanites in terms of the shifting sex role differentiation within the family. He notes conflict between husband and wife in number of children desired. In an urban environment, status is positively related to desired family size for men, but inversely related for women; as the husband and wife come to share family size decision making equally, the pressures exerted by each have a tendency to cancel one another, so no association between status and fertility obtains.

Hutchinson (1961) used a sample of men and women from eight cities in southern Brazil in 1959–1960 to study the effects of intergenerational occupational mobility on completed family size. Examining the relationship for the entire sample, he found average family size of persons nonmobile at origin much greater than that of the upwardly mobile; however, fertility of the nonmobile at destination was lower than for those who had been upwardly mobile. Average family size of the downwardly mobile also lay between status of origin and destination.

Hutchinson next turned his attention to Goldberg's finding that among two-generation Detroit urbanites, mobility has no effect on fertility. He divided his sample into city-born and rural-born and found that for each group the results were the same as those for the entire sample. Hutchinson further considered only two-generation urbanites and again found support for the intermediate fertility thesis. Thus, he found nothing to support Goldberg's suggestion that the relationship between social mobility and fertility was because of rural–urban migration. To explain why his analysis in Brazil *did* reveal a relationship, Hutchinson used Goldberg's explanation as to why the latter found no relationship. He suggested that the urban Brazilian population seldom had egalitarian marital relationships. In Brazil, traditional sex roles had yet to be affected by social and economic change in rural or urban environments. The significance of Hutchinson's work lies in his inference that the relationship between social mobility and fertility might be culture bound; to the extent that cultures differ on such factors as conjugal relationships, a mobility–fertility relationship may or may not obtain.

3   Summary of the Intermediate Studies

To summarize the intermediate mobility–fertility studies, we present a typology (Table 1) indicating the sample investigated, concepts of mobility and reproductive behavior used, hypotheses tested, and findings for each of the works.[9] The study of social mobility and fertility has been approached from divergent perspectives using a variety of data sources and samples. The concepts of mobility and reproductive behavior have been defined in various objective and subjective ways. Apparently, most researchers, by looking at only one type of social mobility or one aspect of reproductive behavior, have viewed their particular measurements as sufficient to test for the presence or absence of a relationship. We infer that most investigators have assumed social mobility and fertility are each unidimensional concepts—an assumption we will later question. Furthermore, different predictions about the nature and direction of the relationship have been made. Given such diversity of approach, it is not surprising that different researchers have reached different conclusions. At best the findings of the intermediate studies are inconclusive about the existence and nature of an association between social mobility and reproductive behavior. Considering only those works revealing a relationship, there has been a tendency to find fertility of the upwardly and downwardly mobile lying intermediate between the nonmobile at origin and at destination.

One common theme in the intermediate studies is what their authors have accepted as indication of the mobility–fertility relationship. All have compared the mean level of fertility of the upwardly or downwardly mobile with that of the nonmobile at origin or destination. The first seven studies in our typology compare fertility of the upwardly mobile with that of the nonmobile at destination. The next six compare fertility of the upwardly mobile with that of the nonmobile at origin and destination. The remaining studies compare fertility of the upwardly and downwardly mobile with the fertility of the nonmobile at origin and at destination. In all cases, the criterion for determining if social mobility affects reproductive behavior is whether there are sizeable differences in mean fertility levels between or among mobile and nonmobile groups. Implicit in this approach is a disregard for the independent effects that status of origin and destination may have in determining fertility levels of the mobile; the approach does not permit

---

[9]In some cases the comments in the hypotheses tested column are rough guesses since it was often difficult to determine exactly what the researcher was setting out to do.

Table 1

Typology of Intermediate Mobility–Fertility Studies (1941–1967)

Study	Sample/data source	Type of mobility	Type of reproductive behavior	Hypotheses tested	Findings
Baltzell (1953)	"Who's Who" and the "Philadelphia Social Register"	Intergenerational (Intergen)	Completed family size (CFS)	Upmobile (U) < nonmobile (N) at destination (D)	Support for hypothesis
Hollingsworth (1957)	British peerage records	Nuptial	CFS	U < N at D	Support for hypotheses
Kirk (1957)	Who's Who in America	Intergen	CFS	U < N at D	Support for hypothesis
Tien (1961, 1965a)	Australian universities faculty	Interoccupation (Inter-OCC)	CFS; Marriage (M)–first birth interval (BI)	U < N at D U interval > N at D interval	U–N same; support for hypothesis 2
Natsis (1966)	United States Baptist ministers	Inter-OCC	M–third BI	U < N at D U interval > N at D interval	Support for hypothesis
Tomasson (1966)	University of Illinois faculty and functional elite in Illinois cities	Inter-OCC	CFS	U < N at D	Support for hypothesis
Perrucci (1967)	United States engineers	Inter-OCC; Intra-OCC	CFS; college graduation–first, second, third BI	U < N at D; U interval > N at D interval	U–N same; support for hypothesis 2

(continued)

Table 1 (*Continued*)

Study	Sample/data source	Type of mobility	Type of reproductive behavior	Hypotheses tested	Findings
Burks (1941)	Genetics Record Office	Inter-OCC: intereducation (Inter-ED)	CFS	U intermediate between origin (O) and D	Support for hypothesis
Bresard and Girard (1950–1951)	French men	Inter-OCC; Inter-ED	CFS	U < nonmobile (N) at O	Support for hypothesis
Lehner (1954)	Roman men	Inter-OCC	CFS	U < N at O	Support for hypothesis
Boggs (1957)	California suburb	Inter-OCC	CFS	U intermediate between O and D	Support for hypothesis (with qualifications)
Poti and Datta (1960)	Calcutta urban and West Bengal rural	Inter-OCC	CFS	U intermediate between O and D	Support for hypothesis (with qualifications)
Scott (1958)	English/Welsh male teachers	Inter-OCC; Intra-OCC	CFS	U intermediate between O and D	No differences
Berent (1952)	English/Welsh couples	Inter-OCC; Intra-OCC	CFS	U and downmobile (DN) intermediate between O and D	Support for hypothesis
Kantner and Kiser (1954)	Indianapolis Study	Inter-OCC; Inter-ED	CFS; planned FS (PFS); planning effectiveness (PE)	U and DN < N at O and D; + between mobility and PE	Support for hypothesis 1; PE for mobile intermediate between O and D

Reimer and Kiser (1954)	Indianapolis Study	Intra-OCC; economic tension (ET)	CFS; PFS; PE	U < N at O + D; DN intermediate between O and D; + between U and PE; PE for DN intermediate; − between ET and PES; + between ET and PE	U + DN intermediate between O + D; PE for U and DN intermediate; + between ET and PFS; − between ET and PE
Westoff et al. (1961)	Princeton Fertility Study (PFS)—initial	Inter-OCC; Intra-OCC; Intraincome; drive to get ahead; aspirations for child's education (ACE)	Desired FS (DFS); PE; M−second BI	U < N at O and D; − between income and DFS; − between drive and DFS; − between ACE and DFS	No significant differences
Westoff et al. (1963)	PFS—follow-up	Comparable to initial study	Comparable to initial study	Comparable to initial study	No significant differences
Brooks and Henry (1958)	Northeast Catholic couples with first-grade children in Catholic schools	Intra-OCC	CFS	U and DN intermediate between O and D	Support for hypothesis
Goldberg (1959)	Detroit area study (second-generation urbanites)	Inter-OCC	CFS	U and DN intermediate between O and D	No differences
Hutchinson (1961)	Brazilian urban men and women	Inter-OCC	CFS	U and DN intermediate between O and D	Support for hypothesis, all samples

27

one to assess fertility differences between the mobile and nonmobile after separating out origin and destination effects. Should a researcher take the independent effects of origin and destination into account *before* assessing whether mobility affects fertility? Our next chapter illustrates why authors of many of the more recent studies have argued in favor of doing so.

Chapter 3 | Contemporary Studies of the Social Mobility–Fertility Hypothesis

1 Blau and Duncan's Approach to the Study of Social Mobility and Fertility

In an epoch-beginning work, Duncan (1966) reanalyzes Berent's data to see if they reveal a "true" mobility effect:

> The gist of the argument is that one is not entitled to discuss "effects" of mobility . . . until after he has established that the apparent effect cannot be due merely to a simple combination of effects of the variables used to define mobility (Duncan, 1966, p. 91).

There must be a significant interaction effect of class of origin and class of destination on fertility before a true mobility effect can be said to exist. If mean aggregate fertility for mobile couples is merely the sum of the grand mean effect of status that applies to everyone in the sample, the increment of class of origin regardless of destination and the increment of class of destination regardless of origin, then an *additive* model obtains and no mobility effect exists. Mobility only affects fertility to the extent that mobile couples are influenced by the class of origin and by their newly acquired membership in a different class. If, however, the expected values of average family size calculated on the basis of the additive model differ significantly from the observed values, the deviations indicate a mobility effect and an *interactive* model would better fit the data. The *process* of mobility exerts an effect on fertility above and beyond that explained by past and present social class.

Analyzing Berent's data by calculating effects based on an additive model, Duncan found that the model reproduced the data reasonably well. He concluded:

> Mobility produces no differences in fertility that cannot be fully accounted for by the additive mechanism implied by the model. From this point of view, mobility has no "consequence" to

29

be discussed, except the consequence that the mobile couple combines the fertility patterns of the two classes (Duncan, 1966, p. 93).

Using data from the American Occupational Changes in a Generation Survey, Blau and Duncan (1967) examined the mobility–fertility relationship from Duncan's earlier perspective. The 1962 sample consisted of about 6000 currently married couples, with wives aged 42 to 61, childbearing completed. The measure of fertility was children ever born. Intra- and intergenerational mobility were analyzed by comparing husband's first job with his 1962 job, father-in-law's occupation with husband's first and 1962 jobs, and husband's father's occupation with husband's 1962 job using Bureau of the Census occupational classifications.

Blau and Duncan first analyzed the effect of intragenerational mobility on completed family size and found upwardly and downwardly mobile couples had lower fertility than the nonmobile at origin but higher fertility than the nonmobile at destination. When they calculated the expected values of average family size on the basis of an additive model and compared these to the observed values, they found quite small deviations and concluded that "although the additive model cannot be accepted without reservation, it comes very close to predicting all the effects produced by a simple classification of couples as mobile or nonmobile" (Blau and Duncan, 1967, p. 379). Hence, there was no effect of mobility on fertility. Analyses of the three types of intergenerational mobility generally produced the same results: significant net effects of classes of origin and destination, but no mobility effects.

Blau and Duncan also found that when they excluded couples with present or previous farm backgrounds, differences in average family sizes by mobility experience were sharply attenuated. They commented that perhaps this was evidence of the sphere of applicability of the mobility–fertility relationship. While movement to nonfarm residences from farm backgrounds may be a form of social mobility, in highly industrialized societies where smaller and smaller proportions of cohorts have farm backgrounds, differential fertility by socioeconomic status will cease to manifest itself; thus, social mobility will cease to have even an additive effect on fertility.

Blau and Duncan were the first of the mobility–fertility researchers to offer any substantial theory as to why the fertility of the mobile couples lay intermediate between the nonmobile at origin and at destination. They drew on the reference group theory Blau developed a decade earlier:

Mobile persons are not well integrated in either social class. Without extensive and intimate social contacts, they do not have sufficient opportunity for complete acculturation to the values and style of life of the one group, nor do they continue to experience the full impact of the social constraints of the other. But both groups exert some influence over mobile individuals, since they have, or have had, social contacts with members of both. . . . Hence, their behavior is expected to be intermediate between that of the two mobile classes (Blau, 1956, p. 291).

Subsequent researchers have referred to this explanation as the *acculturation hypothesis*.[1] We emphasize that support for the acculturation hypothesis is not regarded by Blau and Duncan or most subsequent researchers as evidence of an effect of mobility on fertility.

In addition to considering upward and downward movement in general, Blau and Duncan also investigated the relationship between *distance* of intragenerational occupational movement and completed family size. Using a 10-category occupational status scale and measuring mobility by the number of steps up or down from the occupation of origin to that of destination, the researchers divided their sample into the long-distance upwardly mobile, short-distance movers or stable respondents, and the long-distance downwardly mobile. For long-distance mobility, the additive model did not adequately fit the data. Blau and Duncan concluded that exceptional mobility had an independent effect on fertility by depressing average completed family size. To account for this finding, an earlier Blau theory—the *social insecurity hypothesis*—was again invoked and compared to the acculturation hypothesis:

> The hypothesis used to account for the first pattern can also help to explain this second one, different as the two are. For if it is true that the mobile individual is poorly integrated, it follows that not only is there relatively little communication between him and others, but also that he does not receive much social support from them. In the absence of extensive communication, he cannot fully assimilate the style of life of the members of his new social class, with the result that his beliefs and practices are intermediate between theirs and those of the members of his class of origin. Simultaneously, lack of firm social support engenders feelings of insecurity, and this has had the result that the mobile person tends to assume the extreme

[1]Support for Blau's contention that mobile persons are not well integrated in either class of origin or destination comes in such works as LeMasters (1954), who found that in families where one or more members have moved up or down, *social distance* is created because the mobile have been exposed to the different value systems of the two social classes; and Stuckert (1963), who found, in a sample of white married couples in Milwaukee, that mobility is detrimental to extended family relations, involvement with neighbors, and participation in voluntary associations.

Support for the acculturation hypothesis in studies dealing with consequences of social mobility for types of behavior other than fertility is found in Ellis and Lane (1966), Aiken and Goldberg (1969), and Vorwaller (1970). Ellis and Lane conclude that among 126 male matriculants at Stanford University in 1958, those from lower class backgrounds had departed from the attitudes, values, and judgmental decision standards of the lower class but had only partially adopted the various norms and values of the middle-class subculture to which they aspired. Analyzing 1955 data for 611 currently married women in the Detroit metropolitan area, Aiken and Goldberg found rates of kinship contact and involvement for mobile couples lay between the nonmobile at origin and destination. Similarly, using data from two Massachusetts communities and Detroit elementary school children, Vorwaller concludes that social mobility exerts little or no "interactive" effect on persons' affiliations with voluntary associations. "The status effect of social origin and destination account for variations in number of memberships at significant levels, which supports the notion that socialization processes operate during the course of social mobility to mediate responses at expected levels" (Vorwaller, 1970, p. 481).

position, not the intermediate one, in respect to those attitudes that constitute expressions of insecurity (Blau, 1956, p. 292).

Thus, extreme mobility in either direction entails disruptions of established social ties and changes in interpersonal contacts and social relations. The extremely mobile person loses stable social support and becomes insecure; such insecurity inhibits fertility because of physical and emotional stress and disorientation.

A Recapitulation of the Blau and Duncan Approach

What constitutes a mobility effect? We pause here to comment on Blau and Duncan's study and make clear what is or is not a mobility effect. If the fertility of the upwardly or downwardly mobile lies between that of the nonmobile at origin and destination, if the additive model adequately fits the data, or if support is found for the acculturation hypothesis, no mobility effect obtains. If the fertility of the upwardly or downwardly mobile lies above or below that of the nonmobile at origin and destination, if the interactive model better fits the data, or if support is found for the social insecurity hypothesis, a mobility effect does obtain. Thus, we have two bodies of theory, each attempting to explain observed differential fertility by mobility status, yet support for one is not regarded as evidence of an effect of mobility on fertility. At first glance this may seem perplexing.

If fertility of the upwardly mobile is intermediate between the nonmobile at origin and destination, one may argue that these persons have changed status levels and their reproductive behavior differs from that of either former or current status. One may therefore be tempted to conclude that mobility has affected fertility. Yet the term *mobility,* as used by Blau and Duncan and in common parlance, connotes a *process.* If the additive model fits the data, the *process of moving* has not altered fertility behavior; the family size of the upwardly mobile can be correctly predicted simply with a knowledge of the fertility levels of their classes of origin and destination.

If fertility can be accurately predicted from knowledge of one's classes of origin and destination, then the mobility experience itself need not be considered; origin and destination effects account for the fertility of mobile couples. As such, the model predicting fertility behavior is more parsimonious, since only class effects and not the additional mobility effect need be specified. Ideally, to test for an independent mobility effect, a researcher would want to include a model term for class of origin (X_1), a term for class of destination (X_2), and a term for the mobility effect expressed as the difference between classes of origin and destination ($X_1 - X_2$). Such a model, however, leads to identification problems since the mobility term is an exact function of the former two terms. To avoid identification problems the product term (X_1X_2) is therefore used to capture the effect of mobility, independent of origin and destination effects. If the product term is significant, a mobility effect is said to exist. This is what is meant by the statement that if the interactive model—a model which includes the $X_1 X_2$ term—better fits the data, social mobility has an independent effect on fertility.

Some have advised caution when using Blau and Duncan's additive versus interactive approach to the study of mobility and fertility. Hope (1971) notes that in terms of methodology, possible mobility effects cancel each other out, leaving a zero interaction term. "The nub of the argument is that the criteria of departure from additivity is blunt edged; it lumps together likely and unlikely departures in such a way that the former are swamped by the latter" (Hope, 1971, p. 1020). For example, the upwardly mobile may have lower fertility than the nonmobile and the downwardly mobile may exhibit higher fertility than the nonmobile. If so, and differences in the fertility levels of the mobile and nonmobile were assessed using the Blau and Duncan approach, a zero or nonsignificant interaction term would obtain. Reanalyzing Berent's data, Hope shows that when terms for distance and direction moved are included in the model, mobility effects according to Blau and Duncan's criterion do exist.

Namboodiri (1972a) raises the issue of the direction of causality implied by Blau and Duncan's additive model, which assumes fertility is the dependent variable and classes of destination and origin are independent variables. Hence, the model implies that mobility precedes family formation; this is unlikely when mobility is defined as a comparison between husband's father's occupation and husband's occupation at least 20 years after marriage or between husband's first job and his occupation at least 20 years after marriage. Namboodiri suggests that the more appropriate model is a single-stimulus–double-response model which views class of origin as the stimulus and class of destination and fertility as symmetrically related responses. This model makes the more valid assumption that mobility and fertility occur simultaneously. Namboodiri cautions that the model one fits to the data will affect substantive interpretations.

2 Other Studies Following Blau and Duncan's Approach

Despite these cautions about Blau and Duncan's method of examining the mobility–fertility relationship, the approach has gained acceptance by recent researchers. Boyd (1971, 1973) examined the association between career mobility and completed family size for five Latin American cities. Using the CELADE fertility surveys conducted in 1963–1964, data for 600 to 800 once-married and currently married women were analyzed for each city. All had been married for at least 10 years. Boyd found family size in each city inversely related to socioeconomic status; the additive model adequately fit the data for Bogota, San Jose, Panama City, and Caracas where the fertility of the mobile couples lay intermediate between the nonmobile at origin and destination. She concluded that, except in Mexico City, career mobility was not significant in explaining differential completed family size since variation could be attributed to an additive composite of past and present status effects.

Boyd makes a number of noteworthy points in her study. She asks why most of the intermediate studies (see Chapter 2) failed to find that mobility has disruptive consequences for fertility. Most of these works were based on data from developed countries where fertility varies little by socioeconomic status and the stratification system is fluid. Boyd argues that in these societies mobility may not have disruptive behavioral effects since it has become institutionalized and no longer costly. In contrast, less developed countries have high variation in fertility by socioeconomic status and less fluid stratification systems. Mechanisms for mobility are less institutionalized and individual mobility is more the exception than the rule; hence, in these societies mobility might be expected to demand such behavioral modification as fertility reduction. Offsetting the disruptive effect of mobility on fertility may be the significance attached to the family network such that occupational status changes may not severely disrupt social ties. Boyd comments that this situation might explain her failure to find significant interaction effects of mobility on fertility in four of the five cities investigated. However, that Mexico City was the least economically developed and the only one in which the disruptive mobility effect was found suggests to Boyd that her overall premise was correct.

Boyd further develops the theory underlying the mobility–fertility relationship. Like Blau, she notes that social mobility may disrupt integrative social ties leading mobile couples to restrict their fertility, but such social insecurity might also augment fertility as a means for couples to gain reintegration. Upward mobility might lead to fertility restriction not only because of social insecurity but also because raising children requires time, money, and energy that might otherwise be used to improve one's social standing. On the other hand, upward mobility might increase family size because such couples may choose to invest their social gains in more children, especially when they enter into status groups where high fertility is regarded as an important consumptive value. Downward mobility might restrict family size because downwardly mobile couples may be motivated to regain their lost social position or to halt their social demise.

Boyd also considers the very real possibility that fertility affects mobility rather than the reverse; for example, downward mobility may be the result of the selectivity of couples with high fertility. There might even be a reciprocal relationship such that the upwardly mobile restrict their family size in order to rise in social status and, because of relatively small family size, can rise even further. Thus, Boyd outlines several reasons to suspect an interactive effect; however, as she so vividly illustrates, the predicted nature or direction of the effect depends on the theory adopted.

Finally, Boyd outlines what the optimal study of the mobility–fertility relationship might look like:

It appears that if the social mobility hypothesis is to be meaningful the nature of causality must be more explicitly stated, a temporal analysis must be made, and variables of birth intervals must be included. In short, what is needed is a temporal study which utilizes birth intervals as indicative of reproductive behavior and which assesses the aspirations and occupational status at the time of each pregnancy and decisions concerning family size made prior to or after each pregnancy (Boyd, 1973, p. 15).

While limited by the data and unable to meet Boyd's requirements for the ideal study of the mobility and fertility relationship, Bean and Swicegood (1979) further explicate and refine the mobility–fertility association. Examining the relationship between intergenerational occupational mobility and cumulative fertility using data from the 1970 National Fertility Survey (NFS), they argue that completed family size should be partitioned into intended and unintended births. *Intended births* are planned at conception or ones the couple would have had at some future time anyway; *unintended births* are unplanned at conception and ones the couple never intended to have. Thus, the researchers distinguished between demand for children and effectiveness of fertility regulation; they suggest that the two components might respond differently to the force of social mobility.

Bean and Swicegood began by considering alternative theoretical perspectives of the effect of mobility on fertility. Like Boyd, they adopted Blau and Duncan's viewpoint and did not consider the acculturation hypothesis as a mobility effect. Rather, all were associated or commensurate with that which the interactive model implies.

The first theory Bean and Swicegood present is Blau's social insecurity hypothesis; given this perspective one would predict that both upward and downward mobility are negatively related to intended births but positively related to unintended births because strain and disorientation lead to greater contraceptive failure.

The second perspective, social isolation, would lead one to predict that the socially disruptive effects of mobility would cause a couple to increase intended childbearing to compensate for loss of social ties; however, mobility decreases unintended fertility because of the reduced tendency for couples retrospectively to designate births as unintended.

The third perspective, status enhancement, we discussed in connection with Westoff *et al.* (see Chapter 2). Desire of the upwardly mobile to improve their socioeconomic position causes them to want fewer children and take greater care to avoid unintended births, as does desire of the downwardly mobile to recapture their previous position or keep from declining further. Hence, the status enhancement theory would lead one to predict that mobility has negative effects on births.

Bean and Swicegood derive the fourth perspective from Easterlin (1969, 1973, 1975). Relative economic status (ratio of lifetime income to consumption preferences formed in the parental household) is predicted to affect fertility positively because of a decrease in age at marriage and increase in early childbearing. The researchers argue that, assuming relative economic status is higher with upward mobility and lower with downward mobility, the upwardly mobile will have more intended births, because of greater demand for children, and unintended births, because of lower demand for fertility regulation; the downwardly mobile will have fewer intended and unintended births.

Finally, Bean and Swicegood designate a fifth perspective, selectivity, which reverses the direction of causality and views fertility as affecting mobility. According to this theory, high intended and unintended fertility is associated with downward mobility because couples find it difficult to maintain social status with a large number of children; low intended and unintended fertility is associated with upward mobility because couples with fewer children find it easier to rise on the social scale.

To determine which perspective predicts fertility best, Bean and Swicegood limited the NFS sample to currently wed, once-married women who had gone far enough in their childbearing to have been exposed to the risk of having an unintended birth. They measured mobility by comparing occupational status, in terms of Duncan (SEI) scores, of the respondent's father-in-law with that of her husband at interview. The relationships between upward and downward mobility and intended and unintended fertility underwent regression analysis in which both classes of origin and destination, along with a number of background variables, were entered as controls. Orthogonal contrasts representing mobility interaction effects were constructed and treated as the independent variables of major interest.

Using total number of births as the dependent variable, no statistically significant interaction effects are found; nor was there any significant relationship between mobility and fertility when the latter variable was defined as total number of intended births. However, a significant interaction effect did obtain when unintended births were analyzed. The upwardly mobile had on the average 0.2 more unintended births than the nonmobile couples, and the downwardly mobile had nearly 0.3 fewer unintended births than the nonmobile. This finding was consistent with the relative economic status perspective.

In finding support for the relative economic status hypothesis only in the case of unintended births, the researchers comment that it seems that upward mobility does not cause a greater demand for births but rather a relaxation of the perceived need for fertility control. Similarly, downwardly mobile couples do not want fewer children but instead have fewer unintended births by practicing more effective contraception. Bean and Swicegood note that their finding accords well with the notion that unintended fertility is more susceptible to the influence of social and economic conditions than intended fertility, and they suggest that more studies dealing with differential fertility by various social and economic factors should concentrate on the unintended component of childbearing.

While Bean and Swicegood refine the social mobility–fertility association by partitioning *fertility* into two components, Stevens (1981) further explicates the relationship by partitioning *mobility*. She argues that lack of empirical support for a relationship between social mobility and fertility may be because only total mobility has previously been examined. Total mobility is composed of relative (circulation) mobility and mean (structural) mobility, and Stevens hypothesizes that these two types of mobility experiences may affect fertility differently. Relative mobility is the result of an individual's own endeavors, motivation, skill, or luck. Mean mobility is a function of factors beyond the individual's control which move him from a given social origin to a particular social destination (e.g., labor market conditions).

To test for the "dual nature of mobility experiences" Stevens uses data from the Occupational Changes in a Generation Survey. The analysis is restricted to white males, aged 35–64, in their first marriage. She uses two measures of intergenerational mobility—respondent's father's occupation to respondent's first and current occupations—and one measure of intragenerational mobility—respondent's first occupation to his current one. Fertility is measured by completed family size, childlessness, and having three or more children.

Stevens' method of partitioning mobility into its mean and relative components is ingenious, and our brief summary of her study cannot do the technique justice. Essentially, *mean mobility* is defined as the difference between expected destination and observed origin, while *relative mobility* is the difference between observed and expected destination. Expected destination is obtained via preliminary regression analyses. Like Blau and Duncan, Stevens maintains that origin and destination effects should be controlled before searching for mobility effects. She accomplishes this by constraining origin and destination effects to be equal and fitting one class of origin/class of destination term.

Stevens uses Bean and Swicegood's presentation of the five overlapping theoretical perspectives that might account for an effect of mobility on fertility and discusses the predictions each perspective might make with respect to mean and relative mobility (see Table 1). Note that the socialization (acculturation) perspective maintains that origin and destination effects account for the fertility of mobile couples; hence, this perspective is the baseline or null hypothesis against which each of the other four perspectives is assessed. Unlike Bean and Swicegood, Stevens does not consider the selectivity perspective since it reverses the direction of causality and views fertility as affecting mobility.

Of all the different combinations of perspectives that might be used to account for separate mean and relative mobility effects on fertility, Stevens finds the combination of the relative economic status and status enhancement perspectives

Table 1

Summary of Mobility Effects on Fertility[a]

| | Perspective | | | | |
	Socialization up/down	Stress up/down	Isolation up/down	Status enhancement up/down	Relative economic up/down
Origins to first occupation					
Mean mobility	0/0	$(-/-)^b$	$(+/+)$	0/0	$+/-$
Relative mobility	0/0	$-/-$	$+/+$	0/0	$+/-$
Origins to current occupation					
Mean mobility	0/0	$(-/-)$	$(+/+)$	0/0	$+/-$
Relative mobility	0/0	$-/-$	$+/+$	$-/-$	$+/-$
First to current occupation					
Mean mobility	0/0	$(-/-)$	$(+/+)$	0/0	$+/-$
Relative mobility	0/0	$-/-$	$+/+$	$-/-$	$+/-$

[a]Source: Stevens (1981, p. 576); used with permission of the author and the *American Sociological Review*.

[b]Parentheses indicate instances in which perspective does not explicitly predict an effect, but it seems plausible that one might exist.

most appealing. Mean upward mobility is predicted to have a *positive* effect on fertility because additional economic resources provided by mean mobility let an individual indulge his tastes for children. Relative upward mobility is predicted to have a *negative* effect on fertility because a person's socioeconomic aspirations reduce family size through the allocation of economic resources rather than family building.

Stevens finds each type of *total* mobility shows only a modest relationship to family size. However, when total mobility is partitioned, the relative and mean mobility effects for all three types of mobility are strong, significant, and opposite in sign. The effects are strongest for intergenerational mobility from father's occupation to respondent's first occupation. When the probabilities of being childless and of having three or more children are used as the dependent variables, the same patterns are observed. Hence, Stevens concludes that partitioning total mobility is valuable for describing the relationship between social mobility and fertility.

Counter to her predictions, however, Stevens finds mean mobility *negatively* related and relative mobility *positively* related to completed family size. Stevens provides an ad hoc explanation for these unexpected findings. She uses the relative economic status perspective to explain the positive effects of relative mobility on fertility:

Relative mobility taps the contrast between the husband's observed destination and the mean destination of others sharing certain background characteristics. The positive relationship between relative mobility and family size thus implies that if the comparison between the husband's socioeconomic achievement and the mean achievements of his socioeconomic origin group (i.e., those he "started out with") is a favorable one, then those couples are less hampered by economic considerations in their family building. . . . Added or extra economic resources enable [couples] to indulge more fully [their] tastes for children (Stevens, 1981, pp. 582–583).

This finding and the explanation for it are the same as those Bean and Swicegood presented with regard to unintended births.[2]

Stevens has a more difficult time accounting for the negative effect of mean mobility on completed family size:

However, it has been suggested that upward mobility is associated with "over-conformity" to the attitudes and behaviors found in the class of destination. . . . On the whole, the respondents in this sample benefited from the socioeconomic upgrading of the labor force between the time of their father's generation and their own. . . . There is also a negative relationship between fertility and socioeconomic status. Perhaps the respondents adopted the attitudes and behaviors of their destination classes more than would be expected given the dual socialization hypothesis. . . . Alternatively, since contraceptive use varies directly with socioeconomic status . . . the dampening effect of mean mobility on family size could also be a function of the general upward movement into socioeconomic environments in which family planning is more widely known and practiced, allowing couples to limit the number of unintended births (Stevens, 1981, p. 582).

Regardless that Stevens' findings are exactly opposite from her predictions and that she is therefore forced to posit ad hoc explanations for her results, her work stands out as a further attempt to identify the exact nature of the mobility–fertility relationship. Mobility is a function of both changes in social structure and individual ability, and it is important for the advancement of mobility–fertility research to know whether and exactly how this dual nature of mobility differentially affects reproductive behavior.

[2]The social mobility–fertility hypothesis and the relative economic status hypothesis have two distinct origins. We have traced the beginning of interest in the mobility–fertility relationship in Chapter 2. Interest in the relationship between relative economic status and reproductive behavior comes from Easterlin's (1969, 1973, 1975, 1978) macrolevel examination of fertility trends and economic conditions. Several studies (see, e.g., Bernhardt, 1972; D. S. Freedman, 1963; MacDonald and Rindfuss, 1978; Olneck and Wolfe, 1978; Thornton, 1978b; Westoff and Ryder, 1977) are devoted exclusively to testing Easterlin's relative economic status hypothesis at the microlevel of analysis. We do not consider this body of literature in this book; instead, as with Bean and Swicegood's and Stevens' research, we discuss the relative economic status hypothesis only when it has been used as a perspective by which to account for a relationship between social mobility and fertility. The relative economic status research has produced results that are as inconsistent as findings in the mobility–fertility literature. Consistent with the findings of Bean and Swicegood and Stevens, some researchers have found relative economic status positively related to family size. Others have found a negative relationship, no relationship, or a conditional relationship between the two variables. For a quick summary, see Stevens (1981, p. 575).

3 Recent Studies Not Following Blau and Duncan's Approach

Following the third and final round of the Princeton Fertility Study, Featherman (1970) used the data for the entire follow-up period (1957–1967) to reexamine the hypothesis that social mobility is inversely related to family size.[3] Featherman first considered the relationship between the subjective dimension of mobility and fertility by constructing three indexes to measure the desire to be socially mobile. He hypothesized that each index would relate positively to actual achievement but negatively to fertility over the study period. He found, however, that while the indexes were highly correlated with achievement, they were uncorrelated with the number of additional live births couples had between 1957 and 1967.

Turning to the objective dimension of mobility, Featherman assessed the degree to which additional live births during the follow-up period were instrumental in influencing occupational and economic (income) status achieved by the husbands at the second and third interviews. He found cumulative fertility between panel I (1957) and panel III (1963–1967) had a small positive effect on occupation and economic status achieved at panel III after the effects of social background, education, and prior achieved status were controlled. Thus, children induced slightly higher levels of occupational and economic achievement for men who had the same backgrounds and were roughly at the same point in the life cycle. When the number of additional births between panels I and II (1960) and panels II and III were examined, Featherman found the net effect on achievement of additional births in each between-panel period at the terminal interview was very small but positive. He emphasized that the effects, although positive, were not significant. Like his predecessors, he concludes there is little support for a relationship between fertility and mobility in this highly restrictive and selective sample.

In her study of career mobility and fertility in the Philippines, Deming (1974), too, regards childbearing as the independent variable and mobility as the dependent variable. She argues that marriage and childbearing usually occur early in the husband's career and that rapid or high fertility during this time would be expected to be detrimental for subsequent occupational achievement. Similar to Tien (1961, 1965a) and Perrucci (1967), she further argues that by using completed family size as the measure of fertility, many studies have obscured the effects of differential patterns of family formation on mobility.

Deming tests two hypotheses: (1) delayed marriage and childbearing facilitate

---

[3]Earlier investigations of the mobility–fertility relationship using data from the Princeton Fertility Study are discussed in Chapter 2. The third and final contact with couples in the study was made between 1963 and 1967, approximately 10 years after initial contact. By then, the women were at least 36.5 years old and had been married approximately 11 years. For the study of social mobility, only couples who did not intend to have more children were used.

upward mobility by freeing resources that improve chances for occupational achievement; and (2) recognizing that migration might lead to occupational achievement, "delayed marriage and delayed childbearing facilitate geographic mobility which, in turn, increases opportunities for occupational mobility" (1974, p. 155). To test these hypotheses, she used 1968 data from the urban part of the National Demographic Survey of the Philippines. The sample was limited to currently married, once-married women who in 1960 were halfway through their reproductive years (aged 25–34).

Deming constructed five measures of women's childbearing status as of January 1961 to test the first hypothesis. Two measures related to timing of births, two to number of births, and one was a composite of the other four indicators. She measured socioeconomic status by computing interval level scales based on husband's occupation, education, and income in 1960 and 1968. After controlling for a number of background variables, she found little support for the hypothesized relationship. Path coefficients between early childbearing and occupational achievement in 1968 showed the predicted negative effect of early family formation on 1968 occupation, net of 1960 occupation; however, the magnitude of each of the coefficients was quite small. Measures reflecting number of births were more important than those reflecting timing.

Deming considered the possibility that births from 1961 to 1968 served as an intervening variable which modified the direct effect of early childbearing on 1968 occupational achievement. In testing the model, she found the intervening variable did not influence the direct effect of early childbearing on the 1968 status and did not explain any additional variance in occupational achievement. She concluded that while childbearing, however measured, has only a small effect on achievement, the effect is because of early family formation before mobility takes place; early childbearing is the more important fertility component affecting occupational mobility.

Testing the second hypothesis by analyzing a model where migration was included as an intervening variable between previous occupational status and childbearing and subsequent achievement, Deming found the path coefficients were in the expected direction. Longer delay to first birth and fewer early births facilitated migration, and migration affected status achieved in 1968 positively. However, none of the coefficients was large or statistically significant. Did the effect of early childbearing on subsequent occupational achievement differ by migration status? Deming divided the sample into migrants and nonmigrants and performed separate tests of her first hypothesis on each group. The coefficients for childbearing among migrants were negative and fairly large, indicating that early family formation had debilitating consequences for subsequent occupational achievement. Results for nonmigrants were the same as for the total sample.

In summary, like Featherman, Deming finds little evidence that fertility significantly affects mobility. For the total sample, early childbearing has only a minimal negative effect on subsequent status achievement. Only for migrants does delayed childbearing substantially affect occupational advancement. This finding accords well with those of earlier works (see, e.g., Blau and Duncan, 1967; Goldberg, 1959) which also suggest that the sphere of applicability of the mobility–fertility relationship is limited.

Hargens *et al.* (1978) define mobility in terms of career success, as measured by job performance, and present the assumptions on which the prediction of a negative effect of fertility on occupational attainment rests:

1. People with few children devote fewer resources such as time, energy, and money to their families
2. Such individuals can invest some of the surplus resources in occupations, leading to better job performance
3. This performance leads in turn to occupational success (Hargens *et al.*, 1978, p. 155).

The researchers find these assumptions highly problematic when applied to the general population. First, most prior studies focused on men's mobility and it may be unreasonable to assume that additional children require men to spend more time and energy on their families. Second, even if men (or women) with small families do have more time and energy, they may not be able to use these assets toward occupational attainment because most people work fixed hours and under the direction of others. Third, regardless of how much individuals may strive to advance, they are limited by their education and talent. Finally, even if investments of time and energy lead to higher performance, performance hardly perfectly predicts career success.

Nevertheless, the assumptions above and the consequent prediction of a negative relationship between fertility and occupational attainment may be valid for a few selected occupational groups in which children are clearly not economic assets and where increases in time and energy afforded by a smaller family size can be directly invested into job performance. One such group is Ph.D chemists whose work setting encourages scientific productivity and provides considerable flexibility in allocating time and energy for doing research.

Hargens and colleagues thus test the hypothesis that, for a sample of married male and female chemists who hold positions in universities and federal or state government research laboratories, marital fertility will inhibit job performance. Job performance is measured by the number of research articles each chemist published during a given period and by the number of times a chemist's work was cited by other researchers. Fertility is measured by a dichotomy indicating whether the chemist is childless. Results indicate that, controlling for other factors affecting job performance, chemists who have children produce an average of about one and one-half fewer research articles than childless chemists. Contrary to what might be expected on the basis of differential child-care responsibilities between the sexes, the effect of childlessness on research productivity does not differ significantly between male and female chemists.

Hargens and colleagues summarize their findings as follows:

> The results . . . are consistent with the argument that when one examines an occupation in which workers control the allocation of their time and energy, and in which additional expenditures of these resources should enhance performance, marital fertility does have a negative impact on job performance and presumably, in turn, on occupational success (Hargens *et al.*, 1978, p. 159).

Zimmer (1979, 1981a) conducted the final study to be considered in our review. Zimmer's sample was 3098 once-married, currently married women in Aberdeen, Scotland, who gave birth to a child during 1950–1955. Pregnancy histories were collected through 1970 when over half the sample had reached the end of childbearing. Zimmer constructed five measures of social mobility: comparisons between (1) both spouses' fathers' occupations, (2) wife's father's occupation and husband's current occupation, (3) wife's premarital occupation and husband's current occupation, (4) husband's father's occupation and husband's current occupation, and (5) wife's father's occupation and her premarital occupation. The measures of inter- and intragenerational mobility were then related to various aspects of fertility behavior: (1) number of pregnancies, (2) number of children ever born, (3) timing of births from marriage or from first pregnancy, (4) spacing of pregnancies by pregnancy numbers, and (5) the fertility span.

Zimmer's reason for reexamining the mobility–fertility hypothesis using the Aberdeen data was to correct for the "serious methodological shortcomings" of past research. Specifically, Zimmer claims that the Indianapolis Study and Princeton Fertility Study do not adequately test the hypothesis because only the mean levels of fertility of the upwardly mobile, downwardly mobile, and nonmobile are compared. He blames these studies' inability to find much support for a relationship on the failure to disaggregate the nonmobile by status and the upwardly and downwardly mobile by both status of origin and destination. Zimmer argues that one must devise a table of mean levels of fertility by cross-classifying past and current status and comparing each cell mean of the mobile with that of the nonmobile at origin and destination.

While the researchers of the Indianapolis and Princeton studies for the most part used a manual–nonmanual classification scheme, we agree with Westoff's (1981) rebuttal to Zimmer's allegation; Westoff and his coinvestigators did exactly what Zimmer claimed needed to be done.[4] Moreover, all of the intermedi-

---

[4]In his rebuttal to Zimmer, Westoff also responds directly to Zimmer's contention by reexamining the Princeton Fertility Study data. Westoff conducts an analysis which as closely as possible con-

ate studies used this strategy. We further note that this approach does not allow one to separate out the independent effects of origin and destination. Hence, Zimmer's study, like the intermediate studies, does not distinguish between additive and interactive effects which researchers like Blau and Duncan, Boyd, Bean and Swicegood, and Stevens have regarded as appropriate for an analysis of mobility and fertility.

Nevertheless, Zimmer's research is noteworthy for its use of a number of dimensions of social mobility and reproductive behavior to investigate the relationship. Zimmer found the upwardly mobile have fewer children than the nonmobile at origin, and the downwardly mobile have larger families than the nonmobile at origin. Intermediate fertility levels for the upwardly and downwardly mobile compared to the nonmobile at origin and destination obtain regardless of the dimension of mobility considered. The average age of women at given pregnancies varies by mobility status, regardless of the mobility measure used. Upwardly mobile women are older at first pregnancy and downwardly mobile women are younger than the nonmobile at origin. Patterns are similar at subsequent pregnancies, but the size of the age differences are attenuated.

The upwardly mobile are less likely to have their first pregnancy prior to marriage than are the nonmobile at origin; the downwardly mobile are more likely to do so. For all types of mobility, the upwardly mobile delay their first pregnancy longer after marriage than the nonmobile at origin; the downwardly mobile have their first pregnancy sooner than the upwardly mobile or the nonmobile at origin. The same pattern holds for spacing of the first four pregnancies after marriage. The fertility span (length of time devoted to reproduction) also differs by mobility status; the upwardly mobile have a shorter span while the downwardly mobile have a longer span than their respective nonmobile groups at origin. Finally, the high-status nonmobile are the least likely to use sterilization to avoid pregnancy while the low status nonmobile are the most likely to do so. The upwardly mobile are less likely to be sterilized than the nonmobile at origin and the downwardly mobile are more likely than the nonmobile at origin.

Zimmer summarizes his findings by noting that regardless of the dimension of mobility or fertility investigated, the reproductive behavior of the upwardly mobile women is such that they have lower fertility than the nonmobile at origin or the downwardly mobile, while the downwardly mobile have consistently higher fertility than women from the same origin status who are either nonmobile or upwardly mobile. The reproductive behavior of the mobile lies between that of the nonmobile at origin and destination. Without regard to Blau and Duncan's

forms to that which Zimmer presents for the Aberdeen data. Based on this reanalysis Westoff reaffirms his earlier conclusion; he finds no evidence of a relationship between social mobility and fertility in the Princeton data.

argument as to what should be regarded as a mobility effect, Zimmer concludes that social mobility has a very large effect on fertility, and states:

> Our data have consistently shown that the fertility behavior of any status group results from the additive impact of the combination of statuses associated with the given status group. There is a marked tendency for mobile women, regardless of the direction of movements, to adopt the fertility pattern of the status group into which they move through marriage but the impact of status level on origin is only partially overcome (Zimmer, 1979, p. 190).

Zimmer maintains that even though low status of origin will continue to affect fertility, improvements in status will, in a single generation, result in lower fertility. Provided there is an inverse relationship between socioeconomic status and fertility in a given population, couples who rise in status will partially adopt the lower fertility patterns of the high-status groups; if more upward than downward mobility occurs, the fertility level of the population will decrease. We emphasize, however, that this need not be interpreted as an effect of an individual's upward mobility on reproductive behavior.

4 Summary of the Contemporary Studies

Having reviewed the recent studies,[5] we now consider the contributions they have made to the investigation of the mobility–fertility relationship. Many of these works have distinguished between the effects of the *process* of social mobility on fertility and that of the *additive combination* of classes of origin and destination on reproductive behavior. This distinction brings out various theoretical perspectives and as such has enlarged the body of theory underlying the mobility–fertility relationship. Many recent studies further support the notion that the mobility–fertility association may be limited in its sphere of applicability; the relationship may not be expected to obtain in all cultures, under all social conditions, or, when mobility is defined in terms of career success, for all occupational groups. Distance moved has been introduced as a factor to be accounted for when examining the relationship. In contrast to the intermediate studies which for the most part assumed that mobility affects fertility, the recent works have made it clear that the direction of causality is in question. The suggestion that reproductive behavior be defined not only in terms of completed family size but also in terms of such components as early and later childbearing or intended and unintended births has been proposed, as has the suggestion that total mobility be partitioned into its mean and relative components. Additional emphasis has been given to the need for examining the relationship between the

---

[5]Additional studies pertaining to the methodology needed to examine the mobility–fertility relationship are discussed in Chapter 5.

subjective dimension of mobility and fertility. And, variables such as migration have been proposed as factors mediating the mobility–fertility relationship.

All of these comments, suggestions, or attempts may be regarded as contributions to the advancement of our knowledge of the existence and nature of a relationship between social mobility and fertility. At the same time, they are indicative of a hodge-podge of empirical works, each approaching the problem from a different perspective and arriving at different conclusions. In the next chapter we synthesize these seemingly contradictory research findings and theories to develop a more coherent body of theory on the social mobility–fertility relationship.

Chapter 4 | The Social Mobility–Fertility Hypothesis Reconsidered: Synthesis and Theoretical Elaboration

The preceding two chapters detailed previous research on the mobility–fertility relationship and traced the development of ideas about this association. In this chapter, we provide a synthesis and extension of existing research and theory. We need a more accurate account of why one would expect a relationship between social mobility and reproductive behavior and a more careful delineation of the causal mechanism through which the association operates.

1 Four Possible Causal Links

We have seen that demographers far from agree about the existence or nature of the relationship between social mobility and reproductive behavior. The accumulated evidence has been inconclusive, if not negative. Indeed, we detect a feeling of exasperation on the part of Blau and Duncan when they comment:

> It is the plausibility of the hypothesis rather than the quality of any supporting evidence that seems to account for its continuing appeal. Although no set of negative results can be definitive—because a different outcome might follow from studies in different populations or with alternative measures of mobility—it appears that at some point the burden of proof may fairly be shifted to the proponents of the hypothesis (Blau and Duncan, 1967, p. 371).

Following the typology Weller (1977) used to discuss the association between female labor force participation and fertility, we posit four possible causal links between social mobility and fertility:

1. The observed relationship is spurious
2. Fertility affects social mobility
3. Social mobility affects fertility
4. Both fertility and social mobility affect each other.

The sections that follow are organized around these propositions.

The Observed Relationship Is Spurious

A relationship between social mobility and fertility can be spuriously produced in two ways. A researcher may fail to consider that childbearing and social mobility are determined by a common antecedent variable. For example, education may determine to what degree a couple is socially mobile, and it may also affect their fertility. An observed association between mobility and fertility might then result from failure to control for education. Most researchers have expressed little concern for this possibility. Because of their methods of analysis, they have been unable to control for (or at least properly control for) a number of background variables that could potentially affect the mobility–fertility relationship. We return to this point in the next chapter.

The relationship also can be spuriously produced in terms of what is to be regarded as a mobility effect. Considerable attention has been given to this question since Duncan first raised it in 1966:

> The gist of the argument is that one is not entitled to discuss "effects" of mobility . . . until he has established that the apparent effect cannot be due merely to a simple combination of effects of the variables used to define mobility (Duncan, 1966, p. 91).

According to this point of view, mobility is more than the sum of the independent effects of status of origin and destination. There must be a significant interaction effect of class of origin and destination on fertility before a "true" mobility effect obtains. It must be established that the process of mobility exerts an effect on fertility above that explained by past and present social class. No claim that a mobility effect exists can be made until one finds that the additive model of origin and destination effects does not adequately fit the data.

If one adopts this definition, then, since none of the studies before Duncan's (1966) controlled for the independent effects of past and current status, the majority of the research previously reviewed represents an inadequate test for a mobility–fertility relationship. The observed relationship between the two variables could be spurious because of failure to define a "mobility" variable accurately. Most of the intermediate studies researchers who claimed to have found a relationship indicated that fertility of the upwardly and downwardly mobile lay intermediate between class of origin and destination. While these studies do not represent rigorous tests that the additive model adequately fits the data, intermediate fertility on the part of mobile couples suggests that this is the case. Hence, these studies indicate that the relationship may indeed be spurious.

More recent attempts to find a true mobility–fertility relationship have also been less than successful. Except for the study by Stevens (1981) and to some extent that by Bean and Swicegood (1979), the "acculturation" hypothesis generally finds support. The mobile are not well integrated into either social class. They have insufficient opportunity for complete acculturation to the values and styles of life of the destination class; neither do they continue to experience the full impact of the lifestyle of their origin. The mobile behave as if they are influenced by the childbearing pattern of the class from which they came and by that of the one they enter; however, the *process* of mobility does not affect their reproductive behavior. Observed differences in mean fertility levels between the mobile and nonmobile are regarded as spurious, caused by the independent effects of past and current status.

Fertility Affects Social Mobility

Despite the inconclusive findings to date, there are reasons to suspect a relationship between the process of mobility and reproductive behavior. One such theoretical perspective posits that fertility affects social mobility. We adopt Bean and Swicegood's (1979) term and refer to it as the *selectivity* perspective. This perspective has its roots in Dumont's (1890) contention that a family must be small in order to rise on the social scale. Early commentators stressed the biological aspects of the relationship, the social promotion of the relatively infertile. There is self-selection of subfecund and involuntarily sterile individuals or couples into the upwardly mobile stream. Why this is so, and how fecundity or infecundity affects downward mobility is left unanswered.

More recently, the strictly biological component of the relationship has been deemphasized and the effect of family size, whether involuntary or voluntary, on social mobility has been stressed. For example, Berent (1952) simply states that persons are able to rise in status because of smallness of families and others are constrained to move down under the burden of large families. Children require resource expenditure (time, money, effort), and couples with high fertility may therefore find it difficult to maintain their social position; couples with low fertility may find it easier to achieve social gains because they have excess resources to use to improve their chances for status achievement.

This explanation, either explicitly or implicitly, guided the work of Featherman (1970), Deming (1974), Hargens *et al.* (1978), and Bean and Swicegood (1979). However, little support for the selectivity hypothesis has been found. Bean and Swicegood find no support for it,[1] and Deming finds early childbearing has debilitating consequences for subsequent occupational achievement only for migrants. Hargens and colleagues find support for the hypothesis, but their sample is limited to one very specific occupational group. Indeed, the purpose of their research is to "discover" an occupational group where the hypothesis may

---

[1]Bean and Swicegood posit the selectivity perspective as one of five alternative theoretical perspectives to investigate in their study of intergenerational mobility and fertility. However, in their regression analyses fertility is always treated as the dependent variable, mobility as the independent. With regard to the selectivity perspective, their models are therefore misspecified, and we contend they do not adequately test this hypothesis.

be applicable. Featherman finds cumulative fertility between 1957 and 1963–1967 has a small, nonsignificant, but *positive* effect on occupational and economic status achieved by 1963–1967. Thus, children induce slightly *higher* levels of status achievement. This accords well with Riemer and Kiser's (1954) suggestion that family responsibilities may stimulate the energy and ambition of some so that they achieve more than those without the handicaps of a family.[2]

Social Mobility Affects Fertility

The vast amount of previous research has been concerned with the effect of social mobility on fertility. Why should the process of mobility affect reproductive behavior? As Bean and Swicegood (1979) astutely observe, four theoretical perspectives are evidenced in the literature: social isolation, stress and disorientation, status enhancement, and relative economic status. Each posits that social mobility accounts for additional variance in fertility above that which is associated with the independent effects of origin and destination status. Each makes a different prediction about fertility of the mobile compared to fertility of the nonmobile.

Social Isolation

The social isolation perspective comes mainly from Blau and Duncan (1967) and predicts that both the upwardly and downwardly mobile will have higher fertility than the nonmobile. The process of mobility is viewed as having socially disintegrative aspects; it disrupts established social relationships and forces people into new, potentially alienating environments. The mobile individual or couple is poorly integrated into the new social class and receives little social support from the former class. Lack of firm social support creates insecurity, causing the mobile couple to assume an extreme position of behavior.

---

[2]A few researchers, taking what we earlier called the "static approach" of analyzing the fertility–socioeconomic status relationship (analyzing fertility differentials according to an individual's status at one point), have also reversed the traditional causal order. Rather than examining the effect of status on fertility, they have investigated the impact of reproductive behavior on a couple's current socioeconomic standing. Using a sample of women in the Detroit metropolitan area who had a first, second, or fourth birth in 1961, Freedman and Coombs (1966a,b) found that the more rapid the timing of births the lower the couple's income and the fewer their financial assets at the time of the study in 1965. Similarly, Polgar and Hiday (1974) found the economic condition of families living in poverty areas of New York City in 1965 adversely affected by an additional live birth within a period as short as 2 years. Controlling for parity and comparing families with one or two additional births with families having no additional births, they found the former have significantly lower subsequent levels of current income, ownership of bank accounts and insurance, and general planning and organization of household activities. Couples having an additional birth(s) were also more likely to receive public assistance.

One behavior extreme is increased fertility. Mobile couples compensate for previously lost social ties with unusually large families. How do large families compensate for lost social ties? The literature is unclear but we suggest two ways. Stuckert (1963) finds socially mobile couples less likely to be oriented toward their extended families and to participate in voluntary associations than nonmobile couples. Perhaps, then, couples see having a large number of children as a means to gain additional persons with whom they may interact. Second, having many children may be regarded as a way for the couple to increase interaction with the community or social class they have entered. The more children there are, the greater the opportunity for couples to be involved in school activities, scouting, communication with neighbors, and so on. Presumably, this is what Boyd (1973) has in mind when she comments that social insecurity might augment fertility as a means for couples to gain reintegration.

Stress and Disorientation

The other extreme position mobile couples may assume because of lost social support and subsequent feelings of insecurity is decreased fertility. The stress and disorientation perspective predicts that both upwardly and downwardly mobile couples will have lower fertility than the nonmobile. According to Blau (1956) insecure feelings inhibit fertility because of physical and emotional stress. While not adequately discussed in the literature, stress may inhibit fertility in several ways. Stress may impair the biological capacity to reproduce (affect fecundity). Alternatively, it may affect a couple's desire for children. Physical and emotional stress may precipitate a feeling of anomie; a couple may not desire to bring children into a world which they perceive to be normless or chaotic.

Lost social ties, such as lack of extended family relations, might also lead to lower fertility of mobile couples because of the reduced availability of child care. The couple may feel that they have no one to rely on when the burden of a large number of children becomes too heavy to bear. Hence, they may elect to use contraception or use it more effectively. We should qualify this remark, however, by noting that Bean and Aiken (1976) found strain and disorientation contributing to greater contraceptive failure.

Status Enhancement[3]

This perspective is by far the most often used to account for an effect of social mobility on fertility. It is either implicitly or explicitly used in all the intermediate studies and finds greatest expression in the Indianapolis Study (Kantner and

[3]The term *status enhancement* as used here represents the name given to one of the four theoretical perspectives to account for effects of social mobility on fertility. Our discussion of the concept in this section should not be confused with our later treatment of female status enchancement, where the concept is construed in far broader terms (see Chapter 6).

Kiser, 1954; Riemer and Kiser, 1954) and Princeton Fertility Study (Westoff *et al.*, 1961, 1963). In general, the perspective posits that childbearing and social mobility are inimical to one another. Certain subtleties to the perspective merit discussion.

The term, *status enhancement,* implies a distinction between those who rise in status (the upwardly mobile) and those who do not (the nonmobile) but says nothing about those who lose status (the downwardly mobile). Indeed, discussion of this perspective has most often compared the upwardly mobile and nonmobile. Westoff (1953), in his seminal study, points out that the disposition to be mobile leads to voluntary limitation of childbearing because of a high degree of rationality on the part of the upwardly mobile—a success orientation, and all that it implies. The desire to improve one's status is an important motive for restricting family size since rearing children absorbs resources and effort which could otherwise be used to rise on the social scale (Espenshade, 1980; Hofferth, 1984; Mincer and Ofek, 1982). Hence, *upward* mobility is predicted to affect fertility negatively because reduced childbearing permits savings or gains in resources to be devoted to attaining higher social positions.

The status enhancement perspective is also framed more in terms of the subjective dimension of mobility than the objective dimension. The argument is that the process of becoming upwardly mobile is a less important cause of lower fertility than the aspiration, perceived opportunity, and motivation to be upwardly mobile. Note the phrases "disposition to be mobile" and "desire to improve one's status" in the preceding paragraph. Note also the working hypothesis of the Princeton Fertility Study, "the socioeconomic and psychological requirements for upward mobility are inconsistent with expenditures of time, energy, and money for children" (Westoff *et al.*, 1961, p. 237), and Perrucci's argument that

> if a socially mobile person does order his life in a manner which serves to enhance his mobility potential, he should be more likely to defer marriage as long as possible after college, to have fewer children, and to have children at more widely separated intervals (Perrucci, 1967, p. 617).

Westoff (1953) states that mobility aspiration is probably the more important factor influencing decisions about family size, while the actual degree of subsequent mobility is at least partially attributable to conditions resulting from these decisions.

That the status enhancement perspective stresses the subjective rather than objective dimension of mobility has important implications for the predicted effect of downward mobility on fertility. Boyd (1971), Bean and Swicegood (1979), and Stevens (1981) maintain that given this perspective, one would predict lower fertility for the downwardly mobile than the nonmobile because the former try to regain lost social position or halt their social demise. This reasoning is not consistent with the perspective's emphasis on mobility aspirations. No one aspires to be downwardly mobile, but those who are probably did not aspire or were not motivated to increase or maintain their former status. Not caring if they lose status, the downwardly mobile are likely to have higher fertility than the nonmobile; they choose to invest their resources in children rather than in activities that will enhance or maintain their prior social status. Thus, we argue that the status enhancement perspective is more in line with a prediction that the downwardly mobile will have *higher* fertility than the nonmobile rather than *lower* fertility.

Relative Economic Status

The final theoretical perspective to account for an effect of social mobility on fertility comes from the work of Easterlin (1969, 1973, 1975, 1978, 1980). Most of Easterlin's work is at the macrolevel, where he attempts to explain fluctuations in United States period fertility rates by formulating a hypothesis that uses the concept of relative economic status, perceived permanent income relative to tastes. *Tastes* are defined as consumption preferences formed while the individual was in the parental household. He hypothesizes that the baby boom was caused by increases in relative economic status for couples in the reproductive ages, while the subsequent decline in United States fertility was caused by decreases in relative economic status.

The hypothesis can be directly applied to microdata such that high relative economic status is predicted to increase a couple's fertility and low relative economic status to decrease it. That is, if perceived permanent income is high relative to tastes for consumer goods formed in the parental household, high fertility is expected. If permanent income is low relative to tastes, low fertility is expected. Easterlin argues that relative economic status will have its greatest effect on age at marriage and the pace of early marital fertility. When the comparison between income and tastes is unfavorable, marriage and family building are delayed; when it is favorable, marriage and family building occur relatively early. To the extent that relative economic status affects age at marriage and the pace of childbearing, it indirectly affects completed fertility (MacDonald and Rindfuss, 1978).

Assuming that the upwardly and downwardly mobile have respectively higher and lower relative economic status than the nonmobile, this perspective predicts, respectively, higher and lower fertility for the mobile (Bean and Swicegood, 1979). The Easterlin hypothesis is one of a family of relative income hypotheses which differ on the reference point for tastes. Thus, there seems to be little problem in treating intergenerational mobility as current status relative to tastes formed in the parental household, and treating career mobility as current status relative to tastes existing at marriage or first job.

The formulation of this perspective is relatively new in the social mobility literature. Bean and Swicegood (1979) are the first to offer it as an alternative hypothesis. However, the relative economic status perspective has its roots in the general concept of relative deprivation, appearing earlier in Riemer and Kiser's (1954) work. These researchers attempted to tap the subjective dimension of mobility by introducing the concept of "economic tension," the difference between actual and desired standard of living. Boyd's (1973) comment that upward mobility may increase family size because couples may choose to invest social gains in more children also indicates the potential applicability of the concept of relative economic status to mobility–fertility research.

Summary of the Alternative Theoretical Perspectives

Each perspective makes a different prediction about fertility:[4]

	Upmobile	Nonmobile	Downmobile
Social isolation	+	0	+
Stress and disorientation	−	0	−
Status enhancement	−	0	+
Relative economic status	+	0	−

Thus, the social isolation perspective predicts that the mobile will have higher fertility than the nonmobile, while the stress and disorientation perspective predicts the reverse. For these two perspectives no prediction is made for fertility differences between the upwardly and downwardly mobile themselves. Status enhancement predicts that the upwardly and downwardly mobile will have, respectively, lower and higher fertility than the nonmobile, while relative economic status predicts the reverse.

In the next chapter we argue that there is a hierarchy of mobility models: a difference in fertility between the mobile and nonmobile, according to direction moved and distance moved. The social isolation and stress and disorientation perspectives suggest a simple mobile/nonmobile contrast is sufficient to describe the effect of mobility on fertility.[5] The status enhancement and relative economic

---

[4]Unlike Stevens (see Table 1 in Chapter 3), we do not disaggregate these predictions according to type of mobility. From Stevens' table, except for status enhancement, each perspective makes the same prediction for mean mobility as for relative mobility. Stevens maintains that the status enhancement perspective is only relevant for relative (individual) mobility. This notion is completely consistent with our argument that the perspective places greater emphasis on subjective rather than objective mobility. We have disagreed with Stevens' contention that status enhancement predicts that the downwardly mobile will have *lower* fertility than the nonmobile.

[5]However, even with these two perspectives, direction moved might need to be considered. For example, in the case of social isolation both mobile groups may have higher fertility than the nonmobile, but the higher fertility of the upwardly mobile may be significantly greater than that of the downwardly mobile.

status perspectives suggest that direction moved must be considered to describe the effect adequately. Implicit in our diagram is the possibility that distance moved needs to be considered. Each + (or −) may be interpreted to mean that the greater the *amount* of social mobility, the higher (or lower) the couple's fertility.

Fertility and Social Mobility Affect Each Other

Many investigators of the social mobility–fertility relationship (see, e.g., Berent, 1952; Boyd, 1971, 1973; Riemer and Kiser, 1954) have recognized some degree of mutual causation between the two variables. Those who have emphasized social mobility's effect on fertility have not ruled out the possibility that the latter might in turn affect the former. Likewise, researchers who have emphasized fertility's effect on social mobility have not dismissed the idea that mobility may affect fertility.

Rather than argue which causal interpretation of social mobility and fertility is correct, it seems more reasonable to acknowledge that both are correct. That there is a degree of reciprocal causation between the two variables stems from both being processes which take time to complete and which can intercept each other in complex ways. Considerable evidence suggests that attitudes and decisions about childbearing change during a couple's reproductive life cycle and depend on the particular economic and noneconomic circumstances at the time they are made.[6] At any given time a couple may aspire to or be preparing for a change in status, and the childbearing decision may reflect this aspiration or preparation. Alternatively, a couple's decision to have a child may reflect having recently changed statuses and the social isolation or perceived gains or losses resulting from the change.

Riemer and Kiser discuss the dynamic aspect of family size decision making:

> Basic attitudes toward prestige, money, and children are probably fairly stable, but a family is built up through a series of more or less deliberate decisions in which long and short term goals and needs must be balanced. Not only basic attitudes or goal orientation enters into the decision to have a child or not to have a child at any particular time, but also considerations of the immediate economic situation and the couple's outlook for the future, and those are notoriously affected by fluctuations in the community economy as well as by the realization or disappointment of personal experiences. Experiences with each successive childbirth and the number of years remaining for postponement of desired births are also variable factors in the continual reassessment of how many children there will be and how they will be spaced (Riemer and Kiser, 1954, pp. 213–214).

---

[6]For examples of this line of argument and evidence to support it, see Bumpass and Westoff (1970), Freedman *et al.*, (1965), Hout (1976), Namboodiri (1974), and Simon (1975).

It is reasonable to assume that attitudes, perceived opportunities, and decisions about a change in status may alter over time; these decisions depend on the particular family-size circumstances at the moment they are made. At any given time, a couple may decide to have a child or experience a birth, and because of this decision or experience the moment may or may not be ideal for a change in status. In some cases, the decision about childbirth may leave the couple with no alternative but to change status.

Namboodiri suggests that the mobility–fertility relationship be viewed as a sequential process:

> The probability of a change in parity is influenced by the family's current situational circumstances and the sequence of changes therein up to the point of time in question, and a change, in turn, is considered as affecting the family's chances of changing its situational characteristics (Namboodiri, 1972b, p. 470).

Even this view, however, is a simplification of the complex relationship, for it fails to consider the aspirations or decisions about either childbearing or mobility which may occur before, during, or after either event. At any time in a couple's reproductive life cycle, the decision or actual experience of fertility or social mobility may influence the decision or experience of the other variable. Both past mobility aspirations and decisions and past fertility preferences and decisions can affect subsequent mobility and timing and number of children. These subsequent aspirations and preferences may also be reciprocally related. In short, mobility and fertility are cumulative processes which constantly and perpetually act and react on one another.

2 The Direction of Causality Problem

Recognizing reciprocal causation and being able to deal with it are two entirely different matters. Many mobility–fertility researchers have ended their studies with suggestions for future research; most call for a temporal analysis of the relationship using longitudinal data. Among the earliest advocates, Riemer and Kiser state,

> Consideration of the time sequence—the time at which shifts in socio-economic status occur, the stage of career at which marriage takes place, the timing of births within marriage in relation to status changes—is necessary in order to assess the significance of fertility as a selective factor in upward and downward mobility, and conversely, to assess the degree to which fertility reflects the socio-economic status of childhood and youth, acculturation to a new status, or the severity of the struggle to improve or maintain status at various stages of marital life (Riemer and Kiser, 1954, p. 212).

Similarly, Boyd's ideal would be a temporal study using birth intervals as indicators of reproductive behavior and assessing aspirations and occupational status at each pregnancy and decisions about family size made before or after each pregnancy (Boyd, 1973, pp. 14–15). Boyd calls for a data set which to our knowledge has never been and perhaps never can be collected. Not only should complete information about the objective dimensions of fertility and mobility be gathered, but also reliable data on the subjective dimensions of reproductive behavior and mobility for each important moment of a couple's lifetime.

Lacking highly detailed longitudinal or cross-sectional data containing complete histories of the two variables of interest, researchers have recently resorted to using various methodological techniques designed to evaluate direction of causality. Empirical testing of the reciprocity of a relationship is most pronounced in female labor force participation–fertility research. Waite and Stolzenberg (1976) and Smith-Lovin and Tickamyer (1978) use two-stage least-squares analysis to demonstrate the simultaneous effects of labor force participation on fertility and vice versa and to gain insight into which is the dominant causal path. This technique has yet to be applied to the mobility–fertility association. Moreover, Cramer (1980) provides evidence that it may not be the solution to the bidirectionality problem, even if it were.

A related problem is that most examinations of the mobility–fertility association have used extant data sets designed and collected for other purposes. As such, the data have been inadequate for testing many hypotheses addressing the relationship between mobility and reproductive behavior, including causal direction. For instance, cross-sectional data without complete pregnancy and status-change histories of respondents have forced many researchers to use number of live births as a measure of fertility and occupations of spouses and their relatives at a few points in time as indexes of social mobility.

Hence, one drawback of most studies is that they have been static analyses of two dynamic processes. Social mobility can take a long or short time to be completed; it can be completed with or without interruptions, and possibly never completed. Children ever born is a fairly insensitive index of the process of reproductive behavior. It is a cumulative measure of fertility that refers to past as well as current behavior. Children usually come one at a time, over short or long intervals. Many studies have suffered to the extent that number of live births does not reflect birth timing, perhaps the more important component of a mobility–fertility relationship. Tien (1961), Natsis (1966), Perrucci (1967), and Deming (1974) argue that a relationship is most likely to obtain between mobility and the *pattern* of family building.

In sum, most studies have been unable to address the issue of causality even in its most rudimentary form because the data have been cross-sectional, lacking complete pregnancy and work histories. Use of the Blau and Duncan approach to analyze the mobility–fertility relationship precludes a straightforward application of two-stage least-squares analysis to evaluate causal direction because of how mobility is defined. Mobility is considered the interaction effect independent of the main effects of origin and destination statuses. As such, mobility does not easily lend itself to being treated as a dependent variable, required in analyzing nonrecursive models.

If future investigators wish directly to address the issue of direction of causality, they must follow Riemer and Kiser's advice and conduct their analysis using longitudinal data. This will probably require a major research effort designed exclusively for studying the mobility–fertility association. Without such a study, future researchers may have to assume the causal direction of the relationship. Assuming mobility is the independent and fertility the dependent variable is consistent with the vast majority of previous research and, from a demographer's perspective, perhaps the most interesting causal direction to evaluate. However, that mobility may occur subsequent to most or all of a couple's childbearing is a possibility, and to this extent models will be misspecified. These models are *strictly* applicable only on the assumption that mobility occurs before starting a family. That some theoretical perspectives used to account for an effect of mobility on fertility emphasize the aspirational or perceptual dimension of change in status may, however, ameliorate the implied direction of causality. Overall, the results of models specifying that mobility affects fertility should be interpreted with caution and the awareness that they might reflect the impact of fertility on mobility.

3   The Concept and Dimensions of Social Mobility

We have yet to provide a formal definition of the term *social mobility*. Barber's conceptualization is among the most straightforward:

> We have been using the term social mobility to mean movement, either upward or downward, between higher and lower social classes; or more precisely, movement between one relatively full-time, functionally significant social role and another that is evaluated as either higher or lower (Barber, 1957, p. 356).

Demographers and sociologists agree that Barber adequately represents the most general meaning of the term. More problematic, however, are the meanings or operational definitions of two concepts in the above definition—*social class* and *movement*.

How one best measures a person's social class is an issue scholars have long debated. Both theoretical and empirical reasoning have been applied in trying to resolve this debate.[7] We will not dwell on this issue. Instead, we merely point

---

[7]For a sample of the literature relevant to the question of how one operationalizes the concepts of social class and social mobility, and particularly whether occupation is an adequate measure, the interested reader is referred to Bibby (1975), Breiger (1981), Duncan (1968), Featherman and Hauser (1973), Featherman *et al.* (1974, 1975), Goodman (1969), Haer (1957), Hatt (1950), Hazelrigg

out that mobility–fertility research has defined an individual's or couple's position in terms of income, education, or occupation. As our literature review shows, occupation has most often been treated as an adequate single index of social class, and indexes of social mobility have been developed by comparing persons' changes in occupational position.

Use of occupation to measure social position is best justified on its practicality:

> The most practical procedure is to use a single measurement (rather than a complex index), and one that is simple and can be supplied by the son concerning both himself and his father. Furthermore, it should have relatively stable meaning from one generation to the next (and preferably, one country to another). Almost all researchers have used occupation . . . (Kahl, 1957, p. 252).

Aside from practicality, many researchers subscribe to Robert Hauser's opinion:

> Occupational mobility is a fundamental indicator of the temporal aspect of social stratification. . . . The centrality of occupational roles in the organization of contemporary and especially industrial societies is coupled with strong commonalities across time and space in the differential access of occupational incumbents to social (including economic and political) rewards. . . . In this way occupational incumbency may be viewed as a proxy or index of social standing and occupational mobility as an index of . . . social mobility.
>
>   . . . There is substantial consensus that measurements of occupational mobility across or within generations may provide insights into the openness or rigidity of a society and the interactions of that openness or rigidity with demographic metabolism and social organization. That is, a mobility regime consists of a set of rules or processes governing access to social positions which is articulated with the flow of persons through the life cycle and the social organization of production. . . .
>
> Not only does occupation have broad validity as a proxy for social standing, but occupations are a salient feature of everyday life. Thus social surveys can be used to obtain valid measurements of social mobility *qua* occupational mobility between and within generations, . . . and these survey-based measurements can be compared across time and place. . . . Crude as it is, the concept of occupational social standing may be as close as we have come to a common metric in which the social mobility regimes of differing societies or populations may be compared. . . . For example, the comparative measurement of income inequality is conceptually no less treacherous than that of occupational inequality, and consumption differentials will complicate efforts to measure and compare intergenerational economic mobility (Hauser, 1972, pp. 1–2).

Hence, there are theoretical and practical reasons for treating the concepts of social mobility and occupational mobility as interchangeable. Based on Hauser's argument, researchers should feel fairly confident that occupational mobility

---

(1974), Hazelrigg and Garnier (1976), Hodge (1981), Hodge and Siegel (1968), Hope (1971), Hout (1983, 1984), Inkeles and Rossi (1956), Kahl and Davis (1955), Lawson and Boek (1960), Lipset and Zetterberg (1956), McGuire (1950), Miller (1961), Mitra (1966), Morris and Murphy (1959), Pullum (1975), Schnore (1961), Treiman (1970, 1975, 1977), Tumin and Feldman (1957), and Yamaguchi (1983).

reflects a substantial portion of changes in individuals' functionally significant social roles.

Even if the term *social mobility* is narrowed and redefined as *occupational mobility,* the concept remains multidimensional. Westoff *et al.* (1960) discuss five fundamental problems in the conceptualization of *movement:* (1) the unit of analysis (individual, family, society), (2) direction (vertical, horizontal), (3) the reference points (intergenerational, intragenerational), (4) the unit of measurement (amount, distance), and (5) visibility (subjective, objective). Given this degree of multidimensionality, it is important to clarify how previous investigators have treated each of the five problems.

The unit of analysis has typically been the female respondent but in most cases social position or the change therein has been regarded as pertaining to the couple, and occupational mobility has been measured in terms of husband's change in status. Mobility has most often been defined in terms of the male position—wife's father's, husband's father's, or husband's occupation—based on the premise that the wife's status depends largely on her husband's status while the reverse is rarely the case. "That a woman works is certainly relevant to her reproductive behavior, but it is usually her husband's status that is of major importance in defining her social position" (Kantner and Kiser, 1954, p. 70). This situation is less likely to be true in modern, industrialized societies when greater numbers of women enter the labor force and for more than the purpose of providing supplemental family income.[8]

The issue of direction and unit of measurement in movement requires little discussion. While not denying that horizontal social mobility, the transition from one social group to another situated on the same level, may affect a couple's reproductive behavior, most studies have focused exclusively on the effects of vertical social mobility, the transition from one social stratum to another.[9] Less interest has also been expressed in the amount of social mobility, the proportion of individuals who are upwardly or downwardly mobile within a given population, than in the distance of mobility, how many steps an individual or couple moves upward or downward. Usually, however, the amount of mobility in a given sample has been examined to get an idea of how fluid or open the stratification system is.

The issue of the visibility of movement has received much attention in mobility–fertility research. Indeed, the status enhancement perspective is largely predi-

[8]Rosenfeld (1978) forcefully makes this point with regard to the United States. Using data from the 1967 National Longitudinal Survey of Work Experience she finds mother's occupation a significant dimension of women's intergenerational occupational mobility and suggests that future studies need to consider the occupations of both husband and wife to determine accurately a family's general social standing and changes therein.

[9]For a good discussion of the "situs" (horizontal) dimension of mobility and its utility for further understanding individual behavior, see Morris and Murphy (1959).

cated on the assumption that the subjective dimension of mobility (aspirations, perceived opportunity, and motivation to be mobile) is more important in accounting for fertility behavior than the objective dimension (the actual process of moving). Researchers involved in the Indianapolis Study (Kantner and Kiser, 1954; Riemer and Kiser, 1954) and the Princeton Fertility Study (Featherman, 1970; Westoff *et al.*, 1961, 1963) argue that fertility and actual achievement depend on the operation of a motivational complex; the disposition to be mobile is a determining condition of family size and socioeconomic achievement.

Westoff (1953) contends that the subjective dimension cannot be entirely deduced from the objective dimension since some aspire but are not mobile and some who are mobile have not had any great aspirations to be so. Westoff *et al.* (1960) later test this hypothesis using data from the Princeton Fertility Study. They factor analyze 22 mobility measures and find 9 orthogonal factors: 5 account for the objective dimensions and 4 for the subjective dimensions. Hence, they conclude it is erroneous to treat the objective and subjective dimensions of mobility as interchangeable.

Some empirical evidence suggests that measures of subjective mobility need to be included in mobility–fertility analysis, but previous research has been less than successful in finding a relationship between this most elusive dimension and reproductive behavior. Riemer and Kiser's (1954) use of "economic tension" failed because of its particular susceptibility to causality problems. Westoff and colleagues' (1961, 1963) measures of the importance attached to mobility values, perception of opportunity for getting ahead, drive to get ahead, and aspirations for sending children to college had little effect on couples' desired or actual family size. Similarly, Featherman (1970) found no relationship between fertility and a couple's primary work orientation, materialistic orientation, and subjective achievement evaluation.

Researchers have blamed their failure to find a relationship between mobility aspirations and reproductive behavior on measurement problems. For example, Westoff *et al.* (1961, p. 250) comment that measuring subjective mobility is at a primitive stage in social research. Unfortunately, whether failure is because of inadequate measurement or simply that aspirations and motivations to be mobile are not as important as has been claimed still remains unanswered. Most research has concentrated primarily on the effects of objective occupational movement. To evaluate the status enhancement perspective, it has therefore been assumed that those who are upwardly or downwardly mobile accurately represent those who aspired to improve their status or who were not motivated to maintain their social position.

One aspect of subjective mobility that can be measured rather easily but which has not received a great deal of attention in mobility–fertility research per se is the respondent's occupational aspirations for her offspring. Westoff *et al.* (1961) argue that many conceive of mobility in terms of the future status of their children and view their own role as that of maximizing opportunities for their children. A couple may perceive that for their children to reach a higher social position than their own, they must take specific steps to provide necessary finances and education. One such step may be to restrict family size to minimize resource expenditures and maximize the resources available to one or a few children. Hence, we might expect couples with high mobility aspirations for their children will have lower fertility than those with more modest aspirations for their offspring.

While previous investigators have been limited in the extent to which they could analyze the subjective dimension of mobility, this is not true for the objective dimension of the concept. Measures of the occupation of the wife's or husband's father, husband at marriage and at interview have been extensively used and allow construction of several indexes of mobility that differ according to the reference point of movement. Westoff *et al.*'s (1960) factor analysis of 22 measures of mobility reveals that it may be a mistake to posit interchangeabilities between husband and wife variables and intergenerational and intragenerational mobility. Orthogonal factors representing different objective dimensions emerge. The researchers suggest regarding each objective measure as a unique, independent component of the general concept of social mobility. Unfortunately, most researchers have used only one or two objective dimensions to examine the effect of social mobility on fertility. Many, after finding or failing to find a significant relationship, have concluded that *social mobility* does or does not affect reproductive behavior. We emphasize that this need not be the case. It seems reasonable to allow for the possibility that one type of mobility will have an effect while another does not. Given the presumed orthogonal nature of the dimensions, it also seems reasonable to expect that one of the four theoretical perspectives might account for the effect of one type of mobility while another perspective may account for the effect of a different dimension. The four theoretical perspectives are not mobility-dimension specific; each may be applied to any type of social mobility.

Stevens' (1981) work comes closest to avoiding the tenuous assumption that examining one or two dimensions is sufficient to test the relationship between social mobility and reproductive behavior. Not only does Stevens examine three objective dimensions, but she also divides each dimension into its relative (individual) and mean (structural) components. She recognizes that, for some, mobility results from their own efforts while, for others, it is a result of changing labor market conditions. This theory is a variation of the Westoff *et al.* contention that social mobility is a multifaceted phenomenon. Moreover, Stevens discusses how each of the four theoretical perspectives may be applied to each of the relative and mean components (see Chapter 3).

In sum, social mobility is multidimensional. Despite the large number of studies exclusively examining the mobility–fertility relationship, we believe this literature has barely scratched the surface in measuring and then relating to reproductive behavior all that is implied by the term, *social mobility*.

4   The Intermediate Variables

As we have pointed out in this and previous chapters, reproductive behavior is also multidimensional. Most researchers have used children ever born as an index of fertility, but it is fairly insensitive to the process of reproductive behavior. Exactly *how* does social mobility affect fertility? In a classic article Davis and Blake (1956, p. 212) posit 11 "intermediate" variables:

  I. *Factors Affecting Exposure to Intercourse ("Intercourse Variables")*.
   A. Those governing the formation and dissolution of unions in the reproductive period.
       1. Age of entry into sexual unions.
       2. Permanent celibacy: proportion of women never entering sexual unions.
       3. Amount of reproductive period spent after or between unions.
          a. When unions are broken by divorce, separation, or desertion.
          b. When unions are broken by death of husband.
   B. Those governing the exposure to intercourse within unions.
       4. Voluntary abstinence.
       5. Involuntary abstinence (from impotence, illness, unavoidable but temporary separations).
       6. Coital frequency (excluding periods of abstinence).
 II. *Factors Affecting Exposure to Conception ("Conception Variables")*.
       7. Fecundity or nonfecundity, as affected by involuntary causes.
       8. Use or nonuse of contraception.
          a. By mechanical and chemical means.
          b. By other means.
       9. Fecundity or infecundity, as affected by voluntary causes (sterilization, subincision, medical treatment).
III. *Factors Affecting Gestation and Successful Parturition ("Gestation Variables")*.
      10. Fetal mortality from involuntary causes.
      11. Fetal mortality from voluntary causes.

Davis and Blake contend that *any* cultural factor must affect fertility via one or more of these intermediate variables; there can be no direct effect of any social or cultural factor on fertility (see also Bongaarts, 1978, on the proximate determinants of fertility).

Mobility–fertility researchers have not been totally unmindful of Davis and Blake's argument. The central theme of the pre-1940 studies was the social promotion of the relatively infertile (see Chapter 2). Also, the stress and disorientation perspective suggests that mobility may impair a couple's biological capacity to reproduce. Some theoretical attempts have been made to relate social mobility to involuntary subfecundity. Aside from the literature on delayed childbearing (Baldwin and Nord, 1984), no empirical research has been conducted that directly examines subfecundity as a cause or consequence of mobility.

A few attempts have also been made to examine mobility's effect on age at entry into sexual unions. Hollingsworth (1957), Perrucci (1967), and Zimmer (1979) include an age at marriage variable explicitly in their mobility –fertility models. Several researchers have also examined directly or indirectly the differential use of contraception between mobile and nonmobile couples. The Indianapolis Study (Kantner and Kiser, 1954; Riemer and Kiser, 1954) distinguishes between planned and unplanned families, and social mobility as it affects effectiveness in family planning is investigated. In the Princeton Fertility Study (Westoff *et al.*, 1961, 1963) the percentage of successful family planners is a dependent variable. Bean and Swicegood (1979) divide fertility into intended and unintended births and therefore obtain some evidence of contraceptive failure. Boyd (1971) assesses the effect of mobility on Latin American women's knowledge and use of contraception. Finally, Zimmer (1979) examines whether the prevalence of voluntary sterilization differs by mobility status.

In general, however, these attempts to consider Davis and Blake's analytical framework have been modest. Much more empirical research could and should be conducted to assess directly the impact of social mobility on the intermediate variables. Such investigations would be helpful in further clarifying whether and exactly how mobility and reproductive behavior are related.

5   Conditional Effects

A common theme throughout much of the research literature is that the existence (or nature) of an effect of social mobility on fertility depends on the societal conditions of a given population. Boyd (1973) provides a detailed discussion. Developed countries tend to have more fluid or open stratification systems. In these societies mobility may not have disruptive effects because mobility rates are high and it becomes institutionalized through education. Mobility is no longer the exception, nor as costly, and hence is not associated with extreme behavioral modifications. Developed countries are also characterized by widespread use of contraceptives and limited variation in fertility by socioeconomic status. Treiman (1970, p. 226) suggests this may reflect the nature of the stratification system. He contends that one outcome of high mobility is increasing behavioral heterogeneity within classes and increasing homogeneity among them.

In contrast, less developed countries display higher fertility levels, differential access to and use of contraceptives, and differential fertility by socioeconomic status. This may reflect the stratification system in these societies, where there are high degrees of discontinuity and large behavioral differences among classes. The stratification system is less fluid. Individual mobility is more the exception than the rule, and mobility mechanisms are not institutionalized by education. Mobile persons are likely to receive little social support, experience much stress, and incur substantial "costs" in moving. Consequently, mobility is more likely to disrupt behavior in more traditional, static, and class-homogeneous societies.

Most mobility–fertility research has been based on data from more developed countries, and many investigators have used the above argument to explain their failure to find a relationship. Boggs (1957) maintains that restriction on fertility is a consequence of social mobility under conditions that demand greater sacrifices in return for higher status. With the urban occupational system come prosperity, higher education, and successful experience in adapting to social mobility. These features minimize the impact of mobility; it becomes an accepted and expected part of urban life and therefore does not elicit such responses as modifications in fertility. Similarly, Westoff *et al.* (1961) talk about middle class suburbia with its emphasis on the family as the basic social unit. The family, and presumably a standard family size, becomes fashionable in the urban environment. Also related to this line of reasoning is Riemer and Kiser's (1954) and Tien's (1961) suggestion that in some countries separate analyses for two or more marriage cohorts might be necessary. The effect of mobility on fertility might be pronounced for couples who experienced an economic setback early in marriage.

Freedman cogently argues that the mobility–fertility hypothesis has a limited sphere of applicability:

> [The classical social mobility hypothesis] assumes that the mobile family is one of many individualistic units which rationally restricts family commitments and costs in order to compete successfully in an impersonal and highly individualistic market. Such a model may be applicable to the transitional stage when an urban society is developing indigenous institutions and drawing large masses of immigrants from rural areas. In this situation large numbers of people are unaccustomed to urban institutions and without established precedents or rules to guide their careers. But in the contemporary American scene large numbers have been socialized as indigenous urbanites to expect social change. Change and mobility are an established part of the social structure. The large bureaucratic enterprises, in which more and more people work, institutionalize mobility. People learn to expect and plan for change within reasonable limits as part of the routine of life (Freedman, 1962, pp. 225–226).

Freedman's comments on transitional urban societies and their attraction of masses of rural migrants leads us to consider the place of a migration variable in a social mobility–fertility model. Freedman suggests that the migrant component of a population may cause social mobility to affect fertility. Rural-to-urban migrants most likely experience the disruptive effect of social mobility and therefore modify their behavior severely. Hence, we might hypothesize that the effect of social mobility on fertility differs for different population subgroups— migrants versus nonmigrants—consistent with the findings of Goldberg (1959), Blau and Duncan (1967), and Deming (1974). While focusing more on the migration–fertility relationship, Berry (1983) also finds evidence of conditional effects of mobility on fertility by migration status. At the very least, Freedman's comments suggest that migration should be introduced as a control variable when examining the effect of social mobility on fertility.[10]

---

[10]The relationship between geographic and social mobility is as complex and multifaceted as the social mobility–fertility association. In some studies migration is regarded as a form or dimension of social mobility. In others, migration is treated as either a cause or effect of occupational mobility. For

We should also emphasize the important role of education in the mobility–fertility relationship. Boyd (1973) argues that in developed societies education acts as a mechanism through which mobility is institutionalized. In explaining their failure to find an effect of mobility on family size in a developed country, both Scott (1958) and Tien (1965a) stress this point and note that education acts as a socializing agent. Tien's study reveals that his respondents' mobility is related to their education, and marriage was delayed until after they had obtained professional credentials. Hence, struggle for the mobile to improve their status was at the expense of the university professor's parents rather than at that of the professor's having children. The disruptions incurred to improve their status were over before they assumed any family responsibilities. Similarly, Scott argues that the intergenerationally upwardly mobile and nonmobile male teachers in England and Wales had the same educational experience, and this common standard of education erased any social distinctions between the two groups.

This line of reasoning suggests that in developed countries education, rather than social mobility, will have the dominant effect on fertility. This may also be the case for developing countries as education becomes the driving force underlying the relationship. That is, we should not overlook the possibility that social mobility may operate as an intervening variable in the education–fertility causal chain. It is widely recognized that education has a substantial positive effect on occupational attainment. Blau and Duncan (1967, pp. 152–161) provide one of the best treatments of the effect of education on social mobility per se. They find education has a positive effect on upward intergenerational mobility, but a curvilinear effect on downward mobility. Those who started but did not finish college are more likely to experience downward mobility than those with either more or less education. Whether education is better regarded as an effect that conditions the mobility–fertility relationship or as an exogenous variable that affects reproductive behavior via its effect on a range of status-enhancing variables is a question that the second portion of this work will help clarify.

6   Summary

In this chapter we have looked at why there might be a relationship between social mobility and fertility. We have discussed possible causal links between the variables: (1) the observed relationship is spurious, (2) fertility affects social mobility, (3) social mobility affects fertility, and (4) fertility and social mobility

---

a discussion of the relationship between these two variables, see Berry (1983), Byrne (1975), de Guzman (1975), Freedman and Hawley (1949), Freeman *et al.* (1977), Goldstein (1955), Hiday (1978), Hutchinson (1958, 1961), Macisco *et al.* (1969), Martine (1972), Pihlblad and Aas (1960), Prehn (1967), Ramu (1972), Richmond (1964), and Zelinsky (1971).

simultaneously affect each other. We have also tried to explicate more fully the four theoretical perspectives used to account for an effect of the *process* of mobility on reproductive behavior: (1) social isolation, (2) stress and disorientation, (3) status enhancement, and (4) relative economic status.

While the bulk of previous research has treated social mobility as the independent variable and fertility as the dependent variable, undoubtedly some degree of mutual reciprocity exists between the two. Researchers have been hampered in dealing with the direction of causality problem because the limitations of their data permit only a static analysis of two dynamic processes. Resolution of the causality problem awaits detailed "event history" analysis of the relationship using longitudinal data (Tuma and Hannan, 1984).

We also reiterate that social mobility is a multidimensional concept. Researchers have only scratched the surface in trying to relate all that the term *social mobility* implies to reproductive behavior. Another neglected area in mobility–fertility research is a specification of exactly *how* social mobility affects fertility. Far too little consideration has been given to examining social mobility's effect on the intermediate variables. Finally, numerous researchers have stressed that the effect of social mobility on fertility depends on the societal conditions of a given population. Yet, there has been little empirical testing of these conditional effects. Clearly, an analysis using a comparative framework is needed to investigate this hypothesis further.

Chapter 5 | Methodological Issues in Mobility–Fertility Research

It is now common to define a mobility effect as one beyond the additive effects of status of origin and of destination. Duncan (1966) first proposed this strategy, later elaborated by Blau and Duncan (1967). The strategy separates mobility–fertility research conducted prior to the mid-1960s from more recent studies.

In Chapters 3 and 4 we provided some substantive elaboration of Duncan's argument (1966, p. 91) that researchers are not entitled to discuss "effects" of mobility until they establish that the apparent effect is not a result of merely a combination of effects of the variables used to define mobility. Given the impact that Duncan's contention has had on contemporary mobility–fertility research, we feel it valuable to explicate its methodological basis. We then introduce a procedure that extends Duncan's methodology to allow a systematic search for a mobility model that adequately fits the data. We also examine other recent methods proposed for analyzing the association between social mobility and fertility. The chapter concludes with summary remarks that set the stage for the issues addressed in the rest of the book.

1 The Blau and Duncan Approach

What might a researcher interested in the relationship between social mobility and fertility do with data on the number of children ever born, husband's occupation, and husband's father's occupation for a sample of currently married couples who had completed childbearing? One might classify both the husband's and husband's father's occupations into four broad categories, then cross-classify past and present status, and for each of the resulting 16 cells calculate the mean

Table 1

Mean Number of Live Births per Couple, by Present Social Class and Husband's Class of Origin, Calculated from Berent Data[a]

Class of origin	Present class				
	I	II	III	IV	All
I	1.74 (65)[b]	1.79 (43)	1.96 (23)	2.00 (11)	1.81 (142)
II	2.05 (38)	2.14 (197)	2.51 (150)	2.97 (68)	2.38 (453)
III	1.87 (37)	2.01 (154)	2.67 (431)	3.69 (244)	2.81 (866)
IV	2.40 (5)	3.20 (45)	3.22 (162)	3.68 (220)	3.44 (432)
All	1.88 (145)	2.17 (439)	2.73 (766)	3.56 (543)	2.77 (1893)

[a]Source: Duncan (1966, p. 92).
[b]Numbers per class in parentheses.

fertility for couples residing in that cell. Like Duncan (1966), we use Berent's data to illustrate[1] (see Table 1).

Husbands falling in the same occupational categories as their fathers (main diagonal, upper left to lower right) are regarded as nonmobile, those in higher categories (lower triangle) as upwardly mobile, those in lower categories (upper triangle) as downwardly mobile. There is considerable variation in fertility among all groups. Moreover, the fertility level in a cell representing a particular mobile group differs considerably from the levels in the respective nonmobile at origin and at destination cells. Researchers of the intermediate studies and Zimmer (1979, 1981a) regarded such differences as evidence of an effect of mobility on fertility.

Blau and Duncan, however, question whether presenting a table like the one above and comparing each mobile cell with its respective nonmobile at origin and at destination cells is appropriate in determining a mobility–fertility relationship. Table 1 has 16 combinations of an origin class with a destination class. Suppose that the effect (mean fertility level) of each combination simply sums to (1) the mean effect applying to all couples in the sample, (2) the increment attributable to class of origin, regardless of destination, and (3) the increment attributable to class of destination, regardless of origin. The appropriate model, then, is the additive model

$$Y_{ija} = \bar{Y} + a_i + b_j + U_{ija}$$

---

[1]Berent's (1952) study of the mobility–fertility relationship, using a sample of currently married couples in England and Wales, is discussed in Chapter 2 of this book.

where Y_{ija} = the number of children ever born to the ath wife whose
husband's father's job fell in group i and whose husband's
job falls in group j;

$\bar{Y}$ = the grand mean fertility for all wives;

a_i = the net effect on fertility because of membership in the ith
past class;

b_j = the net effect due to the jth current class; and

U_{ija} = the amount by which the fertility of the ath couple differs
from the expected value, $\hat{Y}_{ij} = \bar{Y} + a_i + b_j$ (Blau and
Duncan, 1967, p. 375).

In brief, the additive model posits a set of row effects (one for each value of i)
and column effects (one for each value of j); it does not posit any cell effects
apart from those given by the sum of the particular row and column effects for a
designated cell. That is, the model assumes no interaction. If the model adequately fits the data (if $Y_{ij} - \hat{Y}_{ij} \cong 0$), it is not necessary to recognize as many
different cell effects as there are cells in the cross-classification of $a \cdot b$ (the
product of the number of rows times the number of columns). If the additive
model adequately fits the data, there is no need to postulate any effect of mobility
on fertility. Couples behave as if they determined their fertility by combining the
fertility pattern of their origin class with that of their destination class in a simple
averaging process (Duncan, 1966, p. 93).

Duncan (1966) reanalyzes Berent's data by calculating effects based on the
additive model. Using multiple classification analysis, the net effects of a_i and b_j
are each expressed as deviations from the grand mean; the weighted sum
(weighted by the frequencies of the classes) of each set of effects is zero. The net
effects Duncan obtains are as follows:

Class	Origin	Destination
I	-0.58	-0.60
II	-0.21	-0.50
III	-0.01	-0.07
IV	0.42	0.66

Thus, for couples intergenerationally upwardly mobile from class IV to class
III, the estimated mean fertility level is 2.77 (grand mean) + 0.42 (origin effect)
− 0.07 (destination effect) = 3.12. This procedure is repeated for the remaining
15 cells (see Table 2).

To assess how well the additive model fits the data, Duncan compares the

Table 2

Average Number of Live Births per Couple, by Present Social Class and Husbands' Class of Origin, Calculated from Berent Data Using Model Based on Assumption of Additive Effects[a]

Class of origin	Present class				
	I	II	III	IV	All
I	1.60 (65)[b]	1.70 (43)	2.13 (23)	2.85 (11)	1.81 (142)
II	1.97 (38)	2.07 (197)	2.50 (150)	3.23 (68)	2.38 (453)
III	2.17 (37)	2.27 (154)	2.70 (431)	3.42 (244)	2.81 (866)
IV	2.59 (5)	2.70 (45)	3.12 (162)	3.85 (220)	2.44 (432)
All	1.88 (145)	2.17 (439)	2.73 (766)	3.56 (543)	2.77 (1893)

[a]Source: Duncan (1966, p. 93).
[b]Numbers per class in parentheses.

expected mean levels of fertility, $\hat{Y}_{ij}$, and the observed mean levels, $\hat{Y}_{ij}$. If all the deviations, $\bar{Y}_{ij} - \hat{Y}_{ij}$, are zero, the additive model fits the data perfectly. Looking at Table 3, one can see that the model does not fit perfectly.

The deviations reveal that the additive model either overstates or understates actual mean fertility for mobility categories. Where signs are minus, the observed number of live births for a given cell is lower than predicted on the basis of the additive model; where signs are plus, observed fertility is greater than predicted.

Even if the deviations are not all zero, it does not necessarily mean there are mobility effects. Large deviations in cells with low frequencies may be mislead-

Table 3

Average Number of Live Births per Couple, Observed Minus Expected Values Calculated from Berent Data[a]

Class of origin	Present class			
	I	II	III	IV
I	0.14 (65)[b]	0.09 (43)	-0.17 (23)	-0.85 (11)
II	0.08 (38)	0.07 (197)	0.01 (150)	-0.26 (68)
III	-0.30 (37)	-0.26 (154)	-0.03 (431)	0.27 (244)
IV	-0.19 (5)	0.50 (45)	0.10 (162)	-0.17 (220)

[a]Source: Duncan (1966, pp. 92–93).
[b]Numbers per class in parentheses.

ing because such observations are subject to sampling error.[2] To decide whether all deviations from the model are attributable to sampling error, compare the variance in fertility explained by the simple, additive model and that explained by the "observed means" model.[3] For example, the additive model may account for 4% of the variance in number of live births, and the observed means model may account for 6% of the variance in the dependent variable. Significance tests can be conducted to see if this increment in explained variance is real. If the increase in explained variance is not significant, the additive model is not rejected as a hypothesis to account for observed fertility variation; the conclusion is that social mobility does not affect fertility significantly. If the increment in explained variance is significant, the additive model does not adequately fit the data; after considering the additive effects of past and current status there is a remainder to be attributed uniquely to mobility.[4]

If the additive model does not adequately fit the data, what can be said about the "effect" of mobility on fertility? As Blau and Duncan note in analyzing the OCG data, one could look at the table of deviations and consider, for example, why mobility from class III to class II is accompanied by lower fertility (-0.26) while moving from class IV to class III is accompanied by higher fertility (0.10), and so on. However, some simplification of the data which incorporates the idea of pattern of mobility is desired. "In short, we are not satisfied to observe that significant deviations $\bar{Y}_{ij} - \hat{Y}_{ij}$ occur; it must be shown that these deviations are in some systematic way related to the notion of mobility" (Blau and Duncan, 1967, p. 377).

But what is the most appropriate way to summarize the effect of mobility on fertility? If the additive model is not the best-fitting model, what alternative hypothesis do we accept? Let us assume that in Berent's data a significant portion of variance is left unexplained by the additive model, and, hence, that social mobility does affect number of children ever born. Is this because *all* mobile couples (upwardly and downwardly mobile combined) have higher (or lower) fertility than nonmobile couples? Using Blau and Duncan's procedure, we divide Berent's sample into the mobile and nonmobile. For each group the observed means are multiplied by their cell sizes, summed, and then divided by the total number in the group. The same procedure is performed on the table of means calculated on the basis of the additive model. We get

---

[2]Duncan (1966, p. 93) finds this true for Berent's data.

[3]The observed means model, which we later call the saturated model, predicts the observed table of means perfectly. It has as many effect parameters as there are cells resulting from the cross-classification of past and current status.

[4]Unfortunately, Duncan does not make this test when analyzing Berent's data. The point is not made until Blau and Duncan's (1967) subsequent analysis of the Occupational Changes in a Generation (OCG) data.

	Observed	Expected	Observed − expected
Mobile	2.81	2.78	0.03
Nonmobile	2.73	2.76	−0.03

If we calculate the observed minus expected values, we find for the aggregate of all mobile couples the deviation is 0.03 compared to −0.03 for all nonmobile couples. The mobility effect of 0.06 seems quite small.

Perhaps, however, the mobile/nonmobile dichotomy does not adequately capture the effect of mobility. Consider, for example, the hypothetical case where all cells in a table have an equal number of observations; all deviations in upward mobility cells are of the same magnitude and direction, whereas all deviations in the downward mobility cells are the same size as the upward mobility deviations but in the opposite direction. Aggregating the upwardly mobile with the downwardly mobile produces a deviation of zero and the difference between the mobile and nonmobile may be sharply attenuated. It may be that to summarize accurately the effect of mobility, direction must be considered. If we follow the same procedures as above but divide Berent's mobile group according to direction, we get

	Observed	Expected	Observed − expected
Upward	2.57	2.60	−0.02
Nonmobile	2.73	2.76	−0.03
Downward	3.01	2.94	0.07

Based on the results of this aggregation, we might conclude there is little difference between the fertility of the upwardly mobile and nonmobile but that downwardly mobile couples have 0.10 more children than the nonmobile.

Even consideration of direction may not be appropriate to capture the effect of mobility. Perhaps distance moved needs to be accounted for. We can aggregate couples according to the number of steps they moved.

	Observed	Expected	Observed − expected
Up three steps	2.40	2.59	−0.19
Up two steps	2.60	2.46	0.14
Up one step	2.57	2.63	−0.06

(Continued)

	Observed	Expected	Observed − expected
Nonmobile	2.73	2.76	−0.03
Down one step	3.10	2.93	0.17
Down two steps	2.71	2.95	−0.24
Down three steps	2.00	2.85	−0.85

No pattern emerges for fertility of the upwardly mobile by number of steps moved; however, the farther couples descend in status, the fewer children they have.

Which of the three aggregation procedures should we adopt? How should we summarize the mobility effect? If the additive model does not adequately fit the data, there are at least three alternative hypotheses regarding the effect of mobility on fertility:

1. The fertility of all mobile couples differs from that of the nonmobile
2. The direction of movement must be considered to convey the mobility effect correctly
3. Distance moved is critical in the mobility–fertility relationship.

Aside from looking at the three sets of aggregations, Blau and Duncan make little attempt to test formally the competing hypotheses and determine the best fitting mobility model. They do not add a mobile–nonmobile comparison to the additive model and test to see if it adequately predicts the observed table of means. If it does, it is not necessary to consider direction and distance to understand the mobility–fertility relationship. If it does not, a direction parameter can be included in the model and one can evaluate whether, after controlling for the effects of origin, destination, and being mobile or nonmobile, direction moved is critical in the mobility–fertility relationship. If there is still a significant difference between this model and the observed means model in the amount of variance in fertility explained, then a distance parameter can be added. Using this strategy, one can be sure of expressing the effect of mobility as succinctly and accurately as possible. That is, one can be sure of not making the mistake of calculating and interpreting effects based on a model that does not adequately describe the data.

Before describing our extension of the Blau and Duncan approach in more detail, we note a few of its shortcomings. Users of the approach have traditionally controlled for other factors that might affect fertility by restricting their samples to a select group of respondents. For example, in her analysis of mobility–fertility in urban Latin America using CELADE data, Boyd (1971) confines her sample to currently married, fecund, native-born women, married only once for 10 years or more to native-born males. Such restrictions severely reduce the sample size. In Boyd's case, the sample for each urban place is reduced so much that, even with four-category occupation-at-marriage and occupation-at-interview variables, most cell-by-cell calculations of observed minus expected means are based on very small numbers. Later Boyd wishes to control for education, marital duration, and age at marriage. To maintain consistency with Blau and Duncan's tabular data presentation and method of analysis, she dichotomizes each interval-level variable and collapses occupational status into manual and nonmanual. She calculates mean fertility levels for the four-cell tables resulting from the cross-classification of origin by destination status for each category of each control variable. Only one control can be used at a time, given the reduction in cell sizes that any higher order cross-classification would cause.[5]

Finally, the Blau and Duncan approach does not easily lend itself to any type of causal modeling. One cannot test whether mobility affects fertility directly or indirectly through one of the intermediate variables. Boyd (1971) assesses the effect of mobility on number of live births and on a contraception knowledge and use score. Using the Blau and Duncan approach, she can analyze mobility's effect on either variable; however, she is left to surmise whether, after considering mobility's indirect effect on number of live births via contraceptive use, mobility has any remaining impact on fertility.

2 An Extension of the Blau and Duncan Approach

Our extension of Blau and Duncan's method of analysis essentially involves a more systematic search for a mobility model that adequately fits the data. We illustrate the technique using CELADE data for Mexico City.[6] We focus on intragenerational mobility, comparing husband's occupation at marriage with that at the interview in 1964. Each occupation variable is in a six-category

---

[5]We emphasize that controlling for other factors only by restricting the sample or by dichotomizing interval-level variables is not inherent to the Blau and Duncan approach. For example, if one wished to control for the effect of education one could calculate an "observed" table of means which reflected an adjustment for education. One could also estimate the model, $\hat{Y}_{ij} = \bar{Y} + a_i + b_j + E_d$, by using regression analysis and deriving the net effects of origin and destination adjusted for the covariate, education. The Blau and Duncan procedure could then be carried out in its normal fashion.

[6]These data come from the Centro Latinamericano de Demografia's (CELADE) extensive surveys of social determinants of fertility and family planning practice among women of childbearing age in 10 Latin American metropolises (1963–1965) and rural regions of Colombia, Costa Rica, Mexico, and Peru (1969–1970). The Mexico City sample consisted of 2353 women and contained the type and range of occupational measures and other variables necessary for us to illustrate our procedure. For complete descriptions of the survey instrument, sampling methods, and variables, see CELADE (1974, 1976) and CELADE and Community and Family Study Center (1972).

classification ranging from professional to unskilled worker. The sample is confined to currently married couples. The dependent variable is live births.

Like Blau and Duncan, we begin by specifying the additive model by means of ordinary least-squares regression in which past and present status are effect coded. Effect coding is similar to dummy variable regression. The only difference is that rather than one category of a variable always being assigned a score of 0, it is always coded -1. This merely changes the interpretation of the unstandardized regression coefficients. In dummy variable regression each coefficient represents the difference between the mean of the group assigned 1s in a given vector and that of the group assigned 0s throughout (the reference category).

In effect coding, each coefficient represents the difference between the mean of a particular group and the unweighted mean of all group means. As in dummy variable regression, one effect-coded variable is omitted from the equation to make the set of normal equations solvable[7]:

$$Y = a + b_1C_1 + b_2C_2 + b_3C_3 + b_4C_4 + b_5C_5 + b_6P_1 + b_7P_2 + b_8P_3$$
$$+ b_9P_4 + b_{10}P_5 + e$$

where Y is number of live births; C_1 (professional) to C_5 (skilled manual) are effect-coded variables representing husband's current occupational status; P_1 (professional) to P_5 (skilled manual) are effect-coded variables representing husband's occupational status at marriage; and a is the unweighted grand mean.[8]

The minimum requirement for an analysis of intragenerational mobility and fertility is that we control for marital duration simply by adding wife's age at interview and at marriage to the equation:

$$Y = a + b_1C_1 + \cdots + b_5C_5 + b_6P_1 + \cdots + b_{10}P_5 + b_{11}\text{Age}$$
$$+ b_{12}\text{AgeMar} + e$$

Thus, to control for marital duration we do not have to dichotomize the sample into women married 10–20 years and those wed more than 20 years and analyze the samples separately. We need only add age, age at marriage, or any other interval variable that we wish to control for directly to the regression equation. Results of this regression analysis for Mexico City appear in Table 4.

The net effects of past and current occupational status are not the main points of inquiry. To illustrate the interpretation of the coefficients, however, we note that after controlling for age, age at marriage, and husband's past status, current status tends to affect fertility negatively; excluding the managerial class, the higher the husband's current occupation, the lower the fertility. Professional

---

[7]For a more detailed discussion of effect coding, see Cohen and Cohen (1975, pp. 188–195) or Kerlinger and Pedhazur (1973, pp. 121–128, 141–145).

[8]The constraints placed on the effect-coded variables are that $b_1 + b_2 + b_3 + b_4 + b_5 + b_{C_6} = 0$. Thus, $b_{C_6} = -(b_1 + b_2 + b_3 + b_4 + b_5)$.

Table 4

Regression of Number of Live Births
on Husband's Past and Current Status,[a] Age,
and Age at Marriage—Mexico City

Independent variables	Unstandardized coefficients
Age	0.166
Age at marriage	−0.245
C_1 (professional)	−0.353
C_2 (managerial)	−0.074
C_3 (high supervisory)	−0.283
C_4 (middle supervisory)	0.008
C_5 (skilled manual)	0.345
(C_6) (unskilled manual)[b]	(0.357)
P_1 (professional)	−0.061
P_2 (managerial)	0.006
P_3 (high supervisory)	−0.114
P_4 (middle supervisory)	−0.375
P_5 (skilled manual)	0.048
(P_6) (unskilled manual)[b]	(0.496)
Constant	3.273
R^2	0.34251
Model F	69.068
Degrees of freedom	12/1591

[a] Intragenerational mobility of husbands of all currently married women.

[b] Suppressed category.

class husbands have a mean fertility level 0.35 less than all sample couples, while those in the unskilled manual class have 0.36 more than all couples. The relationship between past status and fertility, after controlling for marital duration and current status, tends to be curvilinear. Those in the middle of the occupational hierarchy at marriage have the lowest fertility; those at either end, and especially at the lower end, have higher fertility. This nonlinear relationship adds justification for effect coding past and current status and treating them as categorical variables rather than measuring them on an interval level scale.

Most of the variance explained in this model is because of the effects of age and age at marriage. This effect is hardly surprising; age and age at marriage have consistently been very powerful predictors of number of children ever born. When past and current status are omitted from the model, 31.2% of the variance in number of live births is explained; thus, past and present status only explain an additional 3%. This increment, however, is significant at the 0.01 level.

With the above coefficients we can create a table of means expected on the assumption of additive effects just as Blau and Duncan do. The only difference is that we have adjusted for marital duration. For example, expected mean fertility for nonmobile couples whose husbands began and remained in the professional class is 3.273 (grand mean) -0.061 (origin effect) -0.353 (destination effect) = 2.859. However, it is not necessary to do so. We are interested in how much variance the model, assuming only additive effects, can explain. In this example, it explains 34.3% of the variance in number of live births. Our next step is to compare this amount with the amount explained by the "saturated" model.

The saturated model will perfectly replicate an observed table of means. It includes as many effect parameters as there are cells in the cross-classification of origin by destination status (in this case, 36 effects). That is, it exhausts all of the degrees of freedom. It is generated by multiplying each of the effect-coded variables representing past status by each representing current status. The resulting 25 interaction terms are than added to the additive model. The regression equation for the saturated model is[9]

$$Y = a + b_1C_1 + \cdots + b_5C_5 + b_6P_1 + \cdots + b_{10}P_5 + b_{11}C_1P_1 + b_{12}C_1P_2 + \cdots$$
$$+ b_{34}C_5P_4 + b_{35}C_5P_5 + b_{36}\text{Age} + b_{37}\text{AgeMar} + e$$

The saturated model yields the total amount of variance that can be explained in fertility with a knowledge of age and age at marriage effects, origin effects, destination effects, *and* interaction (mobility) effects. As such, it provides a gauge by which we can assess the fit of the additive model and all subsequent mobility models. Regressing number of live births on this set of independent variables, we find $R^2 = 0.35609$, model $F = 26.310$, and degrees of freedom = 33/1570.

To see how well the additive model fits the data, we use the formula:

$$F = \frac{(R^2_{y.12...K_1} - R^2_{y.12...K_2})/(K_1 - K_2)}{(1 - R^2_{y.12...K_1})/(N - K_1 - 1)}$$

where N = total number of cases;
$\quad K_1$ = number of independent variables of the larger R^2;
$\quad K_2$ = number of independent variables of the smaller R^2;
$R^2_{y.12...K_1}$ = the squared multiple correlation coefficient for the regression of Y on the K_1 variables (the larger coefficient); and
$R^2_{y.12...K_2}$ = the squared multiple correlation coefficient for the regression of Y on the K_2 variables (the smaller coefficient) (Kerlinger and Pedhazur, 1973, pp. 70–71).

Applying this formula to see if there is a significant difference between the variance explained by the additive versus the saturated model, we get

---

[9]There are 37 rather than 35 effects in the equation because we control for age and age at marriage.

$$F = \frac{(0.35609 - 0.34251)/(33 - 12)}{(1 - 0.35609)/(1604 - 33 - 1)} = \frac{0.01358/21}{0.64391/1570} = \frac{0.00065}{0.00041} = 1.577$$

For 21 and 1570 degrees of freedom, the F ratio is significant at the 0.05 level. We therefore reject the hypothesis implied by the additive model; after considering the additive effects of current and past status there is a remainder to be attributed uniquely to mobility.

To test the hypothesis that mobility affects fertility to the extent that all mobile couples have higher or lower fertility than the nonmobile, we create a mobile/nonmobile contrast variable. If the woman's husband has not changed status since marriage, she is given a 0. If he has moved, she is given a 1. We add this variable (MOBNON) to the regression equation representing the additive effects model (see table 5). The MOBNON coefficient is directly interpretable. It says that, controlling for age and age at marriage, and origin and destination effects, mobile couples have on average almost 0.5 more children than nonmobile couples. The effect is statistically significant at the 0.01 level. Including MOBNON in the model adds a significant amount of explained variance in fertility above that explained by the additive model.[10] Whether this model captures all of the mobility effect is assessed by computing the F ratio of the difference between the R^2 of this model and of the saturated model. The computed value is 1.178, which with 20 and 1570 degrees of freedom is not significant at the 0.05 level. We therefore fail to reject the simplest of all the mobility hypotheses and interpret the mobility effect in terms of a mobile/nonmobile comparison.

Since the above model adequately fits the data, we need not proceed by specifying alternative, more complex mobility models. To illustrate the technique, however, we present the two remaining models. If the mobile/nonmobile comparison does not accurately capture the mobility effect, we can test the hypothesis that direction needs to be considered. We create a variable (UP-DOWN) where the respondent is given a 1 if her husband were upwardly mobile, a -1 if he were downwardly mobile, and a 0 if he were nonmobile. We add this variable to the regression equation specifying the additive effects and the mobile/nonmobile comparison (see Table 6).

Again, the UPDOWN coefficient is directly interpretable. Controlling for age and age at marriage, origin and destination effects, and mobility status, upwardly mobile couples have $2 \cdot 0.115 = 0.23$ more children than downwardly mobile couples.[11] The difference, however, is not significant. Indeed, considering mobility direction adds only 0.008% to the explained variance in number of live

[10]Since only one additional parameter is being added to the original, additive model, the F ratio given for the parameter and the F ratio of the difference between the two R^2s are the same.

[11]The coefficient is doubled because the upwardly mobile are coded 1, and downwardly mobile -1; the coefficient is expressed as a deviation from 0.

Table 5

Regression of Number of Live Births on Husband's Past
and Current Status,[a] Mobility Status, Age,
and Age at Marriage—Mexico City

Independent variables	Unstandardized coefficients	F
Age	0.163	508.680
Age at marriage	−0.243	311.763
C_1	−0.679	
C_2	−0.290	
C_3	−0.315	
C_4	0.012	
C_5	0.542	
P_1	0.339	
P_2	0.203	
P_3	−0.107	
P_4	−0.436	
P_5	−0.145	
MOBNON	0.471	9.527
Constant	3.217	
R^2	0.34643	
Model F	64.830	
Degrees of freedom	13/1590	

[a] Inatragenerational mobility of husbands of all currently
married women.

births that can be achieved simply with knowing whether the couple has been
mobile or not. The F ratio of the difference between the R^2 of this model and of
the simpler mobility model is only 0.208. We therefore reject the hypothesis that
we need to know direction of movement to describe the mobility effect accurately.

We can present the direction of mobility model differently by creating a
variable (UPNON) which contrasts the upwardly mobile with the nonmobile and
a variable (DOWNON) which contrasts the downwardly mobile with the nonmobile. The regression equation is:

$$Y = a + b_1C_1 + \cdots + b_5C_5 + b_6P_1 + \cdots + b_{10}P_5 + b_{11}\text{UPNON}$$
$$+ b_{12}\text{DOWNON} + b_{13}\text{Age} + b_{14}\text{AgeMar} + e$$

We emphasize that this expression of the direction model is exactly the same as
that containing the MOBNON and UPDOWN effects. The amount of variance
explained is the same, as are all coefficients in the model except those representing
mobility effects. For Mexico, the UPNON coefficient is 0.570, the DOWNON
coefficient is 0.339. They indicate that upwardly mobile couples have almost 0.6

Table 6

Regression of Number of Live Births on Husband's Past
and Current Status,[a] Mobility Status, Direction of
Mobility, Age, and Age at Marriage—Mexico City

Independent variables	Unstandardized coefficients	F
Age	0.163	508.561
Age at marriage	−0.243	311.784
C_1	−0.805	
C_2	−0.370	
C_3	−0.351	
C_4	0.025	
C_5	0.611	
P_1	0.468	
P_2	0.274	
P_3	−0.072	
P_4	−0.451	
P_5	−0.214	
MOBNON	0.455	8.462
UPDOWN	0.115	0.208
Constant	3.216	
R^2	0.34651	
Model F	60.184	
Degrees of freedom	14/1589	

[a] Intragenerational mobility of husbands of all currently
married women.

more children than nonmobile couples and downwardly mobile couples have over
0.3 more children than nonmobile couples. Subtracting the two coefficients, we
find the upwardly mobile have 0.231 more children than the downwardly
mobile—the same value yielded by the UPDOWN coefficient. In cases where the
direction model is selected as that which best fits the data, expressing the mobility
effect in this alternative manner may be insightful.

Had the UPDOWN effect been significant, we would have then tested the
difference between the R^2 of this model and of the saturated model. Were this
difference nonsignificant, we would have accepted the direction model as that
which most adequately describes the effect of mobility on fertility. We would
have then interpreted this set of effects. If the difference in R^2s were significant,
however, we would have proceeded to test the third hypothesis.

The third hypothesis posits that distance moved must be accounted for to
describe accurately the mobility effect. Given a six-category classification for
past and current status, couples may have moved a maximum of five steps in
either direction. To include distance effects in our regression equation we again

use effect coding. Couples in each of the first four steps representing upward mobility are contrasted with those having moved up five steps. Similarly, couples in each of the four steps representing downward mobility are contrasted with those having moved down five steps. These eight variables are added to the regression equation specifying the direction model such that:

$$Y = a + b_1C_1 + \cdots + b_5C_5 + b_6P_1 + \cdots + b_{10}P_5 + b_{11}\text{MOBNON}$$
$$+ b_{12}\text{UPDOWN} + b_{13}\text{UP1} + \cdots + b_{16}\text{UP4} + b_{17}\text{DOWN1} + \cdots$$
$$+ b_{20}\text{DOWN4} + b_{21}\text{Age} + b_{22}\text{AgeMar} + e$$

At this point, depending on the sparseness of the cells in the mobility table, the methodology may break down. It may not be possible to interpret directly the coefficients representing the distance effects. However, the R^2 of the model is unaffected; it accurately represents the amount of variance that can be explained with the additional knowledge of distance moved. Thus, we still have a basis for selecting or rejecting the distance model as that which best captures the mobility effect. For Mexico, the results are $R^2 = 0.35003$, model $F = 42.625$, and degrees of freedom $= 20/1583$. Taking distance moved into account adds only 0.36% to the explained variance in number of live births that can be achieved simply with a knowledge of whether the couple has been mobile or nonmobile. The F ratio of the difference in the R^2 of this model and of the simpler mobility model is only 1.253, which for 7 and 1583 degrees of freedom is not significant. We therefore reject the hypothesis that we need to know distance moved to describe the mobility effect accurately.

Had distance effects been found to contribute significant explained variance, we would have failed to reject this model. In this case, even if the coefficients for the model were uninterpretable directly, we could nevertheless describe the effect of distance moved on fertility. We could calculate a table of means based on the assumption of additive, mobile/nonmobile, direction, and distance effects. We could also calculate the table of means based on the assumption of either additive effects or that implied by the direction model. By calculating the deviations of the former model from either of the latter ones and comparing these deviations from the means along the diagonals, we could get an indication of how couples differ in their fertility according to how mobile they have been.

Finally, it is possible that none of the three models will accurately capture the mobility effect because there may still be a significant amount of explained variance in the saturated model left unexplained in the distance model. It is unlikely one would ever encounter this situation; however, should it be the case, one would be forced to conclude that mobility does affect fertility but this effect cannot be accurately summarized or succinctly described.

The above procedure differs from Blau and Duncan's to the extent that if one finds that the additive model does not fit the data, one can search systematically for the best way to describe the mobility effect. We present three mobility models, each more complex than the former, and test to see which best fits the data. We choose that model which most succinctly expresses the mobility effect while capturing all of the effect. In addition to providing a systematic way to express and then interpret the effect of mobility on fertility, the approach lets one control for as many extraneous factors as necessary. It also lets one examine the causal mechanism through which mobility affects fertility. One can assess whether mobility affects fertility via as many of the intermediate variables for which there are data and then examine whether, after considering these indirect paths, mobility has any additional direct effect on the live births couples have. In this causal analysis approach, however, a researcher is not easily able to treat mobility as an intervening or dependent variable. Like Blau and Duncan's, this approach posits that mobility exists only to the extent that it reflects something other than the additive combination of past and present status. As such, it is not a variable that easily lends itself to being regarded as endogenous in a causal model.

We caution that this method of analysis is by no means definitive. The technique is most appropriate when the investigator accepts Blau and Duncan's definition of what constitutes a mobility effect, is willing to assume that mobility affects fertility and not the reverse, and uses only cross-sectional data. It is also more appropriate when examining objective rather than subjective dimensions of mobility, and when this objective dimension (e.g., occupation) can be meaningfully categorized. When longitudinal or life history data are available, we strongly recommend seeking out or developing other methods for analyzing the mobility–fertility relationship.

3   Additional Methods for Examining the Mobility–Fertility Relationship

Our extension of the Blau and Duncan approach is but one technique to analyze the mobility–fertility relationship. Our detailed description of the procedure provides a foundation for understanding how mobility effects may be conceptualized and examined.

In a series of articles, Hope (1971, 1975, 1981) demonstrates that his technique reveals mobility effects on individual behavior which are undiscoverable using the Blau and Duncan approach. The key to Hope's objection to Blau and Duncan's approach is that the definition of mobility as *interaction* is too narrow; instead, Hope argues, mobility should be defined more broadly as deviation from the linear additive model. The Blau and Duncan model is commonly called the "square-additive" model, where rows and columns represent classes of origin and destination. Hope takes the square table and rotates it 135° to create a "diamond-additive" model. In the diamond model the rows represent mobility ($A - B$, where A is class of origin, B is class of destination) and the columns represent a mean of origin and destination class ($A + B$).

In Hope's model tests of mobility effects are derived from the following equations:

$$\hat{Y} = a + b_1(A + B)$$

$$\hat{Y} = a + b_1(A + B) + b_2(A - B)$$

If the first equation explains more variance in the dependent variable than the second, a mobility effect is said to exist. In Hope's model, mobility is defined as *discrepancy* rather than *interaction*.

Hope's objection to the Blau and Duncan approach is more theoretical than methodological. Whether Hope's definition of mobility (or status inconsistency) and the model derived from it accords better with the sociologist's notion of what should constitute a mobility effect is essentially a theoretical argument of how best to conceptualize mobility. House argues for the Blau and Duncan approach and criticizes the diamond-additive model:

> Hope's diamond model yields evidence of an inconsistency effect whenever the status variables involved have unequal effects on a dependent variable . . . . Obviously Hope has a very different conception than previous analysts of what constitutes status inconsistency and an effect thereof (House, 1978, p. 441).

We will not try to resolve this debate. We merely advise those interested in conducting mobility–fertility research to consider carefully Namboodiri's (1972a) caution that the model one chooses to fit to the data will affect the substantive interpretations.

We note one other technique to examine mobility effects on individual behavior. Sobel (1981) argues that neither Blau and Duncan's square-additive model nor Hope's diamond-additive model parameterizes the main effects of class of origin and destination correctly, such that meaningful departures from the baseline acculturation process can be assessed. He therefore proposes the diagonal mobility model for analysis of mobility effects (independent of origin and destination effects) on fertility and other behavior. Sobel claims that his model correctly establishes a correspondence between sociological theory and statistical method.

Sobel's models are statistically rigorous, and we do not present the methodology here. Instead, we invite the reader to review the technique critically. Sobel's model more closely resembles Blau and Duncan's square-additive model and our extension of it in testing against the null hypothesis of acculturation (additive effects of classes of origin and destination), and provides for a systematic search for the most appropriate and succinct way to describe the mobility effect. The technique consists of a class of models, each of which is designed to test whether the existence, direction, or magnitude of mobility is the most parsimonious way to capture its effect on a particular behavior.

More recently Sobel (1984) expands his methodology and demonstrates how predictor variables other than origin, destination, and mobility may be incorporated into the diagonal mobility models as controls. To illustrate, Sobel re-analyzes data from the 1962 Occupational Changes in a Generation survey, originally examined by Blau and Duncan (1967). Like they did, Sobel finds that while there are origin and destination effects of father's and husband's occupations, there are not intergenerational mobility effects per se on children ever born. The acculturation hypothesis finds support; fertility of mobile couples lies intermediate between that of the nonmobile at origin and at destination. Moreover, the relative effects of origin and destination statuses depend on origin status: "For example, origins and destinations are equally important amongst those from farm origins, but origin status is more central than destination status amongst those with higher white collar origins" (Sobel, 1984, p. 1).

Thus, like so many other studies of the mobility–fertility relationship, Sobel finds that the additive model adequately fits the data. Yet, he considers this finding important in its own right and suggest that instead of focusing narrowly on the mobility effect hypothesis, as in the past, researchers should construct and test more elaborate sociological propositions about the relative and/or differential importance of origins and destinations. In particular, Sobel (1984, p. 22) suggests additional examinations of whether fertility of the mobile more closely resembles that of the nonmobile at origin or at destination, and whether the degree to which fertility of the mobile resembles one of the two nonmobile statuses differs by origin status and/or prevalence of movement from that status.

4 Summary

We have considered the methodologies used to examine the mobility–fertility relationship. It should be clear that, although it seems reasonable to define a mobility effect as independent of class of origin and of destination effects, there is no standard, all-purpose way to do so. The various methodological techniques proposed or used in mobility–fertility research add to this topic's reputation as being multifaceted and complex. It would be most helpful were someone to demonstrate more systematically what differences in inferences about the effects of mobility on fertility are found in a given data set by applying these various techniques. Until this is done, all interested in investigating the mobility–fertility relationship must be aware of the alternative methodologies available and must decide for themselves what they are willing to accept as evidence of a mobility effect.

So, too, must the interested person be aware of the conceptual complexities involved in mobility–fertility research. Our previous chapters were prepared with the objective of untangling and shedding light on these issues. We believe that social scientists will remain at their wits' end in trying to test the social mobility–fertility hypothesis until these conceptual and methodological complexities are addressed in their research.

Based on all evidence to date, we are forced to conclude there is little evidence suggesting that mobility affects fertility per se (by the unsettling process of the move itself). Perhaps, then, in addition to devoting more careful thought to the mobility effects hypothesis, it is time to investigate more broadly defined mechanisms of rising status and their effects on fertility.

Our springboard for the remainder of this book is therefore based on the strong evidence for the acculturation hypothesis. While not attributable to the direct *process* of mobility in itself, this evidence has clearly and consistently demonstrated differential fertility by mobility status. In point of fact, without mobility, there would not be a new destination status to influence the fertility behavior of the individual. Mobility can thus be viewed as a necessary dynamic process for acculturation to have any meaning, let alone effect. As Lopreato *et al.* (1976, p. 5) observe, "if the mobile couples had not been mobile, their fertility rate might have been different. It was mobility that made possible the influence of the new class."

Support for the acculturation hypothesis is also especially germane to population policy, which is a core concern of the second part of the book. Although low status of origin will continue to affect fertility, provided there is an inverse relationship between socioeconomic status and fertility, those who rise in status will partially adopt the lower fertility patterns of their higher status destination groups. And if more upward than downward mobility occurs, the overall fertility of the population will decrease.

While Sobel's (1984) as well as Zimmer's (1981a) recommendations for expanding the theoretical agenda on social mobility and fertility are to devote greater attention to the relative and differential importance of occupational origins and destinations, ours is cast in even broader terms. A fundamental feature of status enhancement is the transition from traditional to more modern attitudes and behavior—a necessary prerequisite for reduced fertility. Whereas an increase in occupational status or prestige may be one mechanism through which more modern fertility attitudes and behavior obtain, it need not be the only or most important mechanism.

In our prior discussion of the role education plays in the mobility–fertility relationship, we suggested it may "drive" or at the very least condition this relationship. We believe that the root cause of the transition from traditional to more modern fertility attitudes and behavior may not lie in status enhancement as measured by a rise on the occupational scale, but rather by a rise in educational attainment—an initial, fostering condition for subsequent, multiple manifestations of status attainment. For this reason, we contend that theoretical development of the notion of educational attainment as the "engine" of status enhancement constitutes one of the most important avenues of investigating the impact of changes in social status on fertility. The remainder of this book is directed to that line of inquiry.

Chapter 6 | Education, Status Enhancement, and Fertility

Our appraisal of research on social mobility and fertility showed that conceptualization and measurement of a woman's status have typically focused on the social standing of her father or her husband. This approach has some legitimacy since, until recent decades, the status of women in most societies was almost always determined by that of her father and husband.

Times are changing. Social scientists increasingly recognize that a woman may derive her status independent of husband or father (Mason, 1984; Safilios-Rothschild, 1982). New conceptualizations of appropriate roles are emerging such as egalitarian marriages, increased participation of women in the mainstream economy, their being single parents, and women's involvement in all aspects of reproductive decision making including their ability to control fertility. With improving transport and communications technology (and corresponding rapid social diffusion), these behavior changes are being experienced in many parts of the world.

1 Education as an Engine of Status Enhancement

For developing countries, women's transition from traditional to more modern attitudes and behavior is generally regarded as fundamental to their status enhancement and a necessary prerequisite for reduced fertility levels (Nag, 1983b; Stycos, 1979). Research on this transition is a most important avenue of investigating the impact of social status changes on fertility. Missing from much of this research, however, is a specific focus on *women* and the factors bringing about their transition from traditional to modern attitudes and behavior. How do women shed older values and beliefs? How do they become involved in institutions of the larger society? How do they improve their position within their household and community? How do they gain greater autonomy in shaping their biological and social destinies? We believe that educating women and extending opportunities to make use of their educational achievements are pivotal in fostering these transitions. A substantial number of scholars share this belief with us (Ainsworth, 1984; Caldwell, 1978, 1980; Chaudhury, 1982; Cochrane, 1979, 1983; Curtin, 1982; Dixon, 1975a; D. S. Freedman, 1963: Graff, 1979; Inkeles, 1974; Wolfe, 1980).

How does education facilitate these transitions and consequently enhance a woman's status? First and foremost, schooling increases a woman's knowledge and competence in virtually all sectors of contemporary life. It broadens her access to information via the mass media and printed material. It develops her intellectual capacities and exposes her to interpersonal competition and achievement. It gives her an opportunity to acquire marketable skills and other personal resources to pursue nonfamilial roles. It raises her image of her potentials and those of her children, and it simultaneously imparts her with a sense of efficacy and trust in modern science and technology which encourages her to control her fate and body (Blood and Wolfe, 1960; Germain, 1975; Holsinger, 1974; Holsinger and Kasarda, 1976; Mason, 1984; Rodman, 1972; Rosen and LaRaia, 1972; Safilios-Rothschild, 1972).

How do these changes associated with increasing women's education manifest themselves in lowered fertility? This question is best answered by identifying the variables that mediate the effects of women's education and explicating the processes by which each influences fertility. This process involves synthesizing the disparate research literature on social and economic fertility determinants into theoretical models which specify the mechanisms by which women's education influences reproductive behavior.

We begin with an overview of empirical findings on the female education–fertility relationship in developed and developing countries. In a theory section we discuss fundamental socioeconomic variables that link education to fertility. Our summary presents a working model, bringing together the basic variables we propose to be instrumental in the female education–fertility causal chain.

Detailed specification of the transmitting structures and processes through which female education influences reproduction require separate chapters. Chapter 7 focuses on employment opportunities outside the home; Chapter 8 on value of children; Chapter 9 on infant and child mortality; Chapter 10 on age at marriage; and Chapter 11 on knowledge and use of contraceptive methods. In each we examine how the particular variable relates to education and fertility and specify the causal processes that we propose interpret the empirical associations reported.

Our models in this chapter and those which follow are presented for heuristic purposes. We make no pretense that they represent the only theoretical interpretations of empirical associations observed. Rather, we hope these models stimulate others to test and amend our specifications to advance research and theory on the social and economic determinants of fertility.

2 Education and Fertility: Basic Associations

The education–fertility relationship in developed countries has been studied extensively [see Cochrane, (1979) and Stout (1984) for literature reviews]. Widespread findings of a negative association have emerged (Berent, 1983; Blake, 1967; Rindfuss and Sweet, 1977). More than a decade ago the Commission on Population Growth and the American Future (1972, pp. 155–156) concluded, "There is an abundant evidence that higher educational attainment is associated with smaller families in the United States. The highest fertility is among the least educated women and the lowest among women with the most education."

Data gathered for the United States as part of the mid-1970s World Fertility Survey (WFS) illustrate the pervasiveness of the association. As shown in Table 1, the ultimate expected number of children of married women is a near uniform negative function of their educational levels, even when holding constant husband's education, family income, and wife's work history, intensity of religious feeling, and marriage cohort. Analysis of Swiss cross-sectional and longitudinal historical data adds further evidence that, controlling for other socioeconomic variables, as the educational level rises, marital fertility declines (van de Walle, 1980).

While most studies in developed nations have shown a linear, inverse relationship between education and fertility, some have reported curvilinear ones. More education is not always associated with fewer children (Freedman *et al.*, 1959; Mason *et al.*, 1971; Wolfe, 1980). Studies based in England and Wales, the Netherlands, Norway, and West Germany have detected a U-shaped relationship (Cochrane, 1979)—the average number of children born tends to be higher among the *least* and *most* educated women.

Cross-national WFS data presented by Berent (1983) illustrate the variability among more developed nations in the functional form of the female education–fertility relationship (see Table 2). As in the United States, the ultimate number of children married women expect monotonically declines with their education levels in Bulgaria, Czechoslavakia, Finland, Italy, the Netherlands, Poland, and Romania. However, France exhibits an L-shaped association and Hungary shows marginal increments in the ultimate number of children wives expect with postsecondary education compared to higher secondary education. Denmark, Great Britain, and Spain, and to some extent, Belgium, exhibit a U-shaped association between the selected fertility indicator and education.

In developing countries, an inverse relationship between education and fertil-

Table 1

Ultimate Expected Number of Children[a] of Married Women by Education Cross-Classified
by Husband's Education, Total Family Income, Wife's Work History, Intensity
of Religious Feelings, and Marriage Cohort—United States, 1976[b]

Sociodemographic variables	Elementary		Secondary		
	Some	Completed	Lower	Higher	Post
Husband's education					
Some elementary	4.39[c]	3.82[c]	3.82[c]	2.99	—[d]
Elementary completed	—	3.11	2.73	2.85	2.41[c]
Lower-high secondary	4.65[c]	3.21	3.03	2.49	2.55[c]
Higher secondary	—	2.70	2.76	2.58	2.43
Postsecondary	—	—	2.72	2.62	2.35
Total family income					
Very low	3.53		2.94	2.89	2.77
Low	3.12		2.87	2.62	2.48
Medium	3.34[c]		2.80	2.63	2.37
High	3.03[c]		2.70	2.57	2.42
Very high	—		2.60	2.32	2.30
Wife's work history					
Currently working	2.76		2.58	2.42	2.23
Worked since marriage/ not currently	3.38		2.90	2.68	2.50
Worked before marriage/never worked	3.69		3.33	2.86	2.71
Wife's intensity of religious feelings					
Catholics					
Strong	—		3.70[c]	3.12	2.96
Moderate	3.73[c]		2.86[c]	2.95	2.46
Weak	3.50		2.91	2.70	2.45
Protestants					
Strong	3.05		2.95	2.58	2.42
Moderate	3.66		3.03	2.46	2.48
Weak	3.05		2.73	2.41	2.25
Wife's marriage cohort					
Pre-1955	4.66[c]	4.49	3.97	3.47	3.35
1956–1960	4.55[c]	3.82	3.44	3.08	2.70
1961–1965	4.55[c]	2.98	2.78	2.62	2.38
1966–1970	4.12[c]	2.78	2.51	2.22	2.08
1971 or later	3.03[c]	2.43	2.36	2.22	1.99

[a]Ultimate expected number of children = the sum of past live births reported by respondent at time of interview and number of additional children she said she expected to have in the future.

[b]Source: Berent (1983, Tables 8, 9, 13, 16, 21).

[c]Based on 10–49 respondents.

[d]Not available, not pertinent, or not applicable.

Table 2

Ultimate Expected Number of Children of Married Women[a] (Standardized by Marriage Duration) by Education Level—World Fertility Survey, More Developed Countries, ca. 1977[b]

Wife's education	Countries[c]													
	BE	BUL	CZ	DEN	FIN	FR	GBR	HUN	ITAL	NETH	POL	ROM	SP	USA
Some elementary	2.17	2.84	3.82		—	3.01	—	3.43	3.13	2.84	3.09	2.41	3.05	4.03
Elementary completed		2.06	2.71	2.46	2.51	2.46	2.55	2.53	2.42		2.77	2.32	2.70	3.12
Lower secondary	2.29	1.88	2.47	2.29	2.43	2.38	2.32	2.06	2.18	2.51	2.40	2.13	2.78	2.85
Higher secondary	2.20	1.84	2.26	2.26	2.41	2.35	2.24	1.91	2.12	2.45	2.17	2.03	2.72	2.60
Postsecondary	2.36	1.72	2.13	2.39	2.32	2.35	2.32	1.93	—	2.42	2.00	1.99	3.03	2.38

[a]Ultimate expected number of children = the sum of past live births reported by respondent at time of interview and number of additional children she said she expected to have in the future.

[b]Source: Berent (1983, Table 6).

[c]Countries: BE (Belgium), BUL (Bulgaria), CZ (Czechoslovakia), DEN (Denmark), FIN (Finland), FR (France), GBR (Great Britain), HUN (Hungary), ITAL (Italy), NETH (Netherlands), POL (Poland), ROM (Romania), SP (Spain), USA (United States of America).

ity has been the most frequently reported (Alam and Casterline, 1984; Bhat-nagar, 1972; Cochrane, 1983; Concepción, 1981; Freedman and Takeshita, 1969; Goldstein, 1972; Heer, 1971; Hermalin and Mason, 1980; Hodgson and Gibbs, 1980; Minkler, 1970; Mitchell, 1972; Rosen and Simmons, 1971; Stycos, 1968; Stycos and Weller, 1967). Depending on the measures used and country context, the strength of association varies, but the pattern is broadly consistent: as female education level rises, fertility declines.

Associations observed, however, like those in developed countries have not always been either linear or monotonic. While the transition from illiteracy to literacy usually depresses fertility, the most substantial reductions often come with increases from elementary schooling (4 to 6 years) to secondary and above (7+) years of education (Carleton, 1967; Cochrane, 1979; Tienda, 1984).

Table 3, presenting WFS total fertility rates by years of schooling for ever-married or ever-in-union women in 5 African, 12 Latin American, and 7 Asian nations depicts this situation. In Kenya, Senegal, the Dominican Republic, Guyana, Bangladesh, and the Philippines fertility rates of women age 15–49 with 1 to 3 years of schooling are higher than those with no schooling. Our reanalysis of the CELADE survey data (1969–1970) for rural regions of Colombia, Costa Rica, Mexico, and Peru likewise showed that controlling for respondent's age, women with small amounts of elementary school education reported more live births than those with no schooling. Cochrane, noting an identical pattern in several Asian and African countries suggests:

> a small amount of education can weaken traditional restraints on fertility such as prolonged breastfeeding, polygamy, and postpartum abstinence without encouraging sufficient contraceptive use to offset these changes (Cochrane, 1979, p. 67).

Of these factors, differential breast-feeding practices appear to be the most important in accounting for the slight rise in fertility among those with small amounts of education in certain developing countries in the Americas, Asia, and Africa. Analysis of WFS data has turned up striking educational differentials in these countries in the likelihood and duration of breast feeding (Ferry and Smith, 1983; Jain and Bongaarts, 1981; Nag, 1983b). Whereas breast feeding was found to decline monotonically with education level in nearly all developing countries studied, some of the most dramatic declines occurred between women with no education and those with 1 to 3 years of schooling. For example, in Haiti, the mean duration of breast feeding among women with no education is 17.0 months compared to 12.7 months among those with 1 to 3 years of education (Ferry and Smith, 1983).

Prolonged lactation protects against conception primarily by extending amenorrhea (i.e., inhibiting the return to ovulation). In the absence of breast feeding, postpartum amenorrhea averages only about 2 months (Knodel, 1982a). With continuous breast feeding, amenorrhea may be extended to a year or more, substantially lengthening birth intervals which, in turn, results in lower completed fertility. Indeed, decomposing differentials in marital fertility using WFS data for 29 developing countries, Casterline *et al.* (1984) find lactational amenorrhea and contraception to be of roughly equal importance.

Whereas breast-feeding differences likely account for most of the perturbed

Table 3

Total Fertility Rate (TFR) of Ever-Married Women or Women Ever in a Union, Age 15–49, by Years of Schooling—World Fertility Surveys, Africa, the Americas, and Asia, ca. 1977[a]

Country	Years of schooling			
	0	1–3	4–6	7+
Africa				
Ghana	6.84	6.67	6.96	5.49
Kenya	8.28	9.21	8.43	7.34
Lesotho	6.24	5.63	5.97	4.76
Senegal	7.32	9.44	6.31	4.47
Sudan	6.47	5.56	4.98	3.37
Americas				
Colombia	7.03	6.04	3.85	2.59
Costa Rica[b]	4.46	4.07	3.11	2.54
Dominican Republic	6.99	7.29	5.37	2.98
Guyana	6.55	6.97	5.56	4.84
Haiti	6.05	4.75	4.06	2.85
Jamaica	6.19	5.92	5.76	4.83
Mexico	8.06	7.47	5.75	3.34
Panama[b]	5.70	5.58	4.12	2.71
Paraguay	8.23	6.61	4.62	2.94
Peru	7.32	6.75	5.06	3.27
Trinidad and Tobago	4.63	3.45	4.13	3.21
Venezuela[c]	7.02	6.36	4.57	2.64
Asia				
Bangladesh	6.07	6.35	6.72	4.98
Jordan	9.34	8.63	6.98	4.91
Korea	5.71	5.46	4.48	3.35
Malaysia	5.30	5.26	4.81	3.19
Pakistan	6.51	5.41	6.12	3.14
Philippines	5.45	6.97	6.15	3.84
Syria	8.81	6.71	5.59	4.08

[a]Source: Alam and Casterline (1984, Table 5).
[b]TFR, ages 20–49.
[c]TFR, ages 15–44.

rise in fertility among women with small amounts of education, other factors such as poor health and nutrition among women with no education may lower their fertility because of their reduced fecundity, higher age at menarche, and increased spontaneous fetal losses (Bongaarts, 1980; Gray, 1983). In addition, as noted above, a slight amount of education may serve to inhibit other traditional constraints on fertility such as taboos on postpartum intercourse. Finally, women with absolutely no education may systematically understate live births. Thus, at least part of the nonmonotonicity in reported fertility may simply reflect measurement error. (On procedures for detecting errors in retrospective reports of births, see Brass, 1979.)

In sum, empirical studies have generally reported negative overall relationships for education and fertility. The strength of association tends to vary among countries and with the fertility and education measures used. A straight (linear) negative relationship is steepest in countries with modest development. In the most and least developed countries, the relationship is weaker and not always monotonically negative. Though this lack of uniformity in empirical findings may be attributed in part to methodological differences (Graff, 1979) or, in some least developed nations, measurement error, it leaves us with uncertainty as to the actual effects of educational advancements. Such uncertainty will prevail until a theoretical basis is developed for the causal linkages between female education and fertility (Graff, 1979; Jain, 1981).

3 Theoretical Explanations

We have argued that increased female education is not only the prime instrument for enhancing the status of women, but it is perhaps the single most important institutional variable amenable to policy manipulation that can help reduce fertility rates in developing nations. Policymakers, however, do not have a clear understanding of *how* education affects fertility. The role of education has frequently been assumed without specification of the causal processes that lead to lower fertility among those women with more education. Close examination of the literature suggests that education affects fertility in distinct ways:

1. *Directly,* by shaping psychic orientations favoring smaller family size
2. *Indirectly,* by influencing a myriad of social, economic, and demographic variables (e.g., employment status, age at marriage, knowledge and practice of contraception) which, in turn, bear on fertility
3. *Jointly,* by interacting with contextual and other factors which condition the effects of female education.

In the sections which follow, we briefly elaborate each of these causal mechanisms.

Direct Effects of Female Education on Fertility

Specifying direct effects of female education on fertility requires a reduced form conceptualization of the education–fertility linkage that excludes certain proximate determinants, particularly those of a biological nature (Bongaarts, 1978, 1980, 1983; Casterline *et al.,* 1984; Davis and Blake, 1956). Even when focusing solely on socioeconomic determinants of fertility, it may be argued that there can be no direct effects and that even the hypothesized effects of highly focused instruction in reproductive behavior, contraception, and population education must be considered indirect owing to the complex and often tenuous link between the teaching act and learning outcome and between these factors and smaller family size. This reasoning holds that all influences of female education on fertility are indirect (Cochrane, 1983; Holsinger and Kasarda, 1976; Peipmeier and Adkins, 1973; Westoff and Potvin, 1967).

While we fundamentally agree with such reasoning, we remain open to the suggestion that female education might directly affect fertility (net of other social and economic causal variables), when the effects are defined as follows. Education has been found to influence a broad spectrum of social–psychological orientations in women, including freedom from tradition, greater faith in science and technology, heightened aspirations for themselves and their children, attitudes and sentiments toward smaller families, and *modern* values that promote use of contraception (Caldwell, 1968b, 1978, 1980; Carleton, 1967; Chung *et al.,* 1972; Dixon, 1976; Fawcett and Bornstein, 1973; Inkeles, 1974; Jaffe, 1959; Mandelbaum, 1974; Stycos, 1979). Education's direct effects on fertility may thus be conceptualized as the environment, curriculum, and content of schooling, all of which expose women to heterogeneous values, promote logical thought processes and inculcate attitudes favoring contraception and restricted family sizes, often noted in the literature on modernization (Fawcett and Bornstein, 1973; Inkeles, 1974; Holsinger and Kasarda, 1976; Oppong, 1983; Palmore, 1974).

Several scholars have looked at associations between education and acquiring modern attitudes and values. Most see modernity in women as a by-product of the process of industrialization (Collver and Langlois, 1962; Fox, 1973; Goode, 1963; Vig, 1977; Wilensky, 1968). As industrialization progresses, women are simultaneously exposed to greater educational opportunities and alternatives to the roles of wife and mother, thus becoming more activistic, future oriented, and open to new experiences.

Rosen and LaRaia (1972, p. 353) have summarized the attitudinal and value changes expected as a woman becomes more "modern":

1. Changes about her sense of worth as a member of a sex perceived as competent and deserving of serious attention
2. Changes in her participation in an egalitarian nuclear family structure em-

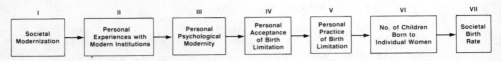

Fig. 1. Sequential block model linking modernization to societal birth rates via individual modernity influences on the individual. Adapted from Miller and Inkeles (1974).

phasizing communication between spouses and placing importance on their equal decision making

3. Changes in the socialization of offspring to be independent and have aspirations
4. Changes in her perception of the world as being controllable through activistic endeavor.

Holsinger (1974) found these attitude and value changes tightly connected to the amount of schooling, while Miller and Inkeles (1974) and Singh (1982) have documented the power of these psyhic changes in reducing fertility. Based on research on modernization and fertility in East Pakistan, India, Israel, and Nigeria, Miller and Inkeles proposed a model specifying the sequential operative structures and processes for individuals which implement causal relations for society (Fig. 1).

Miller and Inkeles' empirical analysis focused on relationships among blocks 2 through 5. They found the psychological orientations favoring birth limitation came primarily from experience with modern institutions—schools, factories, the mass media—and were substantially predictive of accepting birth limitation and practicing birth control. The instrumental nature of these predictive factors led the authors to conclude that structural changes in a society's institutions will have little or no effect on accepting birth limitation without corresponding changes in psychic orientations toward smaller families (a key dependent variable in our reduced form conceptualization).

In like manner, Fox (1973) studied 803 married women in Turkey using behavior and attitude measures of modernism. Modern *behavior* was measured by whether a woman wore short-sleeved dresses, sat with men during visits to her home, shopped alone, talked to men unknown by her husband, went out without her head covered, visited women unknown to her husband, and attended parties or matinees alone. Modern *attitudes* were measured by statements related to gender division of labor, decision making, and separation of sexes in general.

Combining the attitude and behavior dimensions generated four types of women:

1. Free moderns (free behavior, modern attitudes)
2. Free traditionals (free behavior, traditional attitudes)

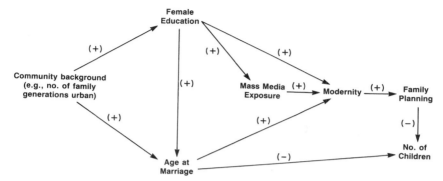

Fig. 2. Modified model of channeling function of psychological modernity. Adapted from Fox (1973).

3. Constrained moderns (constrained behavior, modern attitudes)
4. Constrained traditionals (constrained behavior, traditional attitudes).

Fox asked about family size of women over age 45 and family size expectations of younger women. As anticipated, women with smaller actual or expected families were freer or less constrained than those who had or expected larger families. Eighty percent of free modern women had a small family orientation, compared to 70% of the free traditional, 48% of the constrained modern, and 42% of the constrained traditional women. Virtually identical gradients were found in the percentages who practiced contraception.

Fox modeled the process by which women acquire attributes of modernism in developing societies. Our modified and extended version of her model is presented in Fig. 2.

In this model, community background effects (urban vs rural) on attitudes and behavior are transmitted through childhood education and age at marriage. In rural areas, where early marriage and traditional familial roles are encouraged, female education is considered unnecessary and an intrusion of the profane world into the minds of women. Such views strongly condition the availability of education for women (Fox, 1973, p. 523). Urban settings offer greater encouragement and opportunities for nonfamilial role behavior and thus more support for female education and later marriage.

Consistent with this proposition, Fox found women with rural heritages concentrated in the less-than-primary education category; the majority of women who grew up in urban locales had at least a primary school education. The former tended to marry before age 15, the latter to wait until they were at least 20.

In addition to direct effects of female education on modern attitudes and behavior, education exhibits indirect effects via age at marriage. Fox suggests age at marriage has implications not only for the stage of a woman's personal development on entering into a sexual union, but also for the type of role she plays relative to her husband and kin. Younger marital unions often restrict these nonfamilial influences on women which encourage them to assert their potential for self-development and independence.

The model further specifies that the impact of education on a woman's attitudes and behavior is partly channeled through exposure to the mass media—a major link to the modern world. Attitudes about appropriate role behavior, more egalitarian marriage patterns, participation of women in household decision making, and the notion of the emancipated woman have increasingly come from the mass media, especially, printed.

Overall, Fox contends (and we concur) that education is the key in a woman's transformation from traditional to more modern attitudes and values and from constrained to emancipated behavior:

> Through continued education, women are exposed to new opportunities for broader societal participation, they are presented with alternatives to the traditional wife and mother roles. Since it functions as an introduction to alternative modes of thinking and provides as well a positive orientation to further openness of attitudes and behavior, modern education can be seen as a vital step in the emergence process (Fox, 1973, p. 523).

In numerous other studies, education has been found instrumental in shaping attitudes, values, and preferences for family sizes (Holsinger and Kasarda, 1976; Rosen and LaRaia, 1972; Stycos, 1979). Education is a pivotal factor in developing logical, independent thought, as well as self-interest and personally gratifying goals (Graff, 1979). Indeed, Rosen and LaRaia suggest that education so affects the interior landscape of a woman's mind that it may be used as a proxy for what she believes and how she views her own life.

Thus, our rationale for specifying a direct effect of female education on fertility rests with the contention that it is an overarching socialization process that inculcates modern attitudes and encourages behavior conducive to family size limitation. The causal operators and transmitting factors in the socialization process are specified in Fig. 3.

4   Indirect Effects of Female Education on Fertility

Most concur that the primary effect of female education on fertility comes through its influence on other variables bearing directly on reproductive behavior. At this point, we examine only briefly some socioeconomic variables with important mediating or conditioning roles in the female education–fertility relationship. A more detailed account of the indirect effects of education on each of these and other mediating variables is reserved for subsequent chapters. The linkages to be briefly discussed here include the effect of female education on

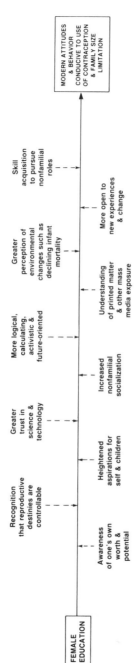

Fig. 3. Causal operators and transmitting processes explaining the specified direct effect of female education on reproductive behavior.

labor force participation, the value of children, age at marriage or at first birth, infant and child mortality, and knowledge and use of contraception.[1]

Labor Force Participation

In many developing nations, the career of an uneducated woman is often restricted to that of housewife and mother; her only way to demonstrate her worth and obtain family and community status is by producing children. The educated woman can achieve status by such alternatives as obtaining employment in offices, factories, and other modern sectors of developing economies (Kasarda, 1971; Mott and Shapiro, 1983; Rothman de Biscossa, 1969; Weller, 1977). Through well-paying jobs open to her because of formal training, the educated woman may become self-sufficient and less inclined to early marriage. Furthermore, married and single women with higher levels of education are more likely to find jobs providing them with satisfactions competing with those derived from having children, such as companionship, recreation, and creative activity, or the financial means to realize them (Baldwin and Nord, 1984; Blake, 1965; Elizaga, 1975; Youssef, 1974).

Value of Children

Educated women can better assess the relative costs and benefits of children. Their education reduces the economic utility of their children in several ways (Arnold et al., 1975; Becker, 1960; Chang, 1979; Friedlander and Silver, 1967; Kagitcibasi and Esmer, 1980; Mason, 1984; Mueller, 1972b; Oppong, 1983; Repetto, 1976a). On one hand, the cost of children increases with mothers' education because the better educated typically have higher educational aspirations for their children and are more likely to view family size in terms of quantity versus quality investment tradeoffs (Mason, 1984; Meeks and Lee, 1979; Michael, 1973; Mueller, 1972a; Rosenzweig, 1978). On the other hand, benefits accrued from children diminish, such as depending on them for future economic assistance (Birdsall, 1974; Cain, 1982). The higher paying jobs of women with more education provide them with growing self-reliance and greater security for old age or widowhood (Mason, 1984; Mueller, 1972b, 1976). Children are no longer the only way to secure position within the family and in society, especially within the husband's family. Educated women are more likely

[1]Labor force participation and the value of children influence demand for children. Age at marriage, age at first birth, and infant and child mortality affect the supply of children. Family planning knowledge and use regulates the outcome of supply and demand.

to be recognized as other than wife and mother. As women become more aware of such alternatives for status and satisfaction, a large family may also be perceived as disadvantageous (Dyson and Moore, 1983; Mason, 1984). Finally, while in school, children's economic contributions to parents through wage or salary employment or household chores are restricted whereas costs of children in school tend to rise (clothing, books, etc.), making larger families economically burdensome (Caldwell, 1980; Kasarda, 1971).

Infant and Child Mortality

In developed and developing countries, infant and child mortality is much lower among families with greater education (Adamchak and Stockwell, 1978; Caldwell, 1979; Caldwell and McDonald, 1982; Hobcraft et al., 1983; Hull and Hull 1977b; Stockwell and Hutchinson, 1975). In developing countries secondary education, in particular, makes a difference in infant and child mortality; rates in the highest educational groups are less than half those of the least educated groups (Caldwell and McDonald, 1982; CICRED, 1983; Hull and Hull, 1977b).

One explanation for the relationships between education and infant and child mortality is that education results in better understanding of hygiene and sanitation (Stephens, 1984; Ware, 1984) and the signs, prevention, and treatment of illness (Caldwell and McDonald, 1982; Hobcraft et al., 1983). Women with higher education may have much more influence on matters related to rearing their children, including decisions about nutrition and health (Caldwell, 1983; Caldwell and McDonald, 1982; Chen, 1983). These factors combined with the favorable social position generally enjoyed by women with higher education increase the probability that expectant mothers and their offspring will be healthy (Arriaga, 1970; Chandrasekhar, 1972; Schultz, 1976).

Thus, women with more education are less likely to experience infant and child mortality. They can recognize that the mortality of their infants and children will be low; they know that they do not need—and are not likely to try—to have additional children for replacement purposes.

Age at Marriage

Studies in developed and developing countries have shown that education is an important predictor of age at marriage or entry into a union and age at first birth (CELADE and CFSC, 1972; Davidson, 1973; Dixon, 1971; Husain, 1970; Hobcraft and Casterline, 1983; Mandelbaum, 1974; McCarthy, 1982; Nag, 1983b; Scanzoni, 1975; Waite and Spitze, 1981; Yaukey, 1973; Yaukey and

Thorsen, 1972). The higher the educational level, the older the age at marriage (Anderson, 1981; Marini, 1978; Smith, 1983) and at first birth (Bloom and Trussell, 1983; Hirschman and Rindfuss, 1980; Rindfuss and St. John, 1983). Older age at marriage in turn is related to more condensed childbearing and lower completed fertility. Where contraception is widely practiced, age at first birth rather than age at marriage has been shown to be the more pertinent variable apropos reproductive behavior (Rindfuss et al., 1980, 1984).

Why is it that the more education a woman has, the older she is when she marries or has her first child? Most importantly, education opens the door to roles other than those of wife or mother. Education, we have noted, fosters awareness and knowledge about alternate adult roles and is the key to acquiring them. Simply put, with more education and correspondingly more alternatives open to a woman, she is more likely to postpone marriage and childbearing (Mason, 1984; Mueller, 1972a,b; Repetto, 1976b; Rindfuss et al., 1984; Smith, 1983).

Knowledge and Practice of Family Planning

In developed and developing countries, knowledge and practice of contraception are linked closely to the educational level of wives and husbands (Berent, 1982; CELADE and CFSC, 1972; Dandekar, 1965; Dow, 1971; Husain, 1970; Janowitz, 1976; Kripalani et al., 1971; Michael, 1973; Miró and Rath, 1965; Rindfuss and Westoff, 1974; Sathar and Chidambaram, 1984; Sen and Sen, 1967). Most research supports an earlier conclusion by Freedman and co-workers (1959, p. 115) that "the more education a wife or husband has, the more likely it is that the couple has used contraception, that they began early in marriage, and that they have planned their pregnancies and avoided more than they wanted."

Family planning information generally comes in pamphlets and other printed media (Cernada and Lu, 1972; D. S. Freedman, 1976). Schooling beyond the primary grades increasingly exposes young women to such media.

Husband–wife communication is essential to effective family planning as well (Brody et al., 1976; Hollerbach, 1983; Mukherjee, 1975). Increased education improves communication between wives and husbands about desired family size (Olusanya, 1971). Women educated beyond minimal levels can better express their feelings and desires about the often sensitive issues of contraception and family size (Carleton, 1967). The effect of husband–wife communication on fertility outcomes can be quite important, as Stycos (1967) has shown. He found Puerto Rican husbands and wives with little or no formal education actually wanted fewer children, but did not practice contraception because of the mistaken belief that their spouses desired additional children.

Related to contraceptive practice is education's primary positive indirect effect on fertility through breast-feeding practices. Breast-feeding duration (lactational amenorrhea) which is often consciously used for birth spacing or limiting purposes is inversely related to education level (Jain and Bongaarts, 1981). In fact, it has been argued that education's effect on differential fertility can be decomposed into two basic components—its positive effect via shorter breast-feeding duration and its negative effect via increased use of modern contraceptive methods (Jain, 1981). Lower fertility among women with greater education is posited to occur as a result of increased modern contraceptive practices more than compensating for education's positive effect via decreased breast-feeding durations.

Summary of Major Indirect Effects

The proposed primary indirect causal linkages in the relationship between female education and fertility can be summarized thus:

- Increased education enhances a woman's prospects for obtaining employment outside the home which competes with bearing and raising children as a career.
- Increased female education reduces the perceived economic utility of children, thus lowering the demand for them.
- Increased female education delays age at marriage and first birth, in turn lowering completed fertility.
- Increased female education indirectly affects fertility by helping women recognize that the mortality of their children will be lower and they need not have additional children as insurance against anticipated losses.
- Increased female education provides directly for or facilitates the acquisition of information on modern contraceptive devices and their use. It increases exposure to mass media and printed materials about family planning, and improves communication between husbands and wives in ways conducive to lower fertility.

These and related propositions will be substantially elaborated in Chapters 7 through 12.

5   Interaction Effects of Female Education on Fertility

In addition to hypothesized direct and indirect effects on fertility, female education interacts with other exogenous variables (and some intervening variables such as labor force participation) so that its influence is conditioned by the presence or levels of other variables. For example, during the 1950s education was found to be differentially related to fertility when comparing active Catholics with Protestants (Westoff *et al.*, 1963). Westoff *et al.* reported that while additional education depressed fertility among non-Catholic and less active Catholic women, the amount of formal education had little or no effect on very active Catholic women. Although the strength of this conditioning variable has diminished in more recent years (Westoff and Jones, 1979), active Catholicism and education in Catholic schools still appear to play a role in influencing the effects of education and other socioeconomic variables (Blake, 1984; Mosher and Hendershot, 1984; Mosher and Goldscheider, 1984).

Another conditioning factor in the female education–fertility causal chain is residence. The urban milieu as the nucleus of social change in developing countries restricts young women less to traditional kinship norms and makes contraception information and material more readily available to those who desire it (Curtin, 1982; Goldberg, 1976). Urban locations also provide women with greater access to employment in modern sectors of the economy and expose them to consumption goods and lifestyle alternatives to bearing and rearing children (Mason and Palan, 1981). Furthermore, the actual and opportunity costs of raising children are higher in urban centers while the economic returns of children to the family tend to be less there as compared to rural sectors (Kasarda, 1971). Thus, education has been shown to have a much more pronounced negative effect on fertility in urban compared to rural settings (Cochrane, 1983).

Moreover, when considering the effect of a married woman's education on fertility, her husband's education is also important (CELADE and CFSC, 1972; Cochrane, 1979; Westoff and Ryder, 1977). A woman's education and her spouse's interact and jointly influence reproductive behavior, such that the amount of fertility reduction expected with additional female education is predicated, in part, on the educational level of her spouse. This should particularly be the case in those societies where social status remains predicated upon husband's standing and where men remain the primary decision makers in a couple's reproductive behavior.

As an important aside, it should be pointed out that female education is related more strongly to fertility than is male education (Chaudhury, 1977; Cochrane, 1979, 1983; Kocher, 1977). Thus, in discussing policy issues, Dixon (1975a, p. 40) contends "investment in female education may have a greater impact on fertility than the same investment in schooling for men." Such a conclusion has found support in the WFS data for less developed countries. Rodríguez and Cleland's (1981) data, for example, show that over the range of education from none to secondary school, there is a difference of 1.9 children for women compared to 1.3 for men. Extending Rodríguez and Cleland's analysis, Cochrane (1983, p. 602) reports that, controlling for pertinent variables, "the effect of female education is still to reduce fertility by almost one child; the effect of male

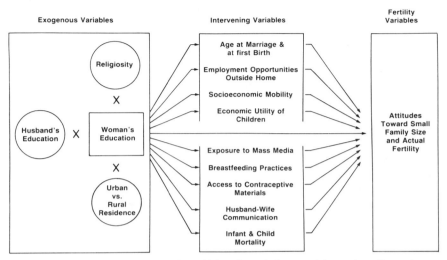

Fig. 4. Causal model to be assessed specifying direct, indirect, and interaction effects of women's education on fertility. × is an expected interaction factor conditioning the effects of female education.

education is one third as large." Moreover, as indicated above, residence was found to interact with both husband's and wife's education so that education's effects are weaker in rural than urban settings.

Figure 4 illustrates a few of the possible factors conditioning the female education–fertility relationship. An extensive presentation of interaction effects is beyond the scope of this book, although in subsequent chapters we discuss some of the more pertinent variables, such as level of economic development, that may condition the effects of education and other socioeconomic variables on fertility. We urge researchers always to consider possible interaction and conditional effects when developing and assessing causal models apropos socioeconomic determinants of fertility.

6   Conceptualizing and Measuring Education

As discussed in our examination of the social mobility–fertility relationship, appropriate conceptualization and measurement of variables are essential for effective analysis. For the researcher interested in examining the relationship between education and fertility, these steps are not as straightforward as they might first appear. For example, several meanings can be attached to the concept "education." To some, education is a process of socialization into society's norms, values, and roles. To others, education is a process of obtaining factual knowledge and acquiring basic skills—in the end, a means to achieve certification of the level of attained learning, which, in turn, determines the opportunity for further advancements in society.

Depending on the aspects of education deemed important by the researcher, different operational definitions will be employed. In much fertility research, number of years of formal schooling completed has been used to measure the extent of exposure to values, norms, and roles in society and the levels of skills attained. If the focus is on acquired skills—the end result rather than the process—education may be conceptualized as literacy and operationalized as ability to read. General newspaper circulation is sometimes used to reflect reading level with higher circulation indicating greater literacy.

A common problem with operational definitions of education is their inability to capture the quality and the content of schooling, particularly in cross-national comparisons of research findings. We have to assume that educational experience is equivalent from country to country (in terms of economic value and opportunities availed) or that the standardized measures we use to summarize educational experience have the same meaning in all cultural settings. Clearly, this is not the case. The severity of violating this assumption is difficult to assess, but the researcher should be aware of the problem and address it whenever possible. (For an excellent discussion of issues involved in the measurement of education, see Hermalin and Mason, 1980.)

Measured effects of female education on fertility may also suffer from sampling bias since much research to date has been confined to ever-married women. Restricting analysis to ever-married women underestimates education's effects because of (1) its positive effect on probability of *never* marrying and (2) its positive effect on postponing marriage until older ages. Thus, for example, reanalyzing WFS data for developing countries presented by Rodríguez and Cleland (1981), Cochrane (1983, p. 596) illustrates that the difference in average total fertility rates between women with no education and those with secondary school education is 3.1 for samples including all women. When samples are restricted to ever-married women, the difference is reduced to just 1.9. Our further assessment of these data reveals that the higher the education completed, the greater is the underestimation of education's true effects when never-married women are excluded.

That the effects of education and other socioeconomic determinants of fertility vary from one place to the next is one of the more important findings to come out of the World Fertility Survey. Variability in the functional form of the relationship means that models incorporating quadratic equations, dummy variables, and logit specifications should be introduced to supplement conventional linear, additive regression analysis of education's effects. Since contextual differences no doubt account for much of the variability in the nature of the relationship (e.g., living standards, availability of family planning services, or direct state intervention), these factors may fruitfully be worked into more general models (perhaps via dummy variables) to help explain comparative differences in the functional form of the relationship (Entwisle and Mason, 1985; Entwisle *et al.,* 1984).

The contextual issue becomes important again when one tries to elaborate means by which education affects fertility. Is it that individual women are taught in school relevant information (on contraceptives, say) and do not share this information with their sisters and neighbors who aren't in school? Probably not. At least some of the impacts of schools operate indirectly through social networks, affecting not only persons who attend schools but also some who do not attend them. To tap the latter effects, education measured for the individual may not be the appropriate variable; rather, forms of network analysis may be required (Rogers, 1979; Marsden and Lin, 1982).

Researchers must further be cognizant of period effects as well as the effects of the sequence and timing of education and childbearing within particular cohorts. As is the case cross-culturally, temporal variations exist in the economic value of education and the foregone options associated with childbearing such that the significance of education for reproductive behavior shifts over time. Likewise, reproductive behavior can affect a woman's educational event histories through disruptions, postponements, and opportunity costs associated with childbearing.

Viewing education as a process with components rather than a cumulative trait may require that we obtain educational histories with the same rigor as we obtain pregnancy histories. Indeed, there is evidence that the effects of education on fertility may vary across the reproductive cycle, and some of those effects are positive (Entwisle *et al.,* 1982). In particular, highly educated women who delay marriage or the birth of their first child may experience a more rapid tempo of family building than their less educated counterparts, even though their completed family size may be smaller. Some support for this notion is apparent in the weaker correlation found between years of schooling and age at first birth than between years of schooling and age at marriage. The implication is that the measured effects of education depend very much on when in the education and reproductive processes one measures them.

Complexities in conceptualization and measurement are not unique to research on the relationship between education and fertility. What might be unique is the significance some attribute to education as both a status enhancement mechanism and a fertility determinant. To present a better informed picture of the importance of education in enhancing the status of women and lowering fertility, we now turn to specifying and elaborating upon the critical socioeconomic factors through which education affects fertility.

Chapter 7 | Labor Force Participation

During recent decades, the number and proportion of women who are economically active have rapidly increased in most developed nations. In the United States alone, the number of working women has more than tripled since the end of World War II (Waite, 1981). The increase has been particularly pronounced for working mothers. Over half the children in the United States under age 18 now have mothers who work away from home (Baldwin and Nord, 1984; Grossman, 1983)—10 times the number recorded in 1945. Likewise, more than half of the mothers of preschoolers are now in the work force. Other industrialized nations report similar statistics and all indications are that the upward trend in female labor force participation will continue (Schwartz, 1982).

The degree of labor force participation for women is markedly affected by the amounts of their education. Highly educated women have higher participation rates and remain in the labor force longer than women with little education (Baldwin and Nord, 1984; Davidson, 1977; Elizaga, 1975; Kreps, 1976; Marini, 1984; Mott and Shapiro, 1983; Nerlove and Schultz, 1970; Smith-Lovin and Tickamyer, 1978). Fertility levels, in turn, are typically lower among working women, and lowest among those working women with the highest levels of education completed (Carleton, 1967; Elizaga, 1975; Jones, 1982).

In this chapter we look at the mediating role of labor force participation in the education–fertility relationship. Before elaborating theories and specifying causal operators, we review empirical findings from industrially developed and developing nations. Because zero-order associations in the United States and other developed nations have been so consistent, we note only representative studies before referring the reader to more extensive reviews. The mixed findings for developing nations along with factors influencing empirical inconsistencies will be discussed in greater detail.

1   Findings in Developed Countries

Repeatedly, research has documented that working women have smaller completed family sizes than nonworking women. In the United States this relationship has held for more than 30 years. Analyzing data from the 1951 Indianapolis Fertility Study, Pratt and Whelpton (1958) found work experience negatively related to actual and desired family size. Ridley (1959) and Namboodiri (1964), using data from the 1955 Growth of the American Families Study (GAF), found working women expected smaller completed families than nonworking women, and those who worked longer had fewer children.

Kupinsky (1971) examined the 1/1000 public use sample from the 1960 United States Census and 1960 GAF study data. In both data sets labor force participation was negatively related to fertility. Kupinsky used number of children ever born as a fertility indicator and present labor force participation as a work indicator. He found the fertility of current workers lower than that of women with only some work experience, who in turn had lower fertility than those who had never worked. The GAF sample allowed assessment of the relationship between plans to work and current and expected fertility. The largest difference in number of children ever born was found between women currently at work and those not planning to work. The fertility of women who planned to work some time in the future fell between the levels of the other groups.

An updated cross-national illustration of the general relationship between indicators of women's work status and fertility within developed nations is presented in Table 1. These data derived from the World Fertility Surveys in the latter half of the 1970s show the clear negative association between employment and childbearing, whether employment is categorized by work history, proportion of time worked since marriage, or full- versus part-time work. Additional analysis of the data by Jones (1982) reveals a strong negative association remaining between childbearing and women's work history even after controls are introduced for wife's level of education, urban versus rural residence, husband's occupation, and income.

Extensive citations of other studies reporting a negative relationship between female labor force participation and fertility in the United States and other developed nations appear in Cochrane (1979), Freedman (1961–1962), Hawthorn (1970), Kupinsky (1977), and Standing (1983). The vast majority of these cited studies likewise show this relationship holding whether fertility is measured by number of children ever born, expected or desired number of children, *and* regardless of the employment measure used.

Table 1

Average Number of Live Births, Standardized by Marriage Duration, Cross-Classified by Work History, Proportion of Time Worked since Marriage, Employment Status, Full- or Part-Time Work, and Place of Work—World Fertility Surveys, ca. 1977[a]

	Countries[b]													
	BE	BUL	CZ	DEN	FIN	FR	GBR	ITAL	NOR	POL	ROM	SP	USA	YUG
Work history														
Currently working	1.54	1.75	1.88	1.86	1.78	1.64	1.60	1.74	1.90	2.01	1.96	2.11	1.81	1.78
Not working, worked since marriage[c]	2.03	2.11	2.35	2.25	2.07	2.24	2.11	1.96	2.23	2.18	2.25[e]	2.32	2.22	1.93
Worked only before marriage or never[d]	2.11	2.19	3.01	2.10	2.30	2.56	2.27	2.15	2.40	2.36		2.56	2.58	2.50
Proportion of time worked since marriage[f]														
Less than one-third	—	—	2.39	—	2.21	—	—	—	2.31	2.29	—	2.41	—	—
One to two-thirds	—	—	2.16	—	1.80	—	—	—	2.00	2.02	—	2.17	—	—
More than two-thirds	—	—	1.75	—	1.69	—	—	—	1.63	2.04	—	2.07	—	—

Full-time or part-time work[g]

Part-time	1.83	—	—	1.98	2.02	—	1.89	1.87	2.23	—	—	2.24	2.08
Full-time	1.42	—	—	1.82	1.75	—	1.33	1.69	1.74	—	—	2.10	1.77

Place of work

At home	1.87	—	—	2.21	2.20	—	1.82			1.90	2.03	—	—
Away from home	1.42	—	—	1.83	1.69	—	1.74	1.74	—	1.96	2.14	—	—

[a]Source: Jones (1982, Table 10).

[b]Countries: BE (Belgium), BUL (Bulgaria), CZ (Czechoslovakia), DEN (Denmark), FIN (Finland), FR (France), GBR (Great Britain), ITAL (Italy), NOR (Norway), POL (Poland), ROM (Romania), SP (Spain), USA (United States of America), YUG (Yugoslavia).

[c]For Denmark, includes all women not working who had worked previously.

[d]For Denmark, restricted to women who had never worked.

[e]Separate statistics not available; number represents combined categories.

[f]Restricted to women who had worked since marriage.

[g]Restricted to women currently working.

111

2 Findings in Developing Countries

Research on developing countries has been far less conclusive than that from advanced industrialized nations. Some studies report an inverse relationship; others suggest a positive relationship; some find no evidence of an association. Gendell *et al.* (1970), examining the relationship between working women and fertility in Guatemala City, report that economically active women had considerably lower fertility than nonworking women. Similarly, in a comparison of fertility in Mexico City and Caracas, Davidson (1977) found employment inversely related to fertility. In both studies, however, only a small proportion of women could be classified as economically active.

Conversely, Peek (1975), studying 4000 Chilean families, found a positive relationship between family size and labor force participation for the modern and traditional sectors when care for younger children was available. Likewise, in a 1% sample of the Korean census, Lee and Cho (1976) report a slight but positive relationship between fertility and women's labor force participation. Working mothers had higher fertility than nonworking mothers, and mothers with many children were more likely to be in the labor force than women with few children. In Korea, female labor force participation is predominantly rural, implying that women are either employed in agriculture or as household workers. This fact also serves as a reminder that cross-national definitions of employment vary, sometimes substantially.

Others have failed to find any evidence of a relationship. Stycos (1965) reported that service workers and housewives in Lima had virtually identical fertility. Controls for social class did not alter the results. Turkish survey data also showed no difference in fertility between working and nonworking women (Stycos and Weller, 1967). Similarly, with respect to the normative rather than the behavioral aspect of fertility, Mueller *et al.* (1971) found no effect of labor force participation on Taiwanese family size ideals when effects of background variables were controlled.

The apparent inconsistencies in empirical findings for less developed countries may be attributed not only to differences in defining employment but also to overall degree of economic development. Most researchers agree that a certain level of economic development is necessary before a relationship emerges between employment and fertility. Once developing countries approach the level of development of industrialized nations, we might anticipate a negative relationship between female labor force participation and fertility to emerge.

Investigations distinguishing between modern and traditional sectors of developing countries lend support to this notion. Goldstein (1972) found that in the modern industrial city of Bangkok fertility of women active in the labor force was lower than that of housewives, but in rural agricultural areas, fertility of employed women was higher. In central Chile, Peek (1975) also found for women employed in the traditional sector no relationship between family size and mothers' working. In the modern sector, employment and fertility were inversely related.

The results from Chile are representative of studies in other countries where cottage industries prevail. Jaffe and Azumi's (1960) classic study of labor force participation in Japan and Puerto Rico found fertility of women in cottage industries identical with that of nonworking women. In contrast, women employed in modern industries outside the home had lower fertility than women working at home or not working. Likewise, in several urban areas of Latin America, Hass (1972) found fertility inversely related to employment outside the home, but not related to home employment. Macrolevel cross-national research correlating child–woman ratios with various female labor force participation rates are consistent with these results and further illustrate the importance of distinguishing place and type of work when examining the female employment–fertility relationship (Collver and Langlois, 1962; Kasarda, 1971).

Results from the more recent World Fertility Surveys in developing nations also suggest the influence of the nature of employment (Alam and Casterline, 1984). Table 2 shows that in most developing countries, employed women have lower fertility rates than women who have not worked. Moreover, women employed by nonrelatives (those most likely to be employed for wages or salaries outside the home) typically have lower fertility rates than women who are family workers or self-employed. This distinction by nature of employment is sharpest and most consistent in the Americas, corroborating the notion that degree of economic development conditions the female employment–fertility association.

In sum, it appears that in countries where women are allowed, if not encouraged, to work outside the home, their economic activity rates and fertility are inversely related. In most developing countries, particularly those with only limited opportunities for women to work outside the home, the evidence is more mixed. However, there are indications that, as developing economies transform from predominantly familial and cottage industries to a more commercial–industrial type (with separation of the work place from the home), increased female labor force participation will result in lower fertility rates (Standing, 1983; United Nations, 1980).

3   The Causal Nature of the Relationship

While there is near consensus that a relationship between female labor force participation and fertility exists, at least in developed nations, there is no agreement on causal direction (Bumpass and Westoff, 1970; Cramer, 1980; Pratt and Whelpton, 1958; Smith-Lovin and Tickamyer, 1978; Waite and Stolzenberg, 1976; Weller, 1977). Those maintaining that fertility is the primary causal vari-

Table 2

Total Marital Fertility Rate[a] in First 20 Years after Marriage (or Union) by Women's Work Status—Selected World Fertility Survey Countries, ca. 1977[b]

Country	Have not worked	Employed by family or self-employed	Employed by nonrelatives
Africa			
Ghana	5.23	5.44	4.28
Kenya	6.93	5.87	6.67
Lesotho	5.42	4.53	4.64
Senegal	6.40	6.05	5.71
Sudan	6.30	5.68	5.52
Americas			
Colombia	5.48	4.86	3.84
Costa Rica	4.15	3.56	3.18
Dominican Republic	6.22	5.59	4.89
Guyana	5.44	5.20	4.05
Haiti	4.79	5.33	4.38
Jamaica	6.66	4.63	4.46
Mexico	6.60	6.08	4.75
Panama	5.22	4.38	3.65
Paraguay	5.49	5.00	3.70
Peru	6.10	6.16	4.88
Trinidad and Tobago	4.05	3.19	2.74
Venezuela	5.44	4.25	4.43
Asia			
Bangladesh	5.42	4.71	4.50
Fiji	4.88	4.03	3.47
Indonesia	5.56	4.28	4.13
Jordan	7.96	7.93	5.82
Korea	4.53	4.95	3.87
Malaysia	5.56	5.32	5.02
Nepal	5.48	5.10	5.17
Pakistan	6.11	5.78	5.95
Philippines	6.27	5.60	5.22
Sri Lanka	4.90	5.05	4.10
Syria	7.32	7.66	6.15
Thailand	4.60	5.00	4.24

[a]Total marital fertility rate = mean number of births to a woman who remained in union during a defined reproductive span.

[b]Source: Alam and Casterline (1984, Table 7).

able base their view on the often-reported finding in developed nations that women with few or no children are more likely to be employed outside the home than women with many children (Blake, 1965). They note that women with large families are less likely ever to be in the labor force than women with smaller families (Kupinsky, 1971; Sweet, 1968). It has been further contended that family size determines not only whether a woman will work but also how long she will remain employed. The decision about the number of children to bear is viewed as preceding the decision to work (Waite, 1975). To the extent that children are valued higher than careers, family size will determine whether the mother will be employed (Smith-Lovin and Tickamyer, 1978).

A number have argued that age of the youngest child in the family best predicts labor force participation. Traditionally, in developed countries, having young children greatly reduced the chances that a woman would work. Studies from the United States, Australia, and Sweden have shown age of the youngest child has a more depressing effect on mothers' working than the number of children in the family (Gendell, 1965; Grossman, 1967; Ware, 1976a). More recent United States findings indicate, however, that this relationship is changing (Mott and Shapiro, 1983). Women today are less likely to avoid employment while they have preschool-age children. In 1978, 39% of mothers with children under age 6 were in the labor force. By 1982, over 50% of mothers with preschoolers were working (Grossman, 1983).

Those who argue that the dominant causal direction is from female employment to fertility point to findings in the United States and elsewhere showing working women *expect* to have smaller families than their stay-at-home counterparts (Jones, 1981). Working women express a smaller ideal family size than nonworking women (Pratt and Whelpton, 1958; Ridley, 1959), and women not currently active in the labor force, but who intend to work in the future, plan fewer children than women who do not intend to work (Ryder and Westoff, 1971a,b; Whelpton et al., 1966; Jones, 1981).

In the United States, the duration of a woman's employment is significantly related to the spacing of her children. Length of time worked since marriage and time between births are positively related. Furthermore, the longer a woman works, the longer the interval between births, resulting in a smaller completed family size (McLaughlin, 1982; Namboodiri, 1964).

As with the social mobility–fertility relationship, investigators of the female employment–fertility relationship are recognizing some degree of mutual causation between the variables. The reciprocal nature of the relationship was noted in the 1960s (see, e.g., Blake, 1965), but not until the mid-1970s did researchers introduce techniques to examine empirically such nonrecursive relationships.

Waite and Stolzenberg (1976), for example, used the two-stage least-squares (2SLS) technique to analyze the simultaneous effects of labor force participation and fertility.[1] They analyzed data from the panel of the National Longitudinal Study of the Labor Market Experience of Young Women (NLS), examining number of intended children and labor force participation plans at age 35. In addition, the model included a number of joint predictors, such as husband's income, wife's age, education, and race. The results showed that, while mutual causation is evident, labor force participation plans were more important in affecting fertility expectations than the reverse.

Smith-Lovin and Tickamyer (1978) also used a nonrecursive model in analyzing labor force participation and fertility with data from the 1970 Explorations in Equality of Opportunity Survey (EEO). They studied actual rather than intended behavior, using number of years the wife worked since marriage and live births during that period as measures of employment and fertility. Other predictors included wife's education, husband's income, and marital duration. Smith-Lovin and Tickamyer found number of children influenced employment after marriage, but postmarriage employment did not alter fertility. Their findings differ considerably from Waite and Stolzenberg's but they are consistent with findings from a similar analysis of the NLS data (Cain, 1979).

Cramer (1980) has suggested that the inconsistent results reported by Smith-Lovin and Tickamyer and Waite and Stolzenberg may be because of the choice of instrumental variables used to identify their models and problems with multicollinearity (high correlations) among the instrumental variables and joint predictors. To illustrate these issues, Cramer performed a sensitivity analysis of alternative instrumental variables using data from the Panel Study of Income Dynamics (PSID). In this analysis, Waite and Stolzenberg's conclusions were supported. Employment plans depressed expected family size, and the reciprocal effect of expected children on labor force participation was trivial. Cramer makes a case for looking at the short-run effects of labor force participation to determine

---

[1]The two-stage least-squares procedure is designed to yield unbiased estimates of the paths involved in the $Y \rightleftharpoons Z$ nonrecursive relationship. Using ordinary least-squares regression to estimate these parameters violates the assumption that the residual variables must be uncorrelated with the predictor variables (Kritzer, 1976). Two-stage least squares rectifies this problem. A new Y variable is computed for analyzing Z as a dependent variable; similarly, a new Z variable is computed for analyzing Y as a dependent variable. Each newly constructed variable is devised by regressing the original Y or Z on other, instrumental variables (W, X). Provided that $W(X)$ satisfies the theoretical requirements that (1) $W(X)$ is an instrument for $Y(Z)$ in the $Y \rightarrow Z$ ($Z \rightarrow Y$) relationship if it causes or is correlated with $Y(Z)$ but does not directly cause $Z(Y)$, (2) $W(X)$ is not caused by either Y or Z, and (3) $W(X)$ is not correlated with the unspecified sources of $Z(Y)$, the new $Y(Z)$ variable will be uncorrelated with the residual variables. The second stage of the procedure involves regressing Y on its instrument and the new Z variable to obtain an unbiased estimate of the $Y \leftarrow Z$ effect, and regressing Z on its instrument and the new Y variable to obtain an unbiased estimate of the $Y \rightarrow Z$ effect. The degree of success for the technique in providing unbiased parameter estimates depends on the degree to which the instrumental variables meet the theoretical requirements noted above. Typically, it is difficult to find instrumental variables that meet these requirements.

to what extent they amass to affect long-run fertility. Only then, according to Cramer, can we determine the nature of significant effects.

Cramer also reexamined the findings of Smith-Lovin and Tickamyer. He questioned their empirical results because of purported problems of multicollinearity, but he adopted their theoretical reasoning. Cramer contends that in the short run, family size will affect employment and that this effect will overshadow any short-term reciprocal effects. However, Cramer argues that in the long-run, the dominant effects are from employment to fertility. Research reported by Mott and Shapiro (1983) support this inference.

Let us conclude this discussion of causal direction with a caveat. Using more sophisticated statistical techniques, such as the 2SLS analysis, to estimate nonrecursive paths in models involving two-way causation entails several methodological and theoretical assumptions about the variables included in the analysis. If any one of these assumptions is violated, the results may be biased or flawed (Alexander *et al.,* 1981; Cramer, 1980). Thus, as with social mobility and fertility, the exact nature of causal relationship still remains ambiguous, awaiting new statistical approaches and better longitudinal measures to disentangle and clarify nonrecursive effects.

4 Theoretical Perspectives and Explanations

Why might employment influence a woman's reproductive behavior, and, conversely, how does this behavior influence her labor force participation? Biological, psychological, economic, and sociological explanations have been offered. Each perspective contributes to our general understanding of the relationship. We begin by discussing factors that condition the presence, direction, or strength of the relationship and then examine key exogenous and intervening variables.

Role Incompatibility

The best-known sociological explanation of the relationship between fertility and labor force participation involves the concept of role incompatibility or role conflict (Jaffe and Azumi, 1960; Stycos and Weller, 1967; Weller, 1968). Role incompatibility exists when bearing and rearing children conflict with a woman's career or other nonfamilial roles. Role incompatibility can stem from normative or time incongruities, or a combination of the two. Normative incongruities arise when society disapproves of nonfamilial roles for mothers. Time incongruities arise when time spent in child care and employment conflict.

Historically, in industrialized nations, the idea of mothers being in the labor force has been less than favorably received. The traditional expectation was that a woman's major roles in life are those of wife, mother, and homemaker (Collver and Langlois, 1962). Nonfamilial employment was thus perceived as normatively incongruent with a woman's domestic responsibilities.

Such negative societal attitudes are rapidly changing. In developed countries, there is increasing acceptance of mothers who work, even when they have young children. Indeed, with larger proportions of women obtaining college degrees and with open, extensive discussion of female liberation and equality of opportunity, many women (including mothers) may feel social pressures (or they may fundamentally desire) to take on nonfamilial work roles.

Concurrently, fathers have become more involved with child care (Ermisch, 1980; Presser and Cain, 1983). However, even with changes in the division of household labor, the woman is still often held solely responsible for the successful operation of the household. Curiously, she is not expected to allow such domestic obligations to interfere with her job performance. With heavy demands on the woman to be successful at both endeavors, the working mother finds herself in a role conflict situation and, typically, the more prestigious the job and the more extensive the educational prerequisites for it, the greater the role conflict (Oppong, 1983; Safilios-Rothschild, 1972; Weller, 1968).

The only way the working mother can alleviate role conflict is to reduce her competing obligations to manageable proportions. Since occupational demands remain fairly rigid while family size can be modified, women tend to opt for smaller families. This option holds even for women able to purchase child care. The negative relationship between labor force participation and fertility has thus largely been attributed to incongruities of dual-role performances. Furthermore, it follows from the formulation of the role-conflict hypothesis that the greater the incongruity between the roles of mother and worker, the greater the differential fertility behavior between women workers and nonworkers.

Normative Incongruities

Although the negative attitude toward mothers' being in the labor force is changing, many women still hold keen perceptions of the normative expectations associated with being a wife and a mother. As late as 1970, 80% of married women in the United States under age 45 believed that a woman's top priority should be caring for her home and family and that everyone was better off if men are the achievers outside the household (Cherlin, 1981, p. 62). Predicated on community context, pressure from kin, and economic circumstances, such expectations may play powerful roles in shaping behavior.

Mothers' employment is less normatively proscribed if financial needs dictate it. United States public opinion polls show that women's most important reason for working outside the home is that their family needs their monetary contributions (Inglehart, 1979). Increasingly, women are seeking employment to maintain a certain standard of family living and attain personal aspirations (Yankelovich, 1981). Whereas attitudes toward employment outside the home are becoming more enlightened, these surveys also reflect a continuing belief among many that women must choose between work and children, whether out of volition or financial necessity.

Time Inequities

A closely related dimension of role conflict is time allocation. Being finite, time is the scarcest resource for a working woman (Mueller, 1982; Sweet, 1973). Since employed women typically carry the double responsibility of working inside and outside the home, the time demand may be such that adjustments in one or the other must be made. If the woman cannot restrict the time demands of employment, she is likely to reduce the time demands of being a parent by restricting her family size.

If normative incongruities and time conflicts lead to lower fertility, we should expect that in the absence of both, labor force participation will not be related to family size. Finding no relationship between employment and fertility may be because of role *compatibility* (Jones, 1981; Smith, 1981; Weller, 1968). If a relative or other parental surrogate is available to care for younger children, or if other economically feasible arrangements can be made, then working and child care may be compatible (Mason *et al.,* 1971; Standing, 1983). Also, if being employed does not take the woman out of the home, role incompatibility is less likely. Type of employment is thus an important conditioning factor in the labor force participation–fertility relationship (Hass, 1972; Smith, 1981).

Role-compatible jobs are most likely in the traditional sectors of the economy such as household agriculture or cottage industries (Dixon, 1975a). This helps explain why in some developing countries researchers have failed to find a relationship between labor force participation and fertility. Working and nonworking women have essentially the same fertility because the working mothers are engaged primarily in household employment with little role incompatibility, and therefore bearing and rearing children does not seriously conflict with their economic activities (Jaffe and Azumi, 1960; Kasarda, 1971; Kupinsky, 1977; Standing, 1983; Weller, 1968).

The role incompatibility hypothesis has been criticized for not specifying when fertility and employment are positively related. It does not logically follow from its formulation what will happen in the absence of conflict (Mason and Palan, 1981). Also, the components of what constitutes conflict are subject to change. Strength of the normative component of conflict versus that of the spaciotemporal components are influenced by structural changes. Formulation of the role incompatibility hypothesis does not allow for such changes or for the separate assessment of the impact of the components. For example, child care standards are normatively based. Such norms change over time and depend on household composition as well as financial resources and the internal division of labor (Mason and Palan, 1981).

Finally, the conceptualization of employment has been pointed out as a weakness (Mason and Palan, 1981). Occupational variations are not considered. Observed differences in the fertility of working and nonworking women may be produced by socioeconomic differences rather than differences in labor force participation status. It is therefore necessary to obtain more precise measurement of employment and social status before drawing firm conclusions about the role–incompatibility thesis.

Subfecundity

Fecundity, the biological capacity to reproduce, may also partially explain the relationship between family size and employment. Some argue that subfecund and involuntarily sterile women are selectively recruited into the labor force. Relatively subfecund women, the "slow breeders," are more likely to work than fecund women. This line of reasoning is based on findings like those Freedman *et al.* (1959) reported. Examining United States data, Freedman and his associates found for all age groups, women who work are more likely to be sterile than women not active in the labor force. They thus concluded that a good portion of the relationship between female work and fertility can be attributed to fecundity.

Several investigators have questioned the fecundity hypothesis (Gendell *et al.*, 1970; Stycos and Weller, 1967). Survey data do not adequately measure sterility and we have no empirical evidence that the majority of working women are subfecund. Furthermore, it has been suggested that nuptiality, not fecundity, is the more important aspect.

Data from Guatemala City support the above argument; that is, fertility differences between economically active and inactive women exist because smaller proportions of economically active women are "ever married" (Gendell *et al.*, 1970). Whereas this argument is based on the questionable assumption that marriage is the only appropriate setting for childbearing, the explanation seems a plausible alternative to the subfecundity hypothesis.

Work Commitment

Psychological commitment to work is a third factor purported to explain the relationship between female employment and family size. It is hypothesized that women with a strong desire to work will, a priori, keep their families small

(Freedman *et al.*, 1959; Whelpton *et al.*, 1966). Safilios-Rothschild (1972) suggests that contradictory findings of studies relating women's work to fertility may be because of failure to consider work commitment. Analyzing a sample of working and nonworking women in Greece, she found female employment decreased fertility, and the decrease was much larger for women with high work commitment.

Some researchers have framed the work commitment hypothesis in terms of gender role orientations (Tickamyer, 1979). Women with a modern view of women's roles in society see work as being as desirable as motherhood, and thus, have fewer children or sometimes none. Women with a traditional view of women's roles see work strictly as a financial necessity. If these women restrict their fertility, it is because they must work, not because they wish to work.

Tien (1965a, 1967) offers a more sophisticated argument. He proposes that women committed to a career tend to desire and have fewer children. Tien distinguishes between working wives and working mothers. Working wives occasionally take time off from their main role as career women to bear children. In contrast, working mothers occasionally take time off from their mother role to enter the labor force. Being committed to a familial role, these women are not as likely to lower their fertility as the committed working wife.

In sum, the self-selection of women with strong desires to work into the labor force operates primarily as a conditioning factor influencing the strength of the female employment–fertility relationship. By itself, the psychological explanation "work commitment" should account for only a small proportion of differential fertility among women. As Standing (1983, p. 528) points out, care should be exercised that the concept measured is work commitment rather than retroactive rationalization for having few or no children.

Opportunity Costs

Economists propose that working women have lower fertility because the market wage they would forego by having a child and interrupting their career is too high to give up. Most economists assume that the opportunity cost of children is high for women who must relinquish high salaries to care for their children and less for women who earn lower wages (Da Vanzo, 1972; T. W. Schultz, 1973).

The opportunity cost explanation appears superior to the role incompatibility hypothesis because it specifies the conditions under which a positive relationship can be expected between labor force participation and fertility. If child care is less time intensive than economic activity—when child care substitutes are easily found—then the opportunity cost of child care is low and labor force participation and fertility are positively related (McCabe and Rosenzweig, 1976).

It is assumed that the greater the opportunity costs of childbearing for a woman, the greater the chances that she will have low fertility (Ben-Porath, 1974; Cain, 1966; Weller, 1977), will delay childbearing (Razin, 1980), and will space her children closely to concentrate the interruption of her career (Ross, 1973; Standing, 1983). These assumptions are based on a maximization model where the decision to work or bear children is viewed as a rational one, assessing benefits and costs of each alternative. To the extent that perceived economic benefits of work and opportunity costs of children outweigh the perceived benefits of children, a woman is likely to choose to enter the labor force and restrict her fertility. Essential here is the notion that people are rational, cost-accounting decision makers, actually know the costs involved, and perhaps more important, that fertility is the outcome of such decisions. Empirical testing of these notions is exceedingly difficult. It is highly suspect that assumptions about rational cost-accounting decision making regarding reproductive behavior are appropriate in most developing countries.

Summary

Thus far, we have examined four proposed causal operators that influence or condition the relationship between female labor force participation and fertility: role conflict, subfecundity, work commitment, and the opportunity costs associated with children. See Fig. 1.

Numerous other factors must be considered before we can begin to understand this complex relationship. In the following sections, we focus on some important variables that also influence or intervene in the relationship between female employment and fertility: family decision making, family planning knowledge and use, age and stage in the family life cycle, age at marriage, and education. This list of variables is not exhaustive; however, combined with those discussed above, we believe they explain most of the variation (and contradictions) in observed relationships.

Family Decision Making

Some researchers (see, e.g., Mincer, 1962; Peipmeier and Adkins, 1973) have argued that the observed relationship between female employment and fertility is spurious, attributable solely to common antecedent causes associated with family decision-making structure. Others have dismissed this argument based on their data analysis. Sweet (1968) and Waite and Stolzenberg (1976), for example, find the relationship between female employment and fertility persists even after controls for family decision-making structure are introduced.

Family decision making would seem, nevertheless, to be an important explanatory variable. A married woman's entry into the labor force does much to alter

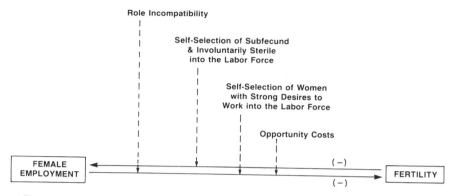

Fig. 1. Factors influencing or conditioning the relationship between female employment and fertility.

her position in the household. Gainful employment allows a woman to contribute financially to the operation of her household, thereby providing her with a sense of independence and more power than the nonworking woman to influence family decisions, including those about family size. Moreover, when women work, they are more likely to perceive themselves as competent and better able to manage their own lives. As modeled in Fig. 2, these outcomes associated with female employment improve women's ability to participate in family decisions, increase her influence in those decisions which, in turn, are likely to lead to reduced family sizes (Cunningham and Green, 1979; Rosen and Simmons, 1971; Weller, 1977).

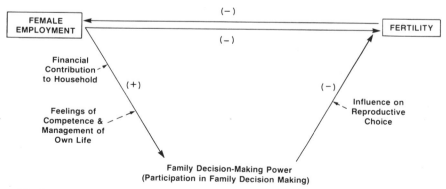

Fig. 2. Family decision making as an intervening factor in the relationship between female employment and fertility.

Family Planning

Family planning is of critical importance to the role incompatibility explanation of the female employment–fertility relationship. Apropos this factor, Stycos and Weller (1967, p. 216) have posited the following contingencies in the female employment–fertility relationship:

| | Mother–worker roles | |
Family planning	Compatible	Incompatible
Available	No relationship	Employment influences fertility
Not available	No relationship	Fertility influences employment

Regardless of the availability of family planning, when mother and work roles are compatible, work and fertility do not influence each other. If family planning is available, women will reduce their fertility if they desire to work in situations where work and large families are incompatible. If family planning is not available and the roles are incompatible, a woman's family size may determine whether or not work is possible. The more children, the more difficult it is for a woman to be employed (Safilios-Rothschild, 1977).

This is a useful but quite narrow interpretation of the possible outcomes in the work–fertility relationship. For example, it appears to limit family planning to modern methods of contraception. As a means of spacing births and ultimately reducing family sizes, we noted that breast feeding is available to most women in good health. If the work situation inhibits breast-feeding intensity and duration, then employment may increase rather than decrease fertility (Van Esterik and Greiner, 1981).

Over the years, research has shown that labor force participation is positively related to favorable attitudes toward contraception and its early, consistent, effective, and purposeful use (Freedman and Coombs, 1966a,b; Pratt and Whelpton, 1958; Ridley, 1959). What mechanisms account for this relationship? Along with enhancing a woman's status, labor force participation gives women more exposure to the outside world, including exposure to ideas and information on contraception. The working mother is more aware of various methods of birth control and their relative effectiveness (Weller, 1977). Given this knowledge and her greater motivation to limit family size for reasons discussed previously, working women are more likely than nonworking women to use effective means of birth control to lower fertility (see Fig. 3). These causal mechanisms (especially those dealing with motivation) substantially will be elaborated in Chapter 11, Family Planning Knowledge and Practice.

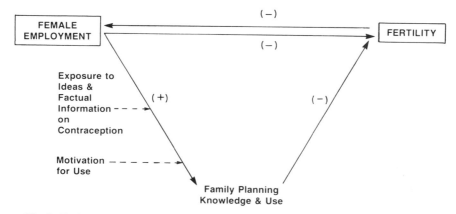

Fig. 3. Family planning knowledge and use as intervening factors in the relationship between female employment and fertility.

Age and Stage in the Family Life Cycle

Understanding the effects of women's age on the relationship between fertility and employment is important for policy as well as theoretical reasons (Waite and Stolzenberg, 1976). Apropos policy, it is useful to know when in a woman's life fertility and employment plans become linked and how well they are sustained over time. If women decide about family size and career goals while still in school, the educational system could be used to inform them about the implications of such decisions. Blake (1969) found fertility and employment plans are typically made at the end of high school, but Tien (1967) and Willis (1973) hold that such plans are not made until marriage.

In specifying theoretical models, it is further necessary to recognize that the employment–family size relationship may change with age, especially as age is associated with family size cycles (Heckman and Macurdy, 1980; Heckman and Willis, 1977). For example, working and having young children at home may be more difficult than working and having adolescents in the household. This varying nature of the relationship may be masked unless women's age and stage in the family life cycle are controlled (Fong, 1976; Hull, 1977).

Age may additionally alter the relationship between fertility and employment via developmental or cohort effects (Bogue, 1969) (see Fig. 4). Developmental effects are associated with emotional and physiological maturation, while cohort effects reflect the cultural conditions facing a generation as it matures. Given that age may affect the relationship in so many ways, we find it surprising that so few researchers have considered age in their analyses, or tried to disentangle its

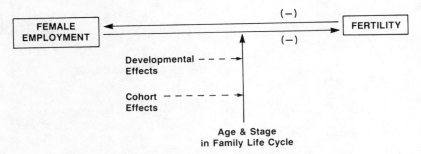

Fig. 4. Age and stage in the family life cycle as factors conditioning the relationship between female employment and fertility.

different aspects such as cohort versus developmental influences. There are exceptions, however.

Waite and Stolzenberg (1976) examined the developmental influences of age. They suggest that as women grow older they become increasingly aware that child care responsibilities might cause them to interrupt their employment, reducing their employability and wage potential. With increasing age, women also learn to reduce the length of their child-care-related employment interruption by bearing fewer children. Waite and Stolzenberg formulate these arguments into the Learning Hypothesis: As women age, the labor force participation effect on fertility becomes increasingly negative.

The Learning Hypothesis was tested and supported by National Longitudinal Study (NLS) data on labor market experience of young women. The sample was 5000 women aged 19 to 29 in 1973. To ensure that the effects of cohort differences in sex role attitudes were not mistaken for the age effects, Waite and Stolzenberg also tested the Liberation Hypothesis: Younger women are more liberal than older women and more tolerant of the idea of mothers with young children being employed. Futhermore, they assessed the Uncertainty Hypothesis: Older women are more certain about the number of children they want because they have more relevant information than younger women who have just started childbearing. Both hypotheses were rejected; Waite and Stolzenberg concluded that the rejection is reassurance that the Learning Hypothesis is plausible.

Tickamyer (1979) examined cohort effects using data from the 1970 United States National Fertility Survey. She expected younger women to hold contemporary sex role attitudes.

> Younger women are more likely to want to work as opposed to having to work and are more likely to hold contemporary sex role attitudes. However, there should be an additional effect due to normative changes in role orientations. Younger women have grown up in a time when it is increasingly acceptable (and even encouraged) for them to have careers and participate in nonfamilial activities, and when family size norms have decreased as well (Tickamyer, 1979, p. 170).

Tickamyer's findings showed a large age-sex role interaction effect in the expected direction: Younger age cohorts favor nontraditional activities and smaller families much more than older age cohorts.

Education

Why is it that working women with little education have higher fertility than those with much education (Elizaga, 1975; Jones, 1982; Nerlove and Schultz, 1970)? Job commitment or motivation might explain this conditional relationship. Women with low education are likely to be in the labor force because of financial need. They are motivated by "push" factors, not for developing a career; the motivation to curtail fertility may therefore be smaller (Shah, 1975).

Difference in sex-role orientation might also account for the relationship among education, employment, and fertility. The more educated a woman, the greater the chance she has been exposed to a modern role orientation and the more likely she is to view work as an alternative to motherhood. In contrast, lesser educated women who tend to have more traditional views of women's roles are more likely to stress the homemaker and mother role. Stronger preferences for work among better educated women place them into greater conflict with their homemaker role or at least reduce their desires for it. As a consequence, such women tend to have fewer children (Kreps, 1976).

Finally, the relationship between education, work, and fertility might be accounted for in terms of opportunity costs. Women with greater education have higher opportunity costs when they forego employment. The larger the salary a woman could receive, the greater the chance that she will enter the labor market and restrict her fertility (Ben-Porath, 1974; Cain and Weininger, 1973). For example, recent United States data on delayed childbearing suggest that women in professional occupations are more likely to have their first child when they are 30 or older than other working women. More than 50% of professional women delayed their childbearing compared to 30% of sales and clerical workers, 6% of service workers, 4% of crafts workers, and 9% of nonworking women (Baldwin and Nord, 1984). Figure 5 illustrates this causal operator and others discussed above.

Age at Marriage

Given that most research has been directed toward the marital setting, age at marriage has been hypothesized as an intervening variable in the relationship between labor force participation and fertility (Hirschman, 1982; Lehrer and Nerlove, 1982). Employment implies a certain degree of financial independence. If an employed woman need not marry to be supported financially, marriage can

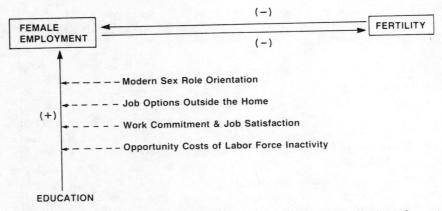

Fig. 5. Education and associated factors influencing the relationship between female employment and fertility.

be postponed. In turn, the number of children a woman is able to bear depends partly on the number of years she is regularly exposed to the risk of childbearing. If this risk is assumed to be equivalent to her fecund years spent in marriage (an assumption we find somewhat questionable), then the longer marriage is postponed, the fewer fecund years remain and, most important, the greater the chance that the woman will have become accustomed to a life style conflicting with childbearing. Figure 6 illustrates these causal operators which will be elaborated in Chapter 10, Age at Marriage and First Birth.

So far, we have looked at some of the most important factors affecting the female employment–fertility relationship. Figure 7 provides a summary model

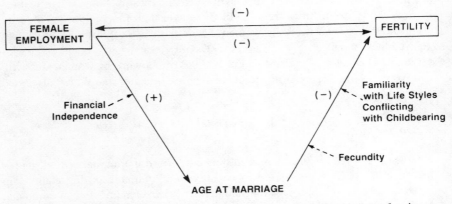

Fig. 6. Age at marriage and associated factors influencing the relationship between female employment and fertility.

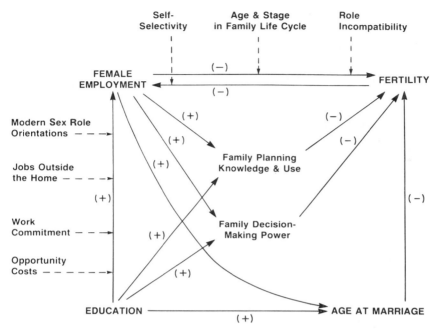

Fig. 7. Summary model specifying primary factors influencing the association between female employment and fertility.

incorporating those factors. Our central position is that women's participation in the labor force and its relationship to reproductive behavior is powerfully influenced by education. In addition to education's effects on career options, education conditions the nature and strength of the female employment–fertility association directly, and indirectly via its influence on family planning knowledge and use, family decision-making power, and age at marriage, all of which intervene in the female employment–fertility relationship.

5 Theoretical and Methodological Issues

Before examining the effects of education on other key variables proposed to shape reproductive behavior, let us note a number of issues that future research on female labor force participation and fertility must address to reconcile inconsistent and sometimes contradictory results. These include conceptual and operational definitions of *employment* and *fertility*, types of data used, and static vs dynamic model specifications.

Measuring employment is perhaps more problematic than measuring fertility.

Most studies distinguish between working and nonworking women. Researchers typically rely on a definition that distinguishes gainful employment from unpaid work. This model might yield reasonable results in industrialized nations; however, as it is male oriented and wage oriented, it is often too crude for developing countries (Anker, 1982; Beneria, 1982; Safilios-Rothschild, 1977). In these countries where women often work occasionally or for in-kind goods and services, some women might incorrectly be classified as nonworking. What effect will this misclassification have on the employment–fertility relationship? Safilios-Rothschild comments,

> Whether or not a woman who works informally and part-time consistently or seasonally defines herself as "working" may have important consequences for her fertility. Most probably women who do not define themselves as working identify themselves primarily with the wife and mother role, although they derive some definite satisfaction from their work involvement. To the extent that such work involvement is compatible with having several children, it may be unrelated to the level of fertility or it may be positively related to fertility, since mothers may use their income to buy extras for their children (1977, p. 363).

Thus, in defining work and in classifying women as working or not working, it is essential to consider the type of work involved and the extent to which it is compatible with child care.

Some studies use attitudinal indicators of employment (intent to work, expected work plans, etc.), while others are based on cumulated years of work experience or current employment—reported behavior. If attitudes and behavior are only weakly associated, inconsistent results are not surprising. Employment plans have little association with actual employment after a birth, subsequent employment, and fertility plans. In contrast, fertility plans are strongly related to actual fertility but not correlated with initial employment, subsequent employment, and employment plans (Cramer, 1980).

A potentially serious problem arises when employment is measured as current employment status and when this indicator is related to a measure of cumulated fertility. Unless we are dealing with women past their childbearing years, we cannot be sure we are dealing with completed family size. Furthermore, current employment status gives no indication of work history. We assume women are stable in their employment behavior, that they conform to a bipolar mover–stayer model of labor supply. If employed, we assume they are more likely to remain in the labor force than to move in or out (Heckman and Willis, 1977). However, without employment histories we lack appropriate data to test this assumption. We have no information about employment patterns, especially as they relate to their childbearing.

Until the relatively recent arrival of the National Longitudinal Study of the Labor Market Experience of Women (NLS) and the Panel Study of Income Dynamics, most studies relied on either census information or cross-sectional survey data. Since the latter were gathered for purposes unrelated to examining the relationship between employment and fertility, these data sets do not provide pertinent information about job motivation, commitment, involvement, and sex-role orientation. Thus, researchers are often prone to draw theoretical inferences about causes of reported female employment–fertility associations without proper empirical support.

Another shortcoming of cross-sectional survey data is the lack of *reliable* fertility and work histories, forcing investigators to use measures defined at specific times rather than over intervals. With less than adequate temporal data, most studies have been based on a static model of the employment–fertility relationship. Increasingly it is being realized that the static model does not adequately describe reality (Bagozzi and Van Loo, 1978; Gurak and Kritz, 1982; Hout, 1978; McLaughlin, 1982; Namboodiri, 1974, 1975, 1983; Rosenzweig, 1976; West, 1980). Fertility and employment are continuing, dynamic processes. Decisions about work and family size are not set at a single timepoint but are subject to change during the fecund life course. A few successful attempts to capture the sequential nature of these decisions indicate that the connection between employment and fertility is not singularly stable. Different patterns emerge depending, among other factors, on the woman's parity.

For example, West (1980) used the cross-sectional 1970 United States National Fertility Survey which yields temporal information about employment and fertility. Work histories were constructed and related to dates of birth. For young white women, labor force participation and the probability of making the transition to a higher parity were inversely related at low parities; however, at parities higher than two, labor force participation and that probability was positively related.

Jones (1981) used data from the 1970 and 1975 United States National Fertility Studies and a life table approach to study childbearing intentions and work status. She examined parity differences in conception probabilities by employment status and birth intentions. Working women with fewer than two children had low conception probabilities, but nonworking women with fewer than two children had high conception probabilities. At higher parities no difference appeared when controlling for employment status. Among women intending to have more children, no specific parity differences were detected although working women had a slightly lower conception probability than nonworking women.

Cramer (1980) used the Panel Study of Income Dynamics (PSID), which permits a true longitudinal analysis. Fertility and employment were measured during calendar years with 1-year lags, allowing for a dynamic model. According to Cramer, the dynamic model is superior to the static model because "centering the measurements around the time of birth eliminates the confusion caused by timing decisions and directs attention to the important question of who has a baby and does a baby affect wife's employment" (Cramer, 1980, p. 176).

Cramer found prior employment inversely related to fertility, and short-run fertility inversely related to subsequent employment. However, in the long run (as the child reaches school age), the negative effect of fertility on employment diminishes. Furthermore, the effect of a birth on subsequent employment diminishes at higher birth orders. There are no parity differences in the effect of initial employment on fertility.

Other researchers have observed parity differences (Lehrer and Nerlove, 1979; Mott, 1972; Waite, 1977). Hout (1978), Namboodiri (1974, 1983) and McLaughlin (1982) have argued that these differences in fertility determinants probably occur because of the normative expectations surrounding the timing of fertility and the acceptable range of completed family size. For example, in the United States there seems to be strong normative pressure to have two children, while higher birth orders are a declining ideal.

In summary, fertility and employment status must be measured carefully and extensively to ensure valid and meaningful interpretation of their relationship. When studying the relationship between work and fertility, it is essential to recognize that both are continuing dynamic processes. Family size plans and employment plans might change over time as each event is affected by and affects the other. In studying the relationship, longitudinal data sets that allow a focus on reproductive and employment event histories are highly recommended. These data sets should resolve many of the difficulties and ambiguities of ex post facto studies. Unfortunately, with the exception of the NLS and PSID data sets, and possibly the Bureau of the Census' new SIPP (Survey of Income and Program Participation) files, data sets enabling dynamic analysis of social and economic determinants of fertility are difficult to come by. There is a particular need to assemble such data for developing countries where contextual circumstances may result in substantially different individual-level effects than those reported for the United States and other developed nations.

Chapter 8   The Value of Children

There is growing consensus that a better understanding of the benefits and costs of children (actual and perceived) is essential for understanding cross-cultural differences in reproductive behavior (Arnold *et al.*, 1975; Bulatao, 1979a,b; Bulatao and Fawcett, 1983; Lee and Bulatao, 1983; Mueller, 1976; Turchi, 1975). Approaches to studying these benefits and costs as they apply to reproductive choice vary with sociological, demographic, economic, and psychological frameworks used to interpret the value of children (see, e.g., Arnold and Fawcett, 1975; Becker, 1960; Cain, 1982; Caldwell, 1982; Namboodiri, 1972c; Terhune, 1974).

Sociologists and demographers treat value of children primarily at the macrolevel as it relates to the demographic transition. At the core of transition theory is the idea that the value of children changes. Ultimately, if not immediately, the demand for children is reduced. As society moves through the stages of economic development, children's labor contributions become smaller, unnecessary, or obsolete by law. Their value as sources of security in old age and times of misfortune diminishes as society sets up institutional support. At the same time benefits are diminishing, the cost of raising children is increasing, primarily because education becomes important, but also because parents' aspirations for their children rise. As the conjugal family emerges, family ties weaken and it becomes difficult to find substitutes for parental care. Mothers' work in the modern sector of the economy becomes less compatible with childbearing and tends to make large numbers of children dysfunctional.

Economic approaches to understanding the value of children include both macro- and microlevel analyses. At the macrolevel, the focus is primarily on how changing economic conditions affect birth rates. Research examples include cross-national analyses of data on child labor and old age support. For example, Kasarda (1971) found child labor in household production positively associated with fertility. Others have shown how sources of old age security are related to fertility levels (Entwisle and Winegarden, 1984; Hohm, 1975).

In the microeconomic framework, children are viewed as a choice among alternative courses of action. They are assumed to serve a variety of economic and noneconomic functions for parents, and decisions about family size seem to involve a balancing of the costs and benefits of children against possible alternative sources of satisfaction. Couples implicitly make perceived cost–benefit calculations about the number of children they will have and try to maximize their total satisfaction (utility function). Accordingly, couples choose to reduce their fertility when the marginal costs of additional children begin to outweigh their marginal benefits (Leibenstein, 1974).

Psychologists emphasize the emotional relationship between parent and child, the significance of children for validating sex roles or adulthood roles, and social status associated with parenthood (Fawcett, 1972, 1984). While the economic perspective focuses primarily on *actual* costs and benefits of children, the psychological perspective is concerned primarily with *perceived* costs and benefits as they influence reproductive behavior.

Although children have universal characteristics and roles within the family, they are not valued everywhere in the same way. Their value appears to depend on social, economic, and cultural contexts. In the sections which follow, we discuss how actual and perceived benefits and costs of children vary across different contexts to influence reproductive behavior and what role education plays in the association. We shall commence by considering noneconomic as well as economic benefits and costs of children and then specify the causal operators linking each benefit or cost factor to reproductive behavior.

1 Noneconomic Benefits of Children

Noneconomic benefits of children involve the psychic satisfaction parents derive from them. Espenshade (1973, pp. 4–5) and Hoffman and Hoffman (1973, pp. 46–61) identify eight dimensions of psychic satisfaction:

1. Adult status and social identity
2. Expansion of the self, tie to a larger entity, immortality, continuation of the family
3. Morality, subordination of self-interest
4. Primary group ties, group affiliation
5. Stimulation, novelty, fun
6. Creativity, accomplishment, competence
7. Power, influence, effectance
8. Social comparison, competition.

Scrutinizing this list, we see that children provide benefits to parents and grandparents. The nature and importance of these benefits, however, change over time and across cultures, as we shall elaborate below.

Throughout history women have gained passage and status by becoming mothers. Having children is certainly not the only way to demonstrate adulthood or achieve social identity, but lacking knowledge and awareness of alternatives, many younger people desire children for these reasons. In some societies, parenthood and adulthood are virtually synonymous. Children likewise provide parents the opportunity to make personal sacrifices, demonstrate sound judgment and dependability, and show moderation and concern for the well-being of others. These virtues are important when seeking social acceptance and recognition.

Such benefits may be particularly important for women in traditional societies where they have little or no economic autonomy (Dyson and Moore, 1983). Women need children, especially sons, to secure their position in the family (Blake, 1965; Cain, 1984; Wolf, 1972). Where women rely on the conjugal relationship as a source of status, they value children as strengtheners of the marital bond (Kagitcibasi, 1979), particularly in rural settings. In urban settings sexuality is viewed as a more effective insurance against divorce than high fertility (Mernissi, 1975).

Women in developed societies share most of these perceptions of the value of children. A marriage is often considered incomplete without children. Moreover, many women view children as binding husbands and wives closer so that neither considers separation or divorce. Children represent the emotional security associated with traditional perceptions of the family as a stable and permanent institution. Children provide the "sense" of family.

Women in developed societies also stress fulfillment of emotional needs. Children are associated with love, caring, happiness, and satisfaction. They fulfill needs for creativity, achievement, and accomplishment (Espenshade, 1973) and provide companionship. In the words of Blake and del Pinal (1981), children are "interaction goods."

The intergenerational continuation of a family lineage is a powerful incentive for having children (Arnold et al., 1975). In both traditional and modern societies, the desire to carry on the family name through male offspring is important. Children also serve important functions in many religions. In the Confucian tradition male heirs are significant because they ensure the parent's welfare in the afterlife (Lee and Kim, 1977; Williamson, 1976). Similarly, sons perform important rituals in Hinduism and other formal religions (Wu, 1977).

In traditional societies children are of special social value to fathers. Often it is difficult to distinguish the social value from a pure economic value. As Caldwell (1976, 1982, 1983) notes, children may imply social strength for the kin group and such strength may imply economic benefit. Where strength in numbers equals strength in physical security, the father can "throw his weight around" when he has many children. Children become influential social investments for the future.

In traditional societies children are needed to ensure and stabilize the large family system. Studying the net value of intergenerational wealth flows, Caldwell (1983) observes that in pretransition societies with marked age and sex discrimination in work and consumption, high fertility is advantageous to fathers and particularly to grandparents. A large family enables the elders to maintain power relations within the family and existing age and sex roles.

2   Economic Benefits of Children

The economic benefits of children may be conceptualized along two dimensions: children as productive agents and as sources of financial security in old age and emergencies (Leibenstein, 1957). The economic benefits are the child's future contributions to the family income through direct contributions to production and in retirement.

In developed societies, benefits of children as deliberate economic investments are low (Becker, 1960, 1965). Children have lost most of their value as productive agents. In highly developed, monetized economies, economic benefits of children through employment outside the household or productive work within it are no longer significant. Likewise, investing in children as retirement annuities is no longer the major source of old age support. Social Security, retirement plans, and savings have replaced children as the primary source of retirement income in developed societies.

In spite of their low actual economic benefits, research in the United States indicates some parents still perceive children as a source of economic gain. In an analysis of Gallup polls, more than half the respondents perceived children as economic investments, especially women with low educational attainment (Blake and del Pinal, 1981; Hoffman et al., 1978).

At first, it might appear safe to assume that children's economic value is more important in developing countries, particularly in agrarian settings. Children can help out in the family business or with household chores such as tending animals or caring for siblings. Children's participation in household maintenance frees the parents to improve and diversify their economic situation by working in more productive activities. This exchange is particularly important where the major income source is an agricultural crop tied in with landholding size and season (Chaudhury, 1982). Parents who can rely on their children often do not have to hire help.

Researchers have debated the validity of this assumption (see, however, Nugent, 1985). Mueller (1976), examining the economic value of children in developing countries, found the work contributions of children insufficient to prevent them from being a net economic burden to the household. Calculating net productivity of children in India and Taiwan by age and sex, she further concluded that daughters continuously produce less than they consume and sons do not become net producers until age 15. Even at that age, the net benefits produced are not enough to make the overall work contribution positive.

As discussed by Chaudhury (1982), Mueller may not have reached this conclusion had she employed a different approach. Her finding that children are economic burdens in peasant agricultures may stem from failing to include nonagricultural activities in estimates of labor inputs; consider that children render services at very early ages, perhaps as young as five and six; consider that children's work frees parents for other activities; and consider different levels of consumption, such as a bare minimum and a moderate level.

Studying time budget data from Java and Nepal, Nag *et al.* (1980) concluded that, at the aggregate level, the economic value of children to agricultural families is high—especially where planting and harvesting are tied to monsoon rains. In spite of such findings, researchers believe that if policies were drafted to eliminate child labor no significant impact on fertility would be observed. Rather, where children make a significant economic contribution to the family, curtailing child labor would hurt the household. Policies involving minimum age and minimum wages would be difficult to enforce. Instead, it is advocated that the economic structure provide job opportunities for adult females since women's wages have been found to be inversely related to female child labor and fertility (Rivera-Batiz, 1982).

With a lack of institutionalized health and welfare programs, it is also plausible that children are essential sources of old age support and security. This statement is supported by findings from less developed countries in the Value of Children Project (Arnold *et al.*, 1975). Specifically in rural settings, more than 70% of the respondents expected to rely on their children as old age security. However, not all researchers agree that this situation applies universally in developing countries. For example, Vlassoff and Vlassoff (1980) studied ever-married men in India and found that for this subgroup, old age security is not an important motivation for demanding children. They speculate that future contributions are not perceived as important because it requires thinking in terms that are too abstract. Furthermore, they observe that men are able to work and support themselves throughout their lives.

Whether empirically founded or not, the perception of economic security is real to many parents in developing countries. The anticipated economic benefits and expected security children will bring to parents is the most noticeable reason for desiring them. As Asok Mitra observes:

> The observation that investment in children is a costly way of securing old age support is the kind of opinion which supposes that other alternatives are open to the family in good measure which is just not correct for most underdeveloped countries. . . . In an underdeveloped country

it is the peasant's urge to pay a premium on a birth now and thereby mortgage the present for the future that is more important than his urge to maximize the present by discounting the future (Mitra, 1972, p. 70).

In countries lacking risk insurance, credit cooperatives, and public relief employment schemes, children are important assets. They are most valuable in countries where elderly parents live with or rely on their children for immediate day-to-day support (Nag, 1983c). In such countries there is no catering to the consumption needs of the elderly. In rural areas, in particular, daily sustenance needs of the elderly are difficult to meet because they often involve many heavy physical chores (Nugent, 1985).

Where women have no economic autonomy, the insurance value children provide is particularly essential, since for widows, children may be the only source of future income and security (Cassen, 1976). Women with little economic independence are especially likely to prefer surviving sons over surviving daughters. Son preference is evident in data from the WFS. Computing the ratio of preference for boys to girls, Cleland *et al.* (1983) found most Asian and African women prefer sons over daughters. In Latin America and the Caribbean women are more receptive to a balanced sex composition.

Further analysis by Cain (1984) suggest that in countries where son preference is strong, the age difference between spouses is large. In these countries women can expect to spend a significant number of years in widowhood, making the need for old age support even more urgent. In male-dominated societies, females are often denied access to the labor market and to inheritance, so children are their only means of support.

A number of researchers have investigated the impact of public old age security policy on fertility. For example, Entwisle and Winegarden (1984) estimate that a one-percentage-point increase in pension benefits would result in 0.67 fewer children per woman. Other researchers are more conservative in their estimates (Wildasin, 1982). Concern has been voiced that the largest obstacle for policymakers trying to implement social security programs is lack of trust in the political system and government. Parents need to be confident that governments are able to keep their promises of support. Parents need evidence that they will be provided for in the future from sources other than their children. Frequent shifts in regimes and general economic uncertainty make such promises far from convincing.

Furthermore, it is also speculated that the need for old age security is tied to the mortality level in the country or immediate community. On one hand, the higher the level of infant and child mortality, the more children, especially sons, are viewed as necessary to secure old age support (Cain, 1984; Lindert, 1980). On the other hand, if mortality is high, life expectancy is short and parents may not anticipate that they will spend many years in old age (Nugent, 1985). This would render old age security less salient as a motivation for a large family size.

3   Noneconomic Costs of Children

Noneconomic costs are essentially the time, effort, and cognitive distress involved in raising children. Espenshade (1973, p. 6) notes that, among others, "These include the emotional and psychological burdens children impose on parents such as the feeling of being "tied down," anxiety over children's health and future welfare, frustrations over misbehavior, and the like."

We might assume that noneconomic costs of children are less salient in developing countries because standards of child care and maintenance are generally less than in developed countries. For example, feeling "tied down" grows with the development of a desire for goods, services, and leisure pursuits. In developed countries, there is a sense that one should be able to set one's own goals and have the freedom to pursue them (Bulatao, 1982; Oppong, 1983). In developing countries, child care arrangements are more readily available and perhaps more acceptable, given fewer pressures for direct parental care of infants and young children. In developed countries, couples often relegate their parental responsibilities to sources outside the household only with difficulty and at a higher emotional and financial cost.

4   Economic Costs of Children

Direct Costs

Economic costs encompass all the expenses associated with producing and supporting children. Apart from the initial cost of prenatal care and delivery, parents face the recurring expenses of such items as food, clothing, housing, education, recreation, and medical care until the children are grown and have left the household permanently.

Direct maintenance costs of children vary in different economic settings. For example, education tends to be more costly in developed countries as are medical expenses and most sustenance goods.

Several studies have tried to quantify the financial costs of children, primarily in the United States. Relying on data from the United States Department of Agriculture and Consumer Price Index data from the United States Department of Labor, Espenshade (1973) estimated the cost of raising a child to age 18 in the United States. The estimated figures range from $31,675 for a low-cost-plan rural nonfarm family in the North Central United States to $58,225 for a moderate-cost-plan rural nonfarm family in the West. Of this amount, 32.3% goes to housing, 24.3% to food, 16.1% to transportation, 9.5% to clothing, 5.3% to medical care, 1.5% to education, and 11% to other expenses.

An update by Grossman (1978) estimates that in 1977 the direct cost of raising a child from birth through college ranges from $44,200 for families with disposable income between $10,500 and $13,500 to $64,200 for those with disposable income between $16,500 and $20,000

More recent assessments of rearing a child show that the figure is rapidly rising. For the average American family, the cost of raising a son born in 1980 to age 22 (including 4 years of college) is projected to be $226,000; for a first-born daughter, $247,000 (constant 1982 dollars). The cost is higher for a daughter because transportation, clothing, and entertainment expenses are estimated to be higher. These costs represent 24.2 and 26.4% of an average total family income over the 22-year period. For a high-income family, the percentage would be somewhat higher; for a low-income family, it would be lower (Olson, 1983). Two-income families spend 23% more on each child than one-income households. Spending is also higher for women who delay childbearing (Espenshade, 1984).

In summary, direct costs are associated with rearing children virtually everywhere. However, these costs rise with increases in modernization and its pressures for special foods, clothing, consumer goods, and most importantly, for schooling.

Opportunity Costs

In addition to direct maintenance costs, parents, especially the mother, might forego other opportunities while they rear their children. As a result, parents might have to lower their standard of living; they might experience reduced savings and investment opportunities, or the mother might give up income-earning possibilities (Mueller, 1972a, p. 182).

The need to relinquish consumption expenditures and reduce savings and investments depends again on societal context. As Espenshade (1973) points out, there is a tendency to think that children do not affect consumption standards or savings ability in less developed countries. Whether this is actually the case depends on the level of aspirations of the parents. In Taiwan, for example, Mueller (1972b) finds that when aspirations are rising, children become real opportunity costs.

The income a woman foregoes while bearing and rearing children varies according to her employment prior to or during the childbearing period, as well as her work plans in general. Some women would not choose to work even if they had no children, and many women plan to continue working while rearing their children. Also, age of the children must be considered when dealing with the opportunity cost concept. Though this relationship is changing in developed countries, the presence in the household of young children sometimes prevents or at least discourages labor force participation (Bowen and Finegan, 1969).

Grossman (1978) estimated that by staying out of the labor force until her child is 14, an American mother in 1977, on average, foregoes up to $150,000 in earnings, depending on her education. The opportunity cost of rearing a single child through college was estimated at $84,000 for a woman with an elementary school education, $99,000 for one with a high school education, $122,000 for a woman with some college or a 4-year degree, and $143,000 for one with 5 or more years of college. These figures, which no doubt have risen considerably since 1977, were derived by adding to the value of the wife's foregone earnings an estimated $33,000 for direct costs such as food and medical care.

In general, in economies where roles of worker and mother are compatible either because of the nature of the job, child care arrangements, or both, the concept of opportunity cost is less important. The concept appears relevant only if women are prevented from spending more time at a job by the presence of children, or if they lose out on advancement opportunities because of children (Nag, 1983a,c). Furthermore, the concept assumes a rational response to knowledge of these costs.

In the microeconomic theory of fertility, opportunity costs include time spent caring for children and the value of market goods and services used in child rearing. These opportunity costs are viewed according to alternative expenditures and activities foregone. Women are assumed to be the prime providers of child care and opportunity costs can be determined by assessing income-earning potentials, measured in terms of education and labor market experiences (De Tray, 1977). However, as pointed out above and in recent literature (Lindert, 1983; Oppong, 1983; Turchi and Bryant, 1979), these and other assumptions may not be empirically founded in all cultures. Since opportunity costs vary extensively from one culture to another, they need to be delineated with great attention to their complexity (Oppong, 1983, p. 549).

As for time inputs, attention must be paid to alternative uses of time, including leisure pursuits and the time cost of foregone leisure (Lindert, 1978, 1983). The time cost of children depends on the compatibility of job opportunities with child care and the rewards sought from working (other than income). The sources and cost of child care will influence the cost of children.

With material inputs, the type, quantities, sources, and market price must be considered along with alternative investments and expenditures. Moreover, it is important to consider perceptions of child-rearing standards. Attitudes about appropriate roles for women and mothers (Scott and Morgan, 1983) determine time and material inputs in children as do norms, values, and beliefs about who should care for children and how they should be reared (Turchi and Bryant, 1979). Since such perceptions are linked with the level of economic development, we should expect cross-cultural variations.

Table 1 outlines the benefits and costs associated with children whose perception and magnitude no doubt differ substantially across cultures. In developing countries, parents may not have an accurate perception of the financial burden of

Table 1

Value of Children Factors Affecting Reproductive Choices[a]

Positive values	Negative values
Emotional benefits	Emotional costs
Economic benefits and security	Economic costs
Self-enrichment and development	Restrictions of opportunity
Identification with children	Physical demands
Family cohesiveness and continuity	Family costs

[a]Source: Adapted from Arnold *et al.* (1975, p. 8).

raising a child. As the Value of Children Project demonstrated, some respondents had trouble verbalizing their thoughts because they were not accustomed to thinking of children in cost terms. Many simply object to the idea of "pricing" children (Fawcett, 1972) or treating them as consumer durables (Blake, 1969). Overall, in cultures stressing the maternal role, benefits or desirable aspects of children are emphasized. In other cultures where alternatives to the maternal role are available and employment opportunities are expanding, costs associated with children are being shown to influence powerfully reproductive choices (Scott and Morgan, 1983).

5   Education and the Value of Children

How does the actual and perceived utility of children vary by mother's education? First and foremost, with increased education, the need and expectation of economic benefits from children are typically reduced (Arnold *et al.*, 1975; Chang, 1979; Kagitcibasi and Esmer, 1980; Mason, 1984). As discussed in the previous chapter, better educated women are more likely to find employment and to be economically independent. The financial security derived from children in old age or emergencies therefore diminishes in importance. Especially in societies with access to capital markets, educated women are likely to be employed in organizations providing some form of retirement security or unemployment benefits. They are better able to support themselves if widowed and need not depend on their children for financial help. In societies lacking such institutional provisions, children's value as risk insurance may not be affected by their mother's education (Cain, 1982).

The value of children as social investments also diminishes with increasing education (Blake and del Pinal, 1981). Educated women are less likely to see reproduction as being instrumental to achieving social status. A woman capable of earning a living independent of her husband and his kin does not have to secure her position in the family or society by bearing children (Dyson and Moore, 1983; Mason, 1984).

The value of children's work has been assumed to diminish with increases in mother's education. The validity of this assumption depends on the type of employment involved. If no assistance in carrying out a job is required from children, then they have no economic value. However, in developing countries children perform many duties in the home, freeing the mother for other activities (Merrick and Schmink, 1983). Thus, it is unclear whether the labor value of children increases or decreases with changes in the mother's educational level.

Assuming gainful employment and child care are incompatible—which may not hold in many developing countries (Standing, 1983)—the higher the mother's education, the higher her opportunity cost. We saw previously that the income women forego when they choose motherhood over gainful employment increases with their educational attainment. Also, the cost of raising a child increases with higher levels of education, particularly because educational aspirations for children rise (Mueller, 1972a, 1982; Michael, 1974).

Finally, as Caldwell (1983), Oppong (1983), and Mason (1984) point out, educated women may perceive the cost of children as higher because they are seeking alternative sources of satisfaction and status. Children may hinder achievement of such desires. Better educated women are more likely to have a less traditional sex-role orientation, implying that they may seek a job rather than motherhood early in marriage, for example.

We have summarized the theoretical linkages between education and the value of children in Fig. 1. It is worth reiterating that societal context (especially the degree of economic development) will condition the relative importance of the causal operators shown in the education–value of children model.

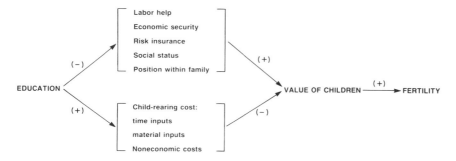

Fig. 1. Theoretical model specifying causal operators linking female education and value of children with fertility.

6   Theoretical and Methodological Issues

Wife's and Husband's Expected Costs and Benefits

When studying the relationship between value of children and fertility, a key question arises: Should one focus on the wife, the husband, or both? A birth is obviously the outcome of actions of both parents. Therefore, it seems logical to incorporate the utility functions of husbands and wives in the research design, although this has often not been done.

Researchers, especially proponents of the microeconomic theory of fertility, have primarily focused on a one-sex utility model of reproductive behavior. The microeconomic theory of fertility assumes that the household head makes fertility decisions. Supposedly, the household head subsumes the utility function of the spouse in his own utility function; the household utility function is assumed to be optimized in the utility function of its head. Though not explicitly stated in the theory, it is further assumed that the male is the household head. Ironically, however, one-sex utility models of reproductive behavior have used data from *female* respondents.

Some researchers object to the one-sex (male or female) utility model, pointing out that our predictive ability of reproductive behavior is enhanced by considering both sexes. The two-sex utility model has been found to predict more variance than single-sex models (Beckman, 1978; Fried and Udry, 1980; Hofferth and Udry, 1976; Osborn and Thomas, 1979; Thomson, 1983). Moreover, the wife's utility considerations may dominate in certain subpopulations, the husband's in others. For example, in the United States, white women dominate reproductive outcome more often than white men. Among blacks, the husband's utility considerations tend to dominate (Fried and Udry, 1980). Thomson (1983) reports that the utility of another child is an individual experience of wives and husbands, not a shared experience of a couple. Emotional utility is important for wife and husband, but for him, economic utility is highly correlated with emotional utility. In general, where traditional sex roles dominate, we should expect to find gender-related differences in perceptions of the value of children. Thus, future research should examine how wives' and husbands' expected costs and benefits jointly enter into the fertility decision-making process.

Parity-Specific Utility Models

Several researchers maintain that parity-specific utility models have stronger predictive power than all-parity models (Namboodiri, 1972b; Terhune, 1974; West, 1980). The nature of fertility decisions varies at different parity levels. Thus, researchers should examine their results, controlling for parity. Possibly noneconomic benefits may have a stronger effect on the decision to have the first child than on the decision to have additional children. Likewise, cost considerations may weigh heavier for children at higher parities.

Bulatao and Fawcett (1983) suggest that perceptions of costs and benefits of children change with changing parity. This is so, they argue, because of the parents' psychological and biological maturation, shifts in household socioeconomic status, and earlier child-rearing experiences.

Perceptions of Utility

Finally, researchers involved in cost–benefit analyses should be sensitive to cultural variations in perceptions of utility. Western researchers have a general idea of what a rational cost–benefit framework encompasses. However, this idea might not be applicable in non-Western cultures. Researchers must be careful when imposing their definition of rationality on countries differing from their own in culture and development. Essentially, researchers must better appreciate the culture and socioeconomic situation of people in developing countries and how their perceptions of the world might differ. In Caldwell's (1983) words, the same economic calculus cannot be used for all societies. Even within cultures, assessing perceptions of utility must be handled with great care. A quotation by Ryder (1983, p. 19) illustrates the subjective complexities involved in quantifying the value of children:

> Thus the time spent on child-rearing is from one viewpoint a cost because it represents forgone opportunities, but from another viewpoint it is a benefit, since it is the vehicle through which many of the satisfactions of child-rearing are derived. Also, the characteristics which make it possible for the child to be a source of pleasure are the same as those which make it possible for the child to be a source of pain. As a third example, acceptance of the burdens of child-rearing is a way to achieve the important pleasure of success in fulfillment of a strong moral obligation.

No doubt, far more sophisticated survey instruments will have to be developed if we are to uncover and disentangle the multiple factors that shape the utility functions of children for parents. Without such instruments, statements about the relative importance of actual or perceived costs and benefits of children in reproductive choices will remain at the speculative level.

Chapter 9 | Infant and Child Mortality

Few will dispute that achieving infant and child mortality reductions is desirable in and by itself. Public and private agencies agree as reflected by their funding and participation in such efforts. Furthermore, since much research points to a positive relationship between infant and child mortality and fertility, reducing mortality looks highly attractive to developing country policymakers in their desire to stem rapid population growth.

Significant cross-sectional correlations reported between lower mortality and lower fertility rates at various historical points in developed countries have led to the assumption that there is a causal link between the two variables. Based on more recent dynamic analyses for developed and developing countries, the picture now appears more clouded: fertility reductions do not always follow mortality reductions. Reductions in mortality may initially result in increased fertility and population growth. Only later do fertility rates decline. How much later depends on cultural conditions and programs implemented. Evidence indicates that health programs reducing mortality must be accompanied by family planning programs and by transformations in socioeconomic structures that encourage parents to practice contraception, if enduring declines in fertility are to occur.

In this chapter we examine empirical investigations of the mortality–fertility relationship in developed and developing countries. We discuss theoretical linkages and transmitting processes to explicate the role infant and child mortality plays in the female education–fertility causal chain. The chapter concludes by addressing a number of methodological issues that bear on research on the relationship between infant and child mortality and fertility.

1 Mortality–Fertility Relationships and Transition Theory

Developed Countries

Until the 1970s, many demographers held that reductions in mortality, especially of infants, preceded and caused fertility reductions. Findings from the European Fertility Project, investigating the social and economic factors underlying fertility decline in more than 700 provinces since the French Revolution, cast doubt on this notion (Coale, 1973).

For example, Knodel (1974) reanalyzed nineteenth-century German data and concluded that the usual description of the demographic transition does not fit. Knodel used a 10% reduction criterion as an indicator of the onset of a mortality decline and fertility reductions. A decline in infant deaths preceded fertility decline in only 34 of 71 German administration areas. In 36 areas, fertility declined earlier, and in one, the declines were simultaneous.

In a similar historical study of Belgium, Lesthaeghe (1975) tried to establish the temporal order of the onset of fertility and mortality declines. In only one of nine provinces were reductions in fertility and mortality simultaneous. In the remaining provinces, fertility declined in 1880, but mortality did not begin to fall until around 1895.

Matthiessen and McCann (1978) have questioned these apparent rejections of the demographic transition model. They contend that although instances may be found where fertility declines precede mortality declines, once both begin to fall, falling mortality further accelerates fertility declines. Moreover, they point out that *infant* mortality may not be the appropriate measure. They argue that if high fertility is a response to actual and anticipated deaths among offspring then *child* mortality is a much better mortality indicator.

Matthiessen and McCann found that in France, Belgium, Scotland, England, and Wales, child mortality started to fall more than 30 years earlier than infant mortality, as it did in the remaining European countries. They contend that using infant mortality to index the onset of the mortality decline causes a systematic advancement of the *measured* date of initiation. Thus, Matthiessen and McCann conclude that if all youthful mortality were considered, the demographic transition model remains an accurate historical description of events in Europe.

Developing Countries

In Latin America, a positive relationship at the macrolevel between infant mortality and fertility has typically been found (Da Vanzo, 1972; Nerlove and Schultz, 1970; Schultz, 1969), and it has been argued that the causal direction of

the relationship is from mortality to fertility. Rutstein and Medica (1975), however, argue that the positive relationship reported in these studies is less than
convincing since the use of aggregate-level data clouds the true nature of the
relationship.

To demonstrate, Rutstein and Medica examined the CELADE family-level
data from rural areas of Colombia, Costa Rica, Mexico, and Peru. They used
Brass and Brass–Sullivan methods to calculate infant mortality rates and parity
progression ratios to measure fertility, thereby eliminating the reverse effect of
fertility on mortality. Rutstein and Medica found previous child deaths generally
did not affect parity progression ratios. Only in Costa Rica and Peru did the
probability of having an additional birth increase with increasing child loss;
moreover, these increases were small and did not occur at all parity levels. In
Colombia and Mexico, the probability of having an additional child *decreased*
with increasing child death. Rutstein and Medica speculate that a woman whose
child dies may herself have health problems that may contribute to the child's
death and her own low probability of having another birth. Thus, they concluded
that for individual biological reasons a mortality decrease does not necessarily
result in a fertility decrease.

Cochrane and Zachariah (1983) report much larger effects. Their analyses of
WFS data indicate that at all parities child mortality leads to a higher probability
of having additional children. The probability is highest if the death occurs to the
last-born child, a recent birth.

Other research based on microlevel data supports this finding. Pebley and her
associates (1979) used 1975 NICAP data (Nutritional Institute of Central America and Panama) to investigate the effect of child death on additional children
desired and found that the more child deaths experienced, the more children the
respondent desired.

Approximately half of the 410 women chosen for study were from semiurban
communities (Petapa); the rest were from urban areas (El Progreso). Pebley *et al*.
chose—perhaps questionably—desired fertility because this measure is unaffected by biological factors and reflects previous experiences with child mortality. Perceived child survival (measuring expectation and predicted to be negatively related to fertility desires) and number of respondent's children who had
died and sibling mortality (measuring experience and predicted to be positively
related to fertility desires) were selected as independent variables. Control variables included residence, education, housing quality, and husband's occupation.

The study is particularly noteworthy for its methodological approach: the basic
assumption that fertility decisions are made sequentially rather than once at an
early stage of marriage. Accordingly, a separate logit analysis was performed for
women with zero to two children, those with three to four children, and with five
or more children to estimate the probability of desiring more children.

Pebley *et al*. found within each parity group, women desiring additional children are likely to be younger, less educated, rural residents, and *more* experienced with child deaths. For El Progreso women with three to four live births, the probability of wanting another child was .63 if one child death and one sibling death had been experienced compared to .39 with no child or sibling death. The same pattern was found in Petapa. For women with five or more live births the difference was not as great, and the probabilities were uniformly small. Pebley *et al.* (1979) concluded that

> The child mortality experience affecting a woman's fertility decisions are not only those of her own childbearing years but also those of her mother's childbearing years, and that these influences are manifested at different stages, as represented by parity levels (p. 135).

These findings suggest that mortality declines must occur over a significant time period—two generations—to reduce a woman's desire for additional children.

Chowdhury *et al.* (1976) followed a different methodological approach to study the child mortality–fertility relationship. In Pakistan, they used a national probability sample of currently married women and in Bangladesh, longitudinal vital registration data of rural women. Fertility and child mortality levels are similar in the two countries: at the time of the study, women gave birth to about six children of whom only four survived the first 5 years of life.

Chowdhury and his associates used birth intervals as their dependent variable. Life tables generated the proportion of women progressing from parity x to parity $x + 1$, again, eliminating the reverse influence of fertility on mortality. Their findings suggest a positive relationship between child death experience and subsequent fertility. In Pakistan, the median interval to the next birth was shorter for women whose child had died than for women with no child death before reaching that parity. Within each parity group, Bangladeshi women with higher previous child loss experienced briefer mean birth intervals. The researchers speculate that this positive relationship between infant mortality and birth interval may be caused by biological factors associated with the ceasing of lactation—a more rapid return to a fecund stage.

Summary

The nature of the infant mortality and fertility relationship is by no means straightforward. According to the demographic transition model, infant mortality influences fertility in that declining mortality brings about declining fertility. Historical data from Europe, we saw, cast doubt on the empirical validity of this contention. At best, the formulation of the transition model is accurate only if the mortality measure is expanded to include both infant and child mortality. Other research suggests that if individual-level data are used, the results of decreasing mortality are less evident than if macrolevel data are used. Moreover, mortality may have to decline over an extended period to affect fertility.

2 Theoretical Explanations

The view that infant mortality is an important fertility determinant is long standing and forms the basis of demographic transition theory (Davis, 1945; Notestein, 1945). (For a succinct explication, see Preston, 1975b). In this framework, the behavioral responses to mortality reductions are clearly formulated. It is assumed that incorporated in the individual decision-making process are accurate perceptions of the existing community mortality level. Given such conditions, an individual will reduce her fertility when she perceives no need to replace a lost child with another or to produce extra children in order to achieve a desired number of surviving offspring. The desired number of children is assumed to adjust down once the chances of survival are evident. Though it evolves only slowly, the desire for smaller families will eventually occur.

Overlooked in the classic formulation of the demographic process of declining fertility is the biological linkage between mortality and fertility. Biological effects are present in particular where breast feeding is common and the only means of protection against pregnancy. Given such conditions, mortality influences breast-feeding duration. Suppressed ovulation due to lactation in turn influences the length of the birth interval and subsequently fertility. Reciprocally, the length of the birth interval affects the health status of the mother as well as the children. We elaborate these important points below.

The Biological Effect

The biological effect of infant mortality on fertility comes primarily as breast feeding stops when an infant dies. The effect is particularly important where the practice of contraception is not widespread (Huffman, 1984; Lesthaeghe, 1982). Lactation inhibits conception by prolonging postpartum amenorrhea. If a woman has been breast feeding, the death of her infant abbreviates postpartum lactational amenorrhea, hastens the return of ovulation, and thereby exposes her to the risk of conception. If the previous child survives the breast-feeding period, the ovulatory suppressant effects of breast feeding result in longer average intervals to the next birth.

Several researchers have assessed the biological explanation. Knodel (1975), examining preindustrial data from France, Germany, Denmark, and Switzerland, found that where breast feeding was common, the biological effect of infant mortality was present. For example, from 1640 to 1780 in Saint Patrice, France, the mean birth interval was 29.4 months if the infant survived, but only 16.5 months if it died—a difference of 1 year. Data from Taiwan also indicate the presence of a biological effect (Heer and Wu, 1975). Respondents with an extended mean length of lactation (longer than 12 months) had fewer subsequent births than those who did not continue breast feeding past 12 months. Other studies have indicated that lactation may lengthen the average duration of amenorrhea by more than 10 months (Casterline *et al.,* 1984; Knodel, 1982a; Potter *et al.,* 1965; Wyon and Gordon, 1971).

What should not be overlooked in discussing biological effects is the reciprocal relationship between birth interval and mortality. Not only the number of children, but also their spacing has an impact on survivorship (Palloni and Tienda, 1983). The interval between conceptions determines the duration of breast feeding. Customarily, weaning takes place at the beginning of a new pregnancy. In the absence of supplementary food sources of similar nutritional value, early weaning is detrimental to the infant. The baby becomes more susceptible to infections and may die.

For the unborn child the health status of its mother is extremely important. The shorter the interval between conceptions, the poorer the mother's health. Maternal depletion is likely to result in a low-birth-weight infant who subsequently is more vulnerable to disease and death. Thus, the health of the children on both sides of the birth interval (often referred to in the literature as the index children) is affected by the length of that interval.

Attempts to separate empirically biological and behavioral effects have so far been inconclusive (Lehrer, 1984). The overall conclusion is that the magnitude of a biological effect is contingent on the extent to which infants are totally or partially breast fed and whether family planning is practiced. Where family planning is widespread, the biological effect to be gained is generally minimal. Only where contraceptive methods are not in use and all infants are breast fed will the biological effect be significant (Bongaarts and Menken, 1983).[1]

The Replacement Effect

Where contraception is widespread, behavioral rather than biological responses to infant mortality may account for its positive relationship with fertility. One possible behavioral response is the replacement effect, reflecting a couple's response to an infant death and occuring whenever the couple attempts to replace that death with the birth of another (Omran, 1971).

There is emerging consensus that the overall replacement effect on fertility is limited since it is based on the assumptions that couples have clear reproductive goals and precise control over their fertility. As Preston (1978, pp. 13–14) points

---

[1]For an up-to-date treatment of the effects of infant breast feeding on the mother, see Popkin *et al.* (1986, Chapter 8).

out, we should not expect more than half of infant deaths to be replaced because most couples are fatalistic about reproduction and have no target number of children. Incidences of fecundity impairment or divorce or death of a spouse might also make control over fertility imperfect.

The replacement effect typically appears in societies where sons are preferred over daughters (Chaudhury, 1982; Heer, 1983; Heer and Wu, 1975, 1978; Khan and Sirageldin, 1977; Rukanuddin, 1982; Welch, 1974). A strong sex-selective replacement effect has been observed in several Asian regions. Heer and Wu (1975), for instance, found Taiwanese parents with two children will have 0.5 more births if they lose a son and a daughter survives, versus 0.04 more births if they lose a daughter and a son survives. Chaudhury (1982) discusses other Asian studies reporting similar results.

Focusing on demand for children as his indicator of fertility, Heer (1983) has raised an interesting methodological issue of relevance to the replacement effect. He points out that the mortality–fertility relationship is not unidirectional. Couples who have lost a child may have wanted fewer children to begin with and in some way may be responsible for the deaths. If so, these couples will demand fewer children than couples who have not lost a child. If parental care is lacking because the child is unwanted and this neglect results in death, such couples will not try to replace the child.

Neglect may be intended and behavioral in the form of poor feeding practice or lack of response to illness (Scrimshaw, 1978; Scrimshaw and Pelto, 1979) or unintended and biological such as working mothers being unable to breast feed or otherwise care for the needs of their children. In contrast to findings from the United States where infant mortality is less among working mothers (Rosenzweig and Schultz, 1983), Caldwell and McDonald (1982) found housewives from 10 Third World countries have persistently lower infant mortality than working women.

Furthermore, high mortality may lower the demand for children because death of a child implies a cost factor in the sense that financial and psychic resources have been wasted. A couple having lost two of six children may demand no more children given the cost factor involved in producing surviving children. On the other hand, a couple having produced only four children without experiencing any deaths may demand more children (Heer, 1983).

In sum, a number of factors condition whether a couple fully compensates for infant and child deaths through additional births. Such replacement is critical for macrooutcomes of policies to reduce infant and child mortality. According to Olsen (1980, p. 429), if replacement is complete, such measures will not affect population growth. However, if replacement is not a variable in the couple's decision making, measures to reduce child mortality may increase population growth.

The Insurance Effect

While the replacement effect is post hoc and related to actual infant or child death, the insurance effect or child survival hypothesis operates in anticipation of an infant death (Taylor *et al.,* 1976). Some have termed this effect the hoarding strategy (see, e.g., Ben-Porath, 1978; Preston, 1975b). Implicit in the insurance effect is the assumption that couples aim for a given number of surviving children at the end of the childbearing years. Though few studies have measured parents' perception of infant mortality (Chaudhury, 1982), the assumption is that couples are aware of the prevailing community level of infant and child mortality and adjust their fertility to take it into account.

Surveys have shown that differences in perceived levels of mortality affect fertility. Heer and Wu (1975) found Taiwan couples perceiving the chances of an infant's survival to age 15 to be less than 0.85 had 0.26 more children beyond the third child than those who perceived the chances to be 0.95 or better. Harman (1970) found a large effect in the Philippines and Snyder (1974) reported one in West Africa, corroborating Heer's (1983) contention that perception of the level of child survival is negatively related to the demand for surviving children and that, depending on the perceived mortality level, the insurance effect could be large, resulting in additional births.

Summary of Effects

So far, we have discussed several mechanisms that may link infant mortality and fertility: the biological effect from cutting short breast feeding; the effect of producing children to replace those who die; and the effect of trying to ensure enough survivors. The biological and behavioral effects may operate jointly, making isolation of any particular effect difficult. It is especially complicated to separate these effects because behavioral factors may influence lactation prac-

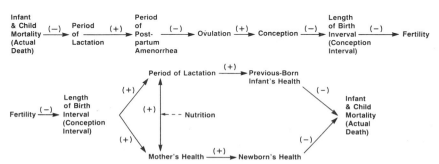

Fig. 1. Biological mechanisms linking infant and child mortality to fertility under the assumption that breast feeding is the sole method of contraception.

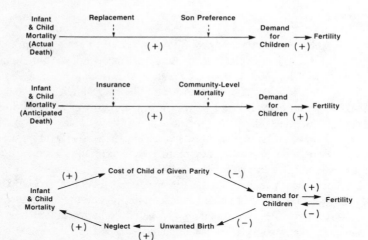

Fig. 2. Behavioral mechanisms linking infant and child mortality to fertility under the assumptions that (1) reproductive goals are clear and (2) control over fertility is possible.

tice; for example, female labor force participation may change feeding practices. With increased work time, lactation may be reduced, thereby shortening the duration of amenorrhea (Lesthaeghe, 1982). If breast feeding is used for fertility control, then it is a behavioral response, not a biological effect (Olsen, 1980). Figures 1 and 2 illustrate the causal operators in the biological–behavioral intervention in the infant mortality and fertility relationship. The strength of these operators, independently or combined, rests on a number of conditions, including, most importantly, the ability to control fertility. Let us now turn to evidence and models of how infant and child mortality is affected by our central exogenous variable—education.

3   The Relationship between Education and Infant Mortality: Basic Findings and Causal Processes

In developing and developed countries, studies of the relationship between education and infant mortality have shown that, in general, children of educated women have higher survival rates than those of less educated mothers. For example, in the 1960s in the United States, infant mortality among women with no more than an elementary education was 76% greater than the rate among infants born to women with 4 or more years of college. There is no evidence that the relationship has become weaker over time (Adamchak, 1979; Adamchak and Stockwell, 1978; Arriaga, 1980; Bertoli *et al.*, 1984).

The effect of education on infant mortality is strongest in countries with

Table 1

Mortality Rates of Infants and Children under Age 5 (per 1000 Births) by
Mother's Education—Selected World Fertility Survey Countries, ca. 1977.[a]

Region/country	Mother's education in years			
	0	1–3	4–6	7+
Africa				
Kenya	181	164	128	111
Lesotho	(224)[b]	215	185	169
Senegal	296	(178)	(113)	(19)
Sudan	146	—	109	—
Americas				
Colombia	146	127	82	49
Costa Rica	157	100	85	45
Dominican Republic	198	140	122	82
Guyana	(83)	(89)	80	64
Haiti	226	(176)	(206)	(89)
Jamaica	(82)	(78)	74	51
Mexico	153	118	87	50
Panama	134	90	52	43
Paraguay	110	88	67	32
Peru	237	171	98	55
Trinidad and Tobago	(74)	(67)	59	43
Venezuela	79	60	60	35
Asia				
Bangladesh	222	198	186	(122)
Fiji	70	67	60	46
Indonesia	193	194	143	77
Jordan	112	83	84	67
Korea	107	94	74	56
Malaysia	67	64	56	18
Nepal	261	(204)	(157)	(136)
Pakistan	208	(143)	(138)	(112)
Philippines	130	118	94	53
Sri Lanka	104	97	80	55
Syria	104	(75)	75	50
Thailand	145	105	110	(38)

[a]Source: Adapted from Hobcraft et al. (1983, Table 3).
[b]Note: Rates based on less than 500 births in parentheses.

Table 2

Infant Mortality Rates and Life Expectancy at Birth Associated with
Brass-Trussell Estimates of Mortality of Children Born to Women Aged
20–24, by Rural–Urban Residence—Indonesia, 1971[a]

	Infant mortality		Life expectancy	
Education	Rural	Urban	Rural	Urban
No schooling	155	160	43.7	42.9
Some primary	142	129	45.8	48.0
Past primary	106	91	52.5	55.6
Past lower secondary	82	61	57.4	62.4
Past upper secondary	68	47	60.8	65.9

[a]Source: Hull and Hull (1977b, p. 47); used with permission of the
authors and The Population Investigation Committee, London School of
Economics.

moderate or low mortality levels (Cochrane, 1979; Cochrane et al., 1980; Shin, 1975; Stockwell and Hutchinson, 1975). In countries with high infant mortality, very few women have received higher education. Thus, mother's education probably cannot play a major role in determining infant mortality, although children born to the few highly educated mothers in such settings are most likely to survive (Hobcraft et al., 1983).

Examining World Fertility Survey data from 28 countries, Hobcraft et al. (1983) found clear indications of the inverse relationship between education and infant mortality (see Table 1). They estimate that infant mortality would drop by 41% and child mortality by 60% if all mothers had 7 or more years of education.

In particular, the mother's secondary education makes a difference in infant mortality experiences. Caldwell and McDonald (1982) report the difference in infant mortality between mothers with primary and secondary education to be twice the magnitude of that between illiteracy and primary education. Similarly, Hull and Hull (1977b) report that in both urban and rural Indonesia, the infant mortality rate for the most educated mothers is less than half that of the least educated group (see Table 2).

How do we explain the negative relationship between education and infant mortality? Sloan (1971) has suggested the following conditions as possible linking mechanisms:

1. Increased awareness of personal hygiene
2. Propensity of the literate to seek medical care for scientific rather than folk reasons
3. Cognitive development enabling consequences of particular acts to be anticipated, particularly those associated with child care

4. Greater efficiency in consumption—the literate tend to pay lower prices for the goods and services they purchase and thus secure more of them from a fixed amount of income.

In addition to the obvious association between education and social position—the association with wealth and power—education is an expression of the knowledge and awareness it takes to realize the importance of hygiene and cleanliness and to take advantage of better sanitation facilities (Stephens, 1984), to break away from traditional explanations of disease (Caldwell and McDonald, 1982), and to recognize signs of illness at an early stage and seek professional help in preventing disease (Hobcraft *et al.*, 1983). Women with higher education not only possess such knowledge and skills, they also carry more weight in making decisions about child rearing and in particular, in daily infant care (Caldwell, 1979, 1983; Caldwell and McDonald, 1982), including allocation of food and water within the family (Chen, 1983). They know when and where to seek help, and because they are in a better position to pay for such help, they will not delay seeking it.

The mechanisms linking education, female labor force participation, and mortality are important since education appears to make a difference in the relationship between employment and infant mortality. Working mothers with less education have been found to experience high infant mortality. However, as Ware (1984) points out, and Caldwell and McDonald (1982) and Mason (1984) also mention, it is not work per se that adversely influences infant survivorship. The type of work makes a difference. If the work situation results in child malnutrition because of its mother's inability to breast feed, then work and mortality are directly related. If sick children are not cared for properly because their treatment would interfere with the work schedule then work would result in child neglect and subsequently higher mortality. Poorly educated women are likelier than women with more education to be working under conditions that would render them unable to care for their children. This situation appears to account for the observed relationship.

Perhaps for all the reasons mentioned above, the highest educational groups are among the first to benefit from improvements in conditions affecting mortality. In Guatemala, between 1959 and 1968, mortality rates declined most rapidly for the highest educational groups and least among those with little or no education (Haines *et al.*, 1983).

Similar illustrations can be provided by focusing on postneonatal (1–11 months) mortality rates. The leading causes of death during these months are infectious conditions, mainly diarrheal diseases, sepsis, and respiratory infections—conditions clearly associated with material level of living. Differences in postneonatal mortality rates by education level are striking. In Mexico the postneonatal mortality rate for illiterate women was 52 per 1000 compared to only 10 per 1000 for women with more than secondary education (Garcia y Garma, 1983).

Since education and contraceptive use are positively related (Cochrane, 1979, 1983), better educated women generally have longer birth intervals than women with less education. A longer birth interval gives the mother more time to recuperate after pregnancy and childbirth. She will be in better health before becoming pregnant again. The better the mother's condition, the lower the likelihood that she will have a premature or low-birth-weight baby. Longer child spacing, therefore, increases infant survival (Mason, 1984).

It is estimated that changes in mortality could be quite significant. Trussell and Pebley (1984) calculate a 10% reduction in infant mortality and a 21% reduction in child mortality if an ideal 2-year birth interval is adopted. These estimates are based on findings from the WFS (Hobcraft *et al.*, 1983) and the Malaysian Family Life Survey (Holland, 1983).

Education is also related to infant and child mortality through feeding practices (Ware, 1984). More educated mothers are less likely to prolong breast feeding or to be forced to rely exclusively on breast milk beyond an age where the child would need supplementary intake. At the same time, since breast milk quantity and quality are also affected by the mother's nutritional and health status, children of better educated mothers are at a further advantage (Cleland and Sathar, 1983; Hobcraft *et al.*, 1983). If mothers rely on artificial feedings, the better educated are most likely to understand the importance of following directions for consuming and storing the products (Millman and Palloni, 1984). In general, better educated mothers are less likely to have malnourished children, especially malnourished daughters. These mothers have more resources for all their children and are also less likely to favor sons over daughters (Ware, 1984).

In summary, education and infant and child mortality are related through nutritional and health factors associated with the lives of mother and child (Chen, 1983). The various theoretical mechanisms linking education to infant mortality are illustrated in Fig. 3. Except for the direct link to family planning, the mechanisms are numerous and difficult to separate. Perhaps the best way to summarize the effects is to adopt the view of Trussell and Hammerslough (1983). Formal education provides more than specific child-rearing and health care skills. It broadens knowledge and alters attitudes and life styles that provide for markedly improved childbearing environments and child care practices.

4   The Role of Infant and Child Mortality in Fertility Reduction

The 1960s and early 1970s were characterized by optimism about the potential influence of infant and child mortality on fertility. Reducing infant and child

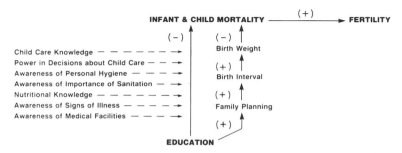

Fig. 3. Theoretical factors linking female education with infant and child mortality.

mortality was considered necessary for acceptance of small family size norms and for effective fertility control (R. C. Freedman, 1963). The view was that as long as many children die in childhood, it was difficult to promote family limitation (Hassan *et al.,* 1971; Taylor *et al.,* 1976).

Starting in the mid-1970s, a concern was voiced that infant and child mortality may not be appropriate variables for policymakers to manipulate to control fertility because such reductions may actually increase the rate of population growth, at least initially. Several studies have provided evidence to substantiate this effect. Working with data from Bangladesh, Chowdhury *et al.* (1976) estimated a 4% fertility reduction if infant mortality were eliminated. However, this reduction would be counterbalanced by a 7% increase in net reproduction as a result of better survival conditions for infants. It was recognized that conditions serving to reduce mortality may encourage population growth. Consequently, some researchers felt that although workable alternatives to produce rapid, substantial fertility reductions were lacking, policymakers should not rely solely on infant mortality despite its attractive feature of being policy manipulable. According to Retherford:

> As a proposed fertility reduction policy for developing countries, child mortality reduction deserves particular scientific scrutiny, not only because its political attractiveness colors policymakers' perceptions of its potential effectiveness, but also because if not pursued as part of a balanced modernization policy, it may render society worse off than before. Unlike most other proposed fertility reduction policies, the failure of this one to obtain the desired fertility response would further increase population growth rates. This in turn might impede the general process of modernization, particularly economic development, itself the fundamental force underlying fertility transition (Retherford, 1975, p. 69).

Retherford was concerned that policies to reduce infant and child mortality be part of a larger socioeconomic development program. Most researchers shared his view. However, some claimed that more rapid and extensive results could be obtained without waiting for socioeconomic transformations. The striking difference of opinion is apparent in the following quotation:

This research attempts to resolve the controversy over the dominant factors affecting fertility by showing that its rapid decline can be assured by drastic control of causes of infant and child mortality through extensive as well as intensive applications of medical technology rather than waiting until such a control is brought into effect by the slow and long process of socioeconomic transformation which may be hard for many countries to generate (Hassan *et al.*, 1971, p. 303).

Today, the debate is not whether health programs to reduce mortality are necessary before family planning is adopted to control fertility or whether such reductions should occur through socioeconomic transformations in order to ensure long-lasting results. Improving the health of all human beings, regardless of the consequences for population size, is viewed as an imperative in itself (Cochrane and Zachariah, 1983).

Since the 1950s, health programs have indeed resulted in worldwide mortality reductions. Corresponding reductions in fertility have not yet been observed. Although demographic transition theory suggests that, in time, such reductions will be achieved, current population pressures in many developing countries imply an urgent need to accelerate this process.

The issue, then, has become discovering the roles infant and child mortality play in childbearing decisions and ultimately, understanding what motivates couples to desire fewer children. In our discussion of theoretical mechanisms linking fertility and mortality, we noted biological and behavioral responses. The biological response suggests that improvements in health may result in lower mortality, but also in higher fertility because pregnancy wastage and fecundity are related to health improvements. The behavioral responses are similarly complex. However, these responses suggest that the desired number of surviving children determines the strength of the relationship between mortality and fertility. Thus, the focus should be on the demand for children.

High mortality leads to high demand for children and consequently to high fertility when parents perceive community health conditions to be such that they have to hoard children in order to be sure enough children survive to adulthood. Similarly, parents will try to replace a lost child to secure a given family size before the end of their reproductive years. Thus, policymakers must provide an environment where health conditions are sound. Parents should feel that it is safe to stop reproducing when they have reached their desired family size.

The desired family may not necessarily be small. Policymakers must therefore focus on the factors that influence the demand for children. This factor was discussed in detail in the previous chapter. Here, we note that old age security may be of relevance. As parents can expect to live longer because of improvements in health, they need reassurance that they will be provided for in old age from sources other than their children. Old age security and financial aid from sources other than children are areas that must be addressed if the demand for large families is to be reduced (Rukanuddin, 1982).

Once smaller family sizes are desired, family planning must be readily available to assure that the number of children can be effectively controlled. In such cases, Heer (1983) and Winikoff (1983) suggest that the relevant groups to target as family planning recipients should be couples who wish to terminate their childbearing because they have reached their desired number of surviving children.

In summary, our assessment of the relationship between infant and child mortality and fertility suggests that mortality reductions lead to fertility reductions by increasing the duration of lactational amenorrhea and reducing the desire to replace lost children or have additional children to insure against future deaths. The demand for smaller family sizes and the adoption of family planning to achieve such demands are likewise produced by the realization that too many children are surviving and that they are too costly to raise (Heer, 1983). Educated women are better equipped to recognize such relationships than women with no or little education. Moreover, not only does education make a significant difference in mortality experiences, but it also appears that it is a key factor in bringing about fertility reductions in response to mortality decline. As a result of improved education, relatively brief time lags between mortality declines and fertility declines have been observed in Taiwan and Puerto Rico (Nerlove and Schultz, 1970; Schultz, 1973). These time lags are much shorter than the ones revealed by historical data from Europe. Thus, with improved mass education, possible increases in population growth resulting from infant mortality reductions will likely be of briefer duration and fertility declines accelerated.

5   Theoretical and Methodological Issues

A number of problems plague research on infant and child mortality. Some problems arise because retrospective data are used and their quality is often questionable. The level of measurement is also a concern. Aggregated data may not reveal the causal mechanisms linking fertility and mortality at the individual level. Other problems are associated with failure to specify properly the models employed to estimate the effects. Most models assume a unidirectional link between mortality and fertility, ignoring the reciprocal nature of the relationship. Finally, lack of control for variables that influence both mortality and fertility may result in reporting spurious relationships and failure to discover important policy-relevant linkages. Let us briefly elaborate these issues.

With the careful preparation and execution of the World Fertility Survey, much improvement has been made in the quality of the data available for analysis. However, the data collected are based on retrospective accounts of events, affecting the accuracy of those reported. Certain events may not have been reported because of variations in definition of *live birth*, the practice of recording events, and the system of recording. Some events are intentionally forgotten, others are simply not recalled.

One lesson learned from the World Fertility Survey is the difficulty encountered in designing questionnaires specific enough to detect cultural variations in practices surrounding death and birth (Hobcraft *et al.*, 1983). In some cultures, conducting funeral services may determine whether or not a death will be remembered at a later date (Ware, 1984). Such errors of omission, added to the problems associated with survey research in general, may result in substantial variance on the measures. Measurement errors of this sort appear to be so critical that results numerous investigators have obtained may be without meaning (Winikoff, 1983).

A related issue is level of measurement. Aggregate-level data have been used in most research. Such data are not nearly as useful as individual-level data in understanding the mechanisms linking infant and child mortality with fertility (Schultz, 1984). However, though individual or microlevel data appear most useful in analyses of the relationship, strict adherence to this level ignores the influence of community-level factors. Environmental conditions such as water quality and the presence of health care programs and facilities would be omitted if data are collected only at the individual level. Therefore, the best strategy in data collecting appears to be a combination of micro- and community-level data.

In addition to aggregation biases some research fails to distinguish clearly cross-cultural variations in the data used. The practice of combining data from less developed countries and contrasting the findings with results from developed countries may disguise important policy linkages because cultural variations go undetected (Ware, 1984).

We previously pointed to the importance of documenting individual perceptions of the chances for survival of children in given environments. Assuming that family planning is possible and practiced, perceptions of survivorship play a significant role in individual family-size decisions. In a similar context we note the scarcity of data on women's roles as they relate to mortality. More information is needed to discover how women's roles in society as well as within the household influence the mortality of children. Household-level surveys should incorporate and emphasize such issues as hygiene and food intake as determined by the distribution of resources within the household. Awareness and knowledge of disease and illness are other issues related to women's roles.

In most empirical studies, mortality is assumed exogenous to the fertility decision. Birth intervals or parity progression ratios are often used to estimate this unidirectional effect of mortality experiences on fertility. Theoretically, we are still uncertain of the mechanisms involved in the mortality–fertility relationship. However, only if mortality is completely outside the realm of the individual will the assumption of unidirectional relationship hold true. Increasingly, it is recognized that fertility has an effect on mortality as well. In our previous discussion, this effect was identified as working through biological and behavioral channels. Biologically, short birth intervals have an adverse effect on mortality. From a behavioral perspective, parents may neglect unwanted children and, thereby, intentionally contribute to their poor health and subsequent death. Thus, allowances must be made for two-way causation, despite problems investigators are likely to encounter in finding instrumental variables to properly identify nonrecursive systems of equations (see footnote 1 in Chapter 7).

Our assessment of the research also pointed to the reciprocal nature of the relationship between lactation and birth interval. Where breast feeding is common and in the absence of other methods of fertility control, it may be assumed that as long as the mother is nursing she is less likely to ovulate and conceive another child. Thus, the longer the duration of breast feeding, the longer the interval between conceptions. However, the interval between conceptions is, in turn, influencing breast-feeding duration (Palloni and Tienda, 1983, 1986). The issue of reciprocity is also present in the relationship between breast-feeding duration and interbirth interval length.

Finally, many studies lack controls for the effects of pertinent variables influencing the infant mortality–fertility relationship. Such omissions may either result in spurious relations or the distortion of associations of interest (Palloni and Tienda, 1986). For example, the literature suggests that maternal education influences both the woman's childbearing pace and the mortality experiences of her offspring (Ware, 1983). Though researchers disagree about the magnitude of the impact, age of the mother at time of birth and her parity are also likely to affect the probability of birth and the birth outcome (Hobcraft *et al.*, 1983; Rutstein, 1983; Trussell and Hammerslough, 1983). In short, associated socioeconomic and demographic variables must be specified and carefully controlled if faulty inferences about infant mortality–fertility relations are to be avoided (Cochrane and Zachariah, 1983; Winikoff, 1983).

Chapter 10   Age at Marriage and First Birth

Interest in the relationship between age at marriage[1] and fertility can be traced to the writings of early population theorists. At the end of the eighteenth century, Malthus argued that delayed marriage is an essential "preventive check" of excessive population growth. Contemporary demographers remain much concerned with the relationship; yet, current research is uncovering as many problems and complexities as it is providing insights.

First is the issue of dealing with the immense cross-cultural and temporal differences in the meaning of the term *marriage* and its relevance to childbearing. In most developed countries, marriage represents a social transition to a formally recognized union initiated by a specific legal or religious ceremony sanctioning coitus and reproduction within that union. Marriage conveys the expectation of frequent sexual activity, with childbearing the normal outcome. Thus, many studies have assumed that the bride's age determines the length of time she will be continuously exposed to the risk of pregnancy.

In many developing regions such as tropical Africa, the Caribbean, and Latin America, however, informal cohabitation and consensual unions involving frequent sexual activity routinely occur in the absence of, or prior to, formal legal or religious ceremonies (Hobcraft and Casterline, 1983). Conversely, in some Asian nations such as Nepal, where child marriages are common, cohabitation and sexual relations do not commence until puberty, often a year or more after the formal marriage event (McCarthy, 1982). In both cases, age at marriage is a poor indicator of the length of time a woman is continuously exposed to the risk of childbearing.

Further complicating age at marriage–fertility analyses is conscious reproduc-

---

[1]In this chapter age at marriage is conceptualized as age at first marriage; for an elaboration of this point see the section on theoretical and methodological issues.

tive control through the increased use of contraceptives and the greater social acceptability and legality of abortion (Bloom, 1984). Where deliberate control of birth timing and spacing is possible, temporal exposure to the risk of childbearing via the marital state loses much of its functional meaning.

Another problematic issue is the significant number of out-of-wedlock births occurring in developed as well as in developing countries. For example, the proportion of first babies born out of wedlock to women aged 15 and over in the United States rose from 16% in the early 1950s to 31% in the early 1980s (O'Connell and Rogers, 1984). In 1983, approximately half of all unmarried women in the United States, aged 20–29, were sexually active and a third of them had been pregnant at least once (Tanfer and Horn, 1985). Such circumstances are not recent phenomena. Historical studies by Laslett (1980) indicate that throughout the past three centuries substantial proportions of European births have been to unmarried women, with the amount typically exceeding 20%.

Finally, high rates of marital dissolution and remarriage pose thorny complications to analyzing age at marriage effects (Henry and Piotrow, 1979). Unstable unions and sequentially different mates affect exposure to the risk of pregnancy in ways yet to be clearly understood.

What is understood from the problems raised above is that age at marriage can no longer be used mechanistically as an exposure variable marking the period during which a woman is at continuous risk of childbearing (Parnell, 1985). For this reason, increased attention is being given to age at first childbirth as the appropriate exposure variable. Bloom (1984, p. 2), outlining the merits of analyzing age at first birth, contends that

1. It is an extremely important social indicator, signalling both the decision to have children and a woman's transition to the role of mother
2. It has important social and economic implications related to a woman's health; her ability and desire to continue in school, her prospects for marital stability, her children's characteristics, and her patterns of labor force participation; geographic mobility; and consumption
3. It has important implications for subsequent fertility and mean length of generation, and, hence, for population growth.

While we, too, will direct attention to the age at first childbirth as a critical variable, there are good reasons not to dismiss age at marriage as a factor of substantial importance. The vast majority of births still take place within marriage or within stable consensual unions. Whereas threshold effects do set its relative significance, age at marriage has been shown to be one of the best predictors of fertility across nations (United Nations, 1983). In countries with limited practice of contraception, a woman who marries young is typically exposed to the risk of pregnancy longer than an equally fecund woman who marries later; consequently, she is likely to produce more children. In countries with widespread contraceptive use, a woman who marries young will typically be exposed to the risk of contraceptive failure and unwanted pregnancy longer than one who marries later. World Fertility Survey data thus show a very close relationship cross-culturally between age at marriage and age at first birth.

Age at marriage is also central to our working thesis that female status enhancement is the sine qua non for reduced fertility. As pointed out by Henry and Piotrow (1979, p. 105), if a woman postpones marriage from age 16 to 19 or from age 18 to 21, she can

1. Stay in school longer and acquire advanced skills and training for income-generating jobs
2. Work before marriage to contribute to her own and her family's income or savings
3. Enter marriage with greater emotional maturity to meet the challenges of family life.

Henry and Piotrow (1979) go on to note, "All these opportunities, which are virtually closed to a girl who marries at 15 or 16, will not only help women understand the value of spacing children and limiting family size later, but also will enable them to play more active roles in family, community, and national development" (p. 105).

Related to age at marriage is the prevalence of marriage and its association with fertility. Mauldin and Berelson (1978), for example, point out that as a general rule of thumb we should expect crude birth rates to be below 35 per 1000 if at least 80% of females aged 15–19 are single. Trussell *et al.* (1982) have demonstrated that in societies where marriage patterns are monogamous and little childbearing occurs among the unmarried, the total fertility rate is a simple product of the proportion married and the marital fertility rate of women at given ages. Their model shows that where there is no deliberate fertility control (contraception is not practiced), each 1-year increase in age at marriage reduces total fertility by 5.4%. As greater reproductive controls are introduced into their model, the amount of change in total fertility resulting from later ages at marriage is reduced accordingly.

Since modern contraceptive means are not uniformly accepted nor widely practiced in many countries experiencing rapid population growth, it is not surprising that policymakers have shown considerable interest in marriage age as a variable to address. Its causal connection to fertility is not simple, however, with numerous demographic and socioeconomic conditions confounding the relationship. We will take a closer look at these conditions, but first let us briefly overview evidence of the basic association in developed and developing countries.

1 Empirical Findings

Developed Countries

Despite some evidence to the contrary (Laslett, 1980), age at marriage and fertility historically were fairly closely linked in presently developed countries. Entry into marriage typically represented a decision to begin childbearing. Thus, age at marriage together with marriage duration represented a good indicator of a woman's effective exposure to childbearing risk (Hobcraft and Casterline, 1983; McCarthy, 1982).

Starting in the late eighteenth century and continuing throughout the nineteenth, women married at increasingly later ages, and, consequently, had fewer children than previous generations. Timing of marriage was negatively associated with its prevalence. The later the average bride's age in a country, the lower the marriage rate; late marriage age was associated with a large proportion of women remaining single throughout their lives (Smith, 1983). During the nineteenth century an estimated 70% of Western European women remained single in their early 20s, and close to 15% never married (Hajnal, 1965). The fertility decline in Western Europe during this period has been attributed largely to this marriage pattern.

By the middle of the twentieth century, age at marriage was still identified as a key variable affecting fertility (Davis and Blake, 1956). Fertility surveys in the 1950s showed the importance of bride's age on fertility (Freedman *et al.*, 1959) as did data from the 1965 and 1970 United States National Fertility Studies (Bumpass and Mburugu, 1977).

In recent years, the age at marriage and fertility relationship appears to have attenuated, at least in developed nations (Bumpass, 1982). Consistent with the Trussell *et al.* (1982) model, knowledge and use of contraception have delayed childbearing and reduced the effects of bride's age. Interest has therefore been shifting to age of entry into motherhood measured by the woman's age at first birth (Bloom, 1982, 1984; Bumpass, 1982; Knodel and van de Walle, 1979; Marini, 1984; Morgan and Rindfuss, 1984). Much of this later research has focused on the interval between marriage and first birth and the relationship between it and subsequent fertility (Rindfuss *et al.*, 1984). Data from the 1973 National Survey of Family Growth (NSFG) reveal that a woman's age at marriage or her most recent birth is closely linked to the timing of the next birth (Ford, 1981). In their analysis of 1976 NSFG data, Millman and Hendershot (1980) find age at marriage affects timing of the first birth, but not of the second. Interestingly, it is the marriage–first birth *interval,* rather than the bride's age per se, which influences timing of the second birth. Again, the magnitude of the effect is conditioned by effective contraception use. Overall, the longer the first birth is postponed, the fewer children in the completed family so that delays in initiating childbearing result in smaller families.

In sum, most research indicates that the younger a woman is at the time of her first birth, the sooner she will have a second and subsequent births. Other things being equal, this implies more generations in less time, a phenomenon that might have greater consequences for population growth than a change in completed family size. It is not just how many children women ultimately bear, but when they begin to bear them that affects a nation's annual fertility rate. Ford, for instance, has noted:

> Given the present low levels of fertility in the United States the timing of births may have more effect than changes in completed family size on annual fertility rates, since changes in completed family size are likely to be small. Even if completed family size does not change at all, if birth intervals become shorter, annual fertility rates will rise temporarily; if birth intervals become longer, annual fertility rates will fall (Ford, 1981, p. 1).

That shorter birth intervals may increase the rate of population growth pertains to developing as well as developed countries. A *ceteris paribus* assumption is necessary, of course, since among other factors, death rates may increase with shorter birth intervals.

Developing Countries

Until the initiation of the World Fertility Surveys in the mid-1970s, scarcity of high quality data on marriage age in many developing countries hindered research on the relationship. Though not without their own measurement problems, the WFS data for many (though not all) developing countries indicate the expected negative relationship: the younger the bride, the more children she bears. Most of Asia conforms to this pattern. India is characterized by young brides and high fertility; Southeast Asia shows moderate age at marriage and moderate fertility; and East Asia has a pattern of late marriage and low fertility. Fertility is high where early marriage is common, and low where late marriage is the norm. The Middle East shows a similar but less pronounced pattern (Henry and Piotrow, 1979; Pebley *et al.*, 1982).

Examining cross-classifications of children ever born by age for 29 developing countries throughout the world, Lightbourne and Singh (1982) show some distinct threshold effects for many nations. Only when first marriage is postponed beyond age 25 are consistent and substantial declines in completed fertility revealed (see Table 1). Up to age 25, women who marry later do not always have fewer children. Indeed, in some African and Asian countries, completed fertility of women who married between the ages of 15 and 20 was higher than that of women marrying before age 15.

Factors such as fecundability damage from early childbirth may be added to

Table 1[a]

Children Ever Born by Age at First Marriage of Women—Selected
World Fertility Survey Countries, ca. 1977[b]

Region and country	Number of children by age at first marriage					
	<15	15–17	18–19	20–21	22–24	25+
Africa						
Kenya	7.9	8.4	8.1	7.4	7.6	6.5
Lesotho	5.5	5.7	5.6	5.1	4.8	2.8
Senegal	6.9	7.4	7.9	5.6	*[c]	*
Sudan (North)	6.5	5.6	6.2	6.0	7.3	4.5
Asia and Pacific						
Bangladesh	6.8	7.0	*	*	*	*
Fiji	7.7	7.3	6.6	5.5	5.3	4.8
Indonesia	5.5	5.5	5.1	5.2	4.8	3.7
Korea, Republic of	6.9	6.2	5.2	4.4	4.1	3.5
Malaysia	5.8	6.8	6.8	6.2	5.8	3.8
Nepal	6.0	5.6	6.1	5.5	5.0	4.6
Pakistan	6.9	7.3	6.3	6.8	*	*
Philippines	8.8	8.7	7.5	7.3	6.2	4.2
Sri Lanka	7.3	7.1	6.3	6.1	5.0	3.5
Thailand	6.6	7.6	7.5	6.3	6.2	3.8
Latin America and Caribbean						
Colombia	9.9	8.2	8.3	8.1	6.3	4.6
Costa Rica	*	9.2	8.0	8.2	6.4	4.8
Dominican Republic	7.9	7.4	7.3	7.0	4.7	4.0
Guyana	7.5	7.0	7.1	6.2	4.9	3.7
Haiti	*	6.8	6.8	6.5	6.1	4.3
Jamaica	7.0	6.3	6.8	5.0	5.4	3.7
Mexico	8.0	8.3	7.9	6.5	6.1	4.2
Panama[d]	7.5	7.3	5.7	5.2	5.0	3.2
Paraguay	7.0	8.7	7.4	6.2	5.1	3.9
Peru	9.1	8.5	7.2	7.0	6.3	4.3
Trinidad and Tobago	7.8	7.0	5.4	4.6	4.3	2.9
Venezuela[d]	8.1	7.7	6.2	6.4	5.1	3.0
Middle East						
Jordan	10.4	8.8	8.2	8.0	6.8	5.7
Syria	8.7	8.5	8.7	7.6	7.8	4.6
Turkey	7.5	7.0	5.9	5.5	4.6	3.5

[a]Source: Adapted from Lightbourne and Singh (1982, p. 27).

[b]Note: Mean number of children ever born to ever-married women aged 45–49 at time of interview, by age at first marriage.

[c]*, Fewer than 10 cases.

[d]Age group 40–44, since 45–49 group not interviewed.

those of nutrition and lactation practices mentioned to explain the initial positive effect of women's age at marriage on fertility in some countries. Table 1 also illustrates so-called "catch-up" effects that operate in speeding the tempo of childbearing for those who marry in their later teens or early 20s.

An early research objective apropos developing countries has been to quantify the amount of fertility decline expected for given increments in age at marriage. Leasure (1963) estimated that in Bolivia an increase of 5 years in mean age at marriage from 22.5 to 27.5 should result in a 27% decline in the birth rate.

Several studies have focused on India. Agarwala (1965) estimated a 30% reduction in births if average age of brides increased from 15 to 19 or 20. Banerjee (1973) reported less substantial fertility reductions for Bihar, India. He estimated a change in average marriage age from 15 to 19 would reduce fertility by approximately 11%, corresponding to earlier estimates of Basavarajappa and Belvalgidad (1968) and Venkatacharya (1968). They reported that an increase in age of Indian brides to 19 or 20 will result in declines in the birth rate not exceeding 10%—only one-third of Agarwala's estimate.

The variance in estimates might be partly attributable to differences in the assumptions on which these studies are based or methods used. Some studies rely on model schedules of fertility associated with given ages at marriage; others use population projection methods with specific assumptions about marriage patterns. Without minimizing the importance of these methodological issues, the essential observation for our purposes is that age at marriage does have a significant impact on a country's fertility level, especially at the early stages of transition (Cho and Retherford, 1974; Mauldin and Berelson, 1978; Rotella, 1984; United Nations, 1983).

We observed above that postponing marriage can also reduce the population growth rate by increasing the span between generations. Coale and Tye's (1961) classic study demonstrates this phenomenon clearly. Examining Malaysian and Chinese fertility in Singapore, Coale and Tye point out that total number of children born to Malaysian women was less than the total born to the Chinese, although the Malaysians had more births annually. This difference resulted from a younger procreation pattern among the Malaysians. By adopting the Chinese schedule, Malaysians could reduce period fertility by 10%. Coale and Tye further applied the Chinese fertility pattern to estimates of the Indian population; this change in the age patterns of fertility reduced births by an amount equal to that achieved by a 20% decrease in period fertility. Their work provides strong analytical evidence that postponing marriage can substantially reduce the birth rate without reducing completed family size (cohort completed fertility). Thus, countries producing five generations in 100 years will increase their population much more rapidly than those producing only three generations, even though their cohort completed fertility is identical (Yaukey, 1973).

2 Theoretical Explanations

It is striking that only a few researchers have tried to provide theoretical explanations for the relationship between age at marriage and fertility. The association can be attributed to biological factors such as fecundity and to sociological phenomena such as norms (including explicit policies mandating the legal age at marriage) and roles.

Fecundity

Age at marriage is sometimes considered the point at which a woman commences a regular or continued risk of becoming pregnant.[2] If we assume childbearing is restricted to married women who make no attempt to limit fertility, then the earlier a woman marries the longer the period she has for childbearing and the more children she will bear (Henry, 1961; Veevers, 1971). When the curvilinear age and fecundity relationship is taken into account, a further explanation for the negative relationship between bride's age and fertility becomes clear. Not only do women who marry late have fewer years in which to bear their desired family, they must also reach their goals during a period of their life course when probabilities of conception are reduced (Jain, 1969; Rindfuss and Bumpass, 1978) and face greater risks of pregnancy wastage (Peel and Potts, 1969). Although fecundity may account for the lower fertility of women who marry much after age 20, for younger women fecundity effects are probably less pronounced (Bloom, 1984; Busfield, 1972).

Some scholars have hypothesized that selection of more fecund women into early marriage might also be a factor of importance. More fecund women might be "caught" by pregnancy and subsequent marriage at an earlier age than less fecund women (Bumpass and Mburugu, 1977). This hypothesis is difficult to test, because measuring subfecundity is so problematic. However, the argument points to a weakness in the assumption that the age at marriage–fertility relationship is unidirectional. Premarital pregnancies play a significant role in young ages at marriage.

Age at menarche has been used as an indicator of fecundity. Ryder and Westoff (1971a) found pregnancy rates higher for women with early menarche than late menarche. More recent data from Belgium, Pakistan, and Malaysia also indicate that early menarche leads to earlier ages at first intercourse, first marriage, and first birth. In Belgium, 15% of the latest maturing women were married by age 20 compared to 30% of the earliest maturing women; 18% of the

[2]The validity of this assumption is discussed in the theoretical and methodological issues section.

former and 36% of the latter had a first birth before age 21. Similarly, Pakistani women who had the earliest age at menarche were much more likely to marry young and give birth at a younger age. In Malaysia, three-fourths of the early-menarche women had a birth within 24 months, compared to one-half of the late-menarche women (Udry and Cliquet, 1982).[3]

Life Cycle and Age Norms

In addition to biological processes such as age at menarche, social processes no doubt account for some of the observed variation in fertility. The sociological meanings attached to age and stage in the life cycle are important (Bumpass and Mburugu, 1977; Rindfuss and Bumpass, 1978). Just as there are norms about appropriate ages for marrying, there are norms about appropriate ages for child-bearing (Udry and Cliquet, 1982; Modell et al., 1978), some associated with early childbearing, others with delayed childbearing.

Norms associated with early childbearing focus primarily on marital status. Rindfuss and Morgan (1983) found an Asian pattern of very short first-birth intervals (9 to 10 months) after marriage, which reflects normative timing in family formation. Subsequent intervals were much longer, so the short first interval seems to be for establishing the social reality of the marriage. Having had that crucial first birth, couples seemed to relax in having subsequent children.

Moreover, most societies view childbearing outside marriage as undesirable. Thus, as Udry and Cliquet (1982) point out, in many developing countries girls are often considered ready for marriage as soon as they show signs of having reached puberty. With age at menarche expected to decline as women's nutrition and health are improved, a widening gap between puberty and desired age at marriage may call for new mechanisms to limit reproduction.

Other norms center around the undesirability of late childbearing. These norms are not necessarily out of concern for the medical risk to mother and child in pregnancy. Rather, it is a question of stage in the life course. A woman might desire to stop childbearing after a given age because she feels she would be out of phase with her peer group or that a birth at this age would be socially unaccept-able. Thus, the childbearing pace of important reference groups is relevant in influencing decisions related to the timing of births. This factor, combined with the fecundity aspect, helps us to understand why the fertility of women who marry late (e.g., after age 25) does not catch up with that of women marrying earlier.

[3]It should be noted that menarche is related to physical health. Late-maturing females may be less healthy and less able to carry a pregnancy to term. The menarche–fertility relationship is more complicated than commonly thought. See Gray (1983).

Exposure to Nonfamilial Adult Roles

Typically, the younger a woman is when she first marries, the fewer chances she has to become acquainted with nonfamilial values and alternative adult roles (Bumpass, 1969, 1982; Bumpass and Mburugu, 1977; Call and Otto, 1977; Presser, 1971). Conversely, the older a woman is at first marriage, the more exposure she is likely to have had to nonfamilial options. She will have a chance to develop a sense of social and economic independence and individual achievement which promote awareness of and desires for alternatives to motherhood. Bearing and rearing children becomes only one of various sources of achieving status and personal satisfaction.

Equally important, how much time she has to develop nonfamilial roles between marriage and first birth will affect her future childbearing. The younger the first-time mother, the less mature she is in evaluating implications of a second birth. The perception of consequences and alternatives differ for women making these decisions when they are in their teens or early 20s, versus early 30s.

These changing perceptions with age underly what we term the *mañana effect* and the *child-reality effect* of delayed childbearing. These effects are especially potent on upwardly mobile women. Gallup surveys in 1971 of white college women aged 18 to 24 showed a strong aversion to childlessness and one-child families (Blake, 1974). When asked about their own preferences and tastes, 89% responded that fewer than two children was too small a family. The same percentage stated that they wanted to have at least two children. Now that these earlier cohorts of college-educated women are entering the final stages of their childbearing years, far larger proportions have remained childless or have only one child (Baldwin and Nord, 1984).

We propose that prior preferences were unfulfilled not only because of the post-1970 rise in divorce but also because women's career responsibilities and consumption patterns led to sequential birth postponent decisions—the mañana effect—to the point where parental age factors and lifestyle opportunity costs eventually dissuaded many career women from beginning a family. The child-reality effect operates on career women who have a first child and then realize that the time, energy, and emotional costs involved in motherhood are far greater than they had anticipated. The thought of having a second child becomes less attractive, especially if both quality of career and motherhood commitments are serious matters to them.

To summarize, the primary linkages between age at marriage and fertility are biological and social (see Fig. 1). If age at marriage is the point at which a woman is first regularly and continuously exposed to the risk of becoming a mother, the biological capacity to bear children, fecundity, is of importance. Age at marriage is then tantamount to the number of fecund years available for marital

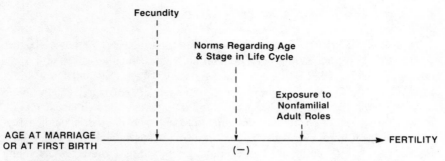

Fig. 1. Causal operators explaining effects of age at marriage or first birth on fertility.

childbearing. Since fecundity decreases with age, age at marriage and fertility will be inversely related. The social meaning of age is also significant. Norms define and sanction the appropriate timing of marriage, age of childbearing, and desired number of children. With increasing age, a woman becomes more aware of such norms and the costs of departing from them. If the social cost of childbearing is perceived to be high, older women can be expected to cease childbearing. Finally, the younger the bride the less experience she has with adult roles other than those of wife and mother. The extent to which these linkages between age at marriage and fertility operate to their full potential depend on several other factors to be discussed next.

3 Exogenous and Intervening Factors

The age at marriage–fertility relationship is affected or mediated by other social and economic factors. Women's education, labor force participation, and contraceptive practice are perhaps the most important factors in this context. We examine each in turn.

Education[4]

Studies conducted in developed and developing countries show education is an important predictor of age at marriage (Scanzoni, 1975; Yaukey and Thorsen, 1972). Indeed, in developed countries, educational attainment has become more strongly linked to age at marriage in recent years (Marini, 1978), with extended

---

[4]In this discussion the primary concern is with the effect of education on age at marriage; however, it should not be overlooked that the relationship is nonrecursive.

postponement particularly common among the highest attainment levels (Smith, 1983). Marini (1978) and Waite and Spitze (1981) report that a woman's school enrollment decreases the probability of marriage at ages 16 through 20, especially immediately after high school completion. Women not pursuing higher education tend to marry shortly after high school.

In developing countries, World Fertility Survey data from Asia, the Pacific, Latin America, and the Caribbean show well-educated women are less likely to be married by the end of their teenage years and have higher mean ages at marriage (Smith, 1983). Analyzing 1976 Malaysian household data, Anderson (1981) estimates a 1-year increase in schooling corresponds to a 1-month delay in marriage. Similar estimates for the United States indicate that an additional year of education increases age at marriage by 0.68 of a year (Marini, 1978).

Studies focusing on age at first birth rather than age at marriage are consistent in assessing education as an important determinant of onset of childbirth (Bloom and Trussell, 1983; Hirschman and Rindfuss, 1980; Rindfuss and St. John, 1983). Education is closely associated with the tendency to delay childbearing and there is evidence that the effect of education has increased across cohorts (Bloom, 1984). Women college students are especially likely to postpone motherhood. Analyzing data from the National Longitudinal Survey of the High School Class of 1972, Rindfuss *et al.* (1984) found that during the 6 years following high school, only 10% of women who went to college or graduate school had become mothers compared to 81% who had become homemakers. An increasing probability is that women in recent cohorts who continue their education beyond high school and delay the birth of their first child will end up with no children at all.

How do we account for the finding that the more educated women marry later and become mothers later? Biological factors associated with age are obviously important, but again, social factors are of substantial significance.

Role acquirement is one sociological dimension affecting the relationship. Education, we have stressed, fosters awareness and knowledge about a range of possible adult roles and is the key to acquiring them. Therefore, the more years of schooling, the more opportunities to acquire roles not defined in terms of early marriage (Mason, 1984; Mueller, 1972a; Repetto, 1976a; Smith, 1983). The more attractive the options, the less likely is motherhood (Rindfuss *et al.*, 1984).

Highly educated women typically do not pursue roles of student and mother concurrently. Following college graduation, they may seek to capitalize on their educational investment by acquiring high-salaried jobs or pursuing a profession. Thus, it is not just the awareness and opportunities that education fosters, but also the purposive behaviors (the economic return of education) and the incompatibility of schooling and early motherhood.

A number of these arguments have been formulated theoretically in terms of what has been called the *new home economics* (Becker, 1981). Rotella (1984, pp. 36–37) provides an excellent summary of the theory's primary assumptions and propositions:

> The "new home economics" sees marriage as essentially a trade relationship which individuals enter in order to increase their lifetime consumption stream. . .
>
> . . . Age at marriage, likelihood of ever marrying and choice of mate should all be related to the variables included in the model. First, since a frequent form of marriage relationship is between a male specializing in market production and a female specializing in home production, reductions in the difference between men and women in their ratios of market productivity to home productivity should reduce economic incentives to be married. Specifically, a rise in women's market productivity should lead to less marriage, whether in the form of higher age at marriage, more divorce, lower proportions ever marrying, or related patterns. This could occur from any of the following changes: increases in female labor force participation (especially in the modern sector), rising women's wages, increases in women's education, or expanded market opportunities because of lower discrimination. In contrast, a rise in men's wages could be expected to increase their incentives to marry since it enhances their market productivity relative to home productivity. Second, because the production of children is costly both in terms of time and goods, increases in the market wages and educational level of mothers (or potential mothers) should lower the demand for quantity of children because of the higher time costs involved. Since "own children" are a likely output of marriage-partnerships, reductions in the demand for children should reduce the incentive to be married.

In developing countries, education and age at marriage may be related through mechanisms such as arranged marriages and dowry size (Mason, 1984). Women with less education are more likely to be involved in an arranged marriage (Caldwell, 1983) and such arrangements usually involve young brides (Dyson and Moore, 1983). Better educated brides often command a higher price, so marriage is postponed while the bride's parents acquire added capital for the dowry (Lindenbaum, 1981). Furthermore, educated women may be such an asset to their parents because of their potential contributions to the family economy that parents may try to delay their daughters' marriages (Mason, 1984; Salaff and Wong, 1977). Finally, since women in many developing countries tend not to marry down in status, the search for equal or higher status mates by highly educated women may be more difficult and take longer than for less educated women (Rotella, 1984).

In developed countries, characteristics of the family of origin may also influence the probability of marriage for a young woman (Otto, 1979; Rindfuss *et al.*, 1984). Here, the more resources within the family—that is, the higher the mother's education and the occupation of the household head—the less chance that the daughter will marry before high school graduation (Carlson, 1979; Waite and Spitze, 1981).

Whereas, the positive relationship between education and age at marriage is well documented, an interesting, yet less well-documented finding, is the interaction effects of education and age at marriage on fertility. Education may affect fertility differently for different ages at marriage. For example, among women who marry later, those with some college education tend to have more children than women with less than a high school education (Bumpass, 1969; Busfield, 1972). Increments in number of years of education completed therefore may not *necessarily* bring about fertility reductions.

Several explanations have been offered for the interaction of education and age at marriage on fertility. As noted previously, fecundity and social awareness of adult roles are essential in understanding the relationship. In addition, aspirations for self and offspring and their achievement through the woman's career or her husband's education have been suggested to explain the interaction effect (Bumpass, 1969; Busfield, 1972).

Differences in education among women who marry at younger ages likely result in variations in their knowledge and use of contraception which might also account for the conditioning effect of education among those who marry early. Simply put, better educated women tend to know more about contraception than women with little education (Lightbourne and Singh, 1982; Ryder, 1973; Sathar and Chidambaram, 1984; Zelnik and Kantner, 1972). Moreover, through awareness of roles and high aspirations for themselves and their children, better educated women also have more incentive to apply such knowledge. As a consequence, although they may marry rather young, they have fewer children than women with low levels of education who marry at the same age.

Differences in knowledge and use of contraception among women of varying

Table 2

Theoretical Classification Specifying Outcomes of the Age at Marriage–Education Interaction with Associated Variables Affecting Fertility

Age at marriage– education conditions	Fecundity	Role awareness	Aspirations for self and children	Ability to realize aspirations	Effective contraceptive use	Expected fertility outcome
Young age at marriage–low education	High	Low	Low	Low	Low	High
Young age at marriage–high education	High	High	High	Moderate	Moderate	Moderate
Old age at marriage–low education	Low	Moderate	Moderate	Low	Moderate	Low
Old age at marriage–high education	Low	High	High	High	High	Low

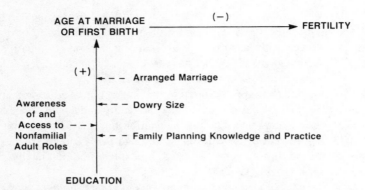

Fig. 2. Causal operators explaining the relationships between education and age at marriage or first birth.

amounts of education do not explain the curious positive association between education and fertility among women who marry later. For these women, deferring marriage allows them to acquire roles that compete with motherhood and develop higher aspirations for self and children. Nonetheless, more highly educated women are usually in a better financial position to realize such aspirations and still have a large family. They have better career opportunities, the potential for better paying jobs, and are likely to marry men with a similar, or higher level of education or high incomes. Thus, even if they choose not to be active in a career, they are more likely than less educated women to be able financially to realize their higher aspirations without lowering their fertility (Busfield, 1972).

In sum, interactions between age at marriage and education not only directly influence reproductive behavior but are also associated with biological and female status conditions that further play critical roles in fertility outcomes. In Table 2 we classify these interactions and associated conditions as they would be expected to shape reproductive behavior. In Fig. 2, we diagram the causal operators discussed above that relate female education to age at marriage or first birth.

Labor Force Participation

The relationship among education, age at marriage, and fertility is further mediated by modern work opportunities available to women. In a socioeconomic structure where few modern jobs are available to women, adult roles other than those of wife and mother tend to be limited. In contrast, if the socioeconomic structure encourages and depends on women workers, female socialization often emphasizes career choice as an alternative to early marriage. Moreover, with

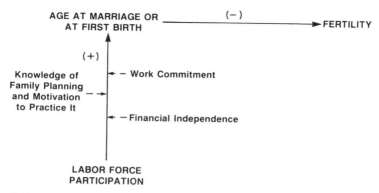

Fig. 3. Causal operators explaining the relationships between labor force participation and age at marriage or first birth.

such choices, the opportunity to learn about family planning and the incentive to use contraceptives effectively are increased. In general, the better the employment opportunities for women and the higher their job commitment, the more effective is their practice of contraception (Salaff and Wong, 1977).

Consistent with the new home economics model, the labor market value of the years spent in school is also very important. The higher the labor market value, the higher the opportunity cost of marrying and leaving the labor force (Becker, 1981; Cochrane, 1979). Where wages for single women relative to married women are high, age at marriage will be later. Similarly, the higher the salaries of men relative to women, the earlier women will marry (Becker, 1981; Smith, 1983). Figure 3 specifies this financial independence operator along with other key factors that help explain the relationship between female employment and age at marriage or at first birth.

Finally, we should mention one likely nonrecursive effect, not specified in Fig. 3. Whereas employment allows marriage to be postponed, it is plausible that delayed marriage provides the opportunity for employment, and may, in fact, necessitate it (Entwisle *et al.*, 1982).

Family Planning Knowledge and Practice

Before use of modern contraceptive methods became widespread, the relationship between age at marriage and fertility was much stronger. The bride's age was a fairly accurate indicator of the initiation of continuous sexual activity and onset and increased likelihood of childbearing. Thus, delaying marriage was a means of achieving a small family size, while early marriage resulted in a large family size. Today, the availability of modern contraceptive technology allows couples who marry early to have families as small as those of couples who marry late. Should we expect to continue to find a negative relationship between age at marriage and fertility?

Our answer is a qualified yes. Since no contraceptive method is 100% effective, the longer exposure period, especially at peak ages of fecundity, involves a higher risk. More importantly, young women appear to be less knowledgeable and less effective users of contraceptives than older women. With formal sex education either absent or inadequate, many young women and men still possess only limited knowledge about birth control. Even if she were knowledgeable, a young woman might be an inconsistent or ineffective user because of normative pressures.

Young women may also be less motivated to use birth control. Being less familiar with possible roles other than wife and mother, or having less time to accumulate skills for alternate roles, younger brides may lack the necessary incentive to control their family size. These factors might help explain why young women are not as effective in controlling their fertility as older women, and, thus, why early marriage often results in larger completed family size even in populations where modern contraception technology is widely available.

Summary

In the preceding sections we focused on the theoretical linkages between age at marriage and fertility, including the biological factor of fecundity and the social factors of norms and roles. We explored the conditioning and intervening factors of education, labor force participation, and family planning. In Fig. 4 we summarize the complex interrelationships among the variables. Education, employment, and family planning are separately and in conjunction instrumental in the relationship between age at marriage or first birth and fertility. Female high school or college graduates are more likely to postpone marriage or childbearing, to become active in the labor force, and to pursue a career. They are more familiar with contraceptive practices and their knowledge and effective use of family planning methods helps them realize their career plans or stay single or childless. In turn the longer the delay of marriage or childbearing, the less time women have in their reproductive span and the more aware they are of alternatives to motherhood. Moreover, the more education they possess, the more attractive are these alternatives. In Chapter 11, we shall elaborate upon the causal linkages involving family planning knowledge and use illustrated in Fig. 4.

4   Theoretical and Methodological Issues

A variety of theoretical and methodological problems arise in analyzing the effects of age at marriage on fertility. One that warrants reiteration is the cross-

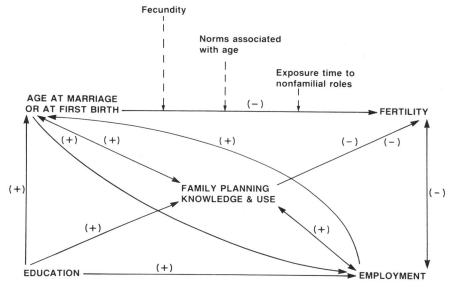

Fig. 4. Summary model specifying primary factors influencing the association between age at first marriage or age at first birth and fertility.

cultural and temporal variation in the meaning and significance of the term *marriage* for cohabitation, sexual activity, and childbirth. As a socially defined event, first marriage may follow cohabitation by a considerable interval (especially in the Caribbean and certain African countries) or cohabitation may not follow until months or even years after the formal marriage ceremony (as in some Asian countries).

In Western nations, marriage has been traditionally viewed as the social sanctioning of sexual relations and reproduction. Societal norms prescribed these activities to the marital state. In recent decades, this normative prescription has been increasingly ignored (Zelnik and Kantner, 1980). For example, 82% of the unmarried women aged 20 to 29 in the United States reported in 1983 that they had experienced sexual intercourse and over half stated they had had intercourse at least once in the 4 weeks preceding the interview (Tanfer and Horn, 1985). Correspondingly, as previously noted, the percentage of all first babies born to women out of wedlock increased from 16 to 31% between the early 1950s and early 1980s (O'Connell and Rogers, 1984). From 1970 to 1980, the number of families headed by women under age 45 in the United States increased by 2.3 million (96%) with the most dramatic rise among blacks (Wilson, 1985). During 1980–1981, more than 70% of first-born babies of black women were conceived out of wedlock (O'Connell and Rogers, 1984).

With the contemporary rise in sexual permissiveness, cohabitation of the unmarried, and out-of-wedlock births, age at marriage has become a dubious indicator of duration of effective risk to childbearing. This, together with the immense cross-cultural differences in the relevance of "marriage" for reproductive behavior would point to age at entry into motherhood (i.e., age at first childbirth) as a much better measure of the length of exposure dimension. Indeed, such temporal and cross-cultural differences in the significance of marriage for reproductive behavior draw into question the representativeness of any fertility survey that is restricted to married or ever-married women.

When focusing on woman's age apropos the timing of either marriage or first childbirth, consideration should also be given to possible period and cohort effects (Hobcraft and Casterline, 1983; Tsui, 1982). The effect of being reared during a particular era or belonging to a given birth cohort may affect the age at marriage or first childbirth and fertility relationship in several ways. We know from evidence in the United States that the prevalence and timing of marriage are closely linked to the overall economic conditions (Easterlin, 1966, 1978; Elder and Rockwell, 1976). A downswing in the economy results in fewer marriages through postponement, while an economic upswing encourages marriage in general and early marriage in particular. Likewise, when cohort sizes are large, it has been hypothesized that competition for available employment is greater and income relative to aspirations lower, resulting in longer delays in marriage and childbearing (Easterlin, 1980). Related macroeconomic explanations have been offered for increases and decreases in fertility rates and trends (Butz and Ward, 1979; Rindfuss and Sweet, 1977).

Recent cohorts vary more than older cohorts in their timing of first birth, not only because of a changing distribution of individual characteristics, but also because particular societal conditions have greater effects on first birth than previously (Bloom and Trussell, 1983). For example, current childbearing age United States cohorts are more likely both to continue practicing contraception and to continue their education after they marry than earlier cohorts were (Marini, 1978).

Only recently have researchers begun to investigate concurrently the effects of age, period, and birth cohort on timing of first entry into marriage or motherhood and fertility. Nevertheless, as Hobcraft and Casterline contend, "In most circumstances the analysis is deficient unless both period and birth cohort are considered simultaneously, with controls for age and duration—despite the difficulties involved" (Hobcraft and Casterline, 1983, p. 7).

Another methodological issue is the assumed unidirectionality in the relationship between education and age at marriage. In treating the education and age at marriage or first birth relationship, we have considered education to be the independent variable. We believe this model is only appropriate for those developing countries with limited opportunity for higher or continuing education for women.

Other patterns of causality may exist. Reasonable arguments support the idea that age at marriage can determine the level of education obtained (Alexander and Reilly, 1981; Call and Otto, 1977). In developed countries, however, the negative impact of age at marriage on educational attainment has diminished (Rindfuss *et al.*, 1980). Although marriage generally terminates schooling for women, in the United States at least one out of every four women, married after 1950, has attended high school or college since marriage (Davis and Bumpass, 1976; Nam and Folger, 1965). As social policy measures facilitate such efforts, we can expect the proportion of women who continue education after entering marriage to become much higher.

Throughout this chapter we have treated age at marriage as synonymous with age at first marriage. In doing so we have not discounted that a woman might marry more than once, giving several ages at marriage to consider. Age at first marriage is most relevant to our discussion because it indicates more accurately the time available for a woman to develop and accumulate alternative roles. In subsequent marriages, the bride's age effect is no longer "pure"; it is con- founded by numerous other experiences, difficult to quantify and unique to the individual. Moreover, the nature of family planning knowledge and practice can be expected to be different for a woman marrying for the first time than for one entering her second or third marriage; presumably, in the latter cases we are no longer dealing with inexperienced women. Findings on the effects of the timing and duration of marital disruption on fertility are inconclusive. The effect may be reduced fertility (Cohen and Sweet, 1974) or no significant effect emerges (Bald- win and Nord, 1984; Thornton, 1978a). Until more concrete evidence accumu- lates, researchers whose models still employ the age at marriage factor should feel justified in regarding age at *first* marriage as the appropriate indicator.

Finally, three seemingly straightforward, yet sometimes overlooked, issues should be noted. First, because of the close empirical association of age at marriage with other socioeconomic determinants of fertility (such as education and labor force participation) reported zero-order correlations and cross-classi- fied distributions likely contain substantial spurious components that overstate the strength of the relationship. The general rule that analyses and causal in- ferences be based on multivariate models is therefore especially pertinent to age at marriage–fertility research. Second, because of lengthening intervals between first marriage and first birth and growing percentages of women in many devel- oped nations not completing their fertility until older ages, substantial bias may be introduced to analyses of age at marriage effects that exclude women who have not completed their childbearing years. Third, mean age at marriage or mean age at first birth may be an unrepresentative indicator of populations that have bimodal distributions of age at marriage or first birth events—for example, those populations with high proportions of teenage pregnancies and high propor- tions of members who delay childbearing until later years.

Chapter 11 | Family Planning Knowledge and Practice

For nearly two decades the right to determine one's family size has been considered a basic human right (United Nations, 1980; United Nations, ESC, 1973). By preventing higher order births and facilitating birth spacing, family planning not only contributes to women's and children's health but also to achieving socioeconomic advancement objectives on personal and societal levels. Yet, many couples fail to exercise their right to determine family size. In 1981, of the 900 million couples of childbearing ages in the world, less than one-half were practicing contraception (United Nations, 1984). Not surprisingly, contraceptive practice is lowest in those developing nations where rapid population growth is posing serious problems (International Conference on Family Planning in the 1980s, 1981).

Why do so many women worldwide not plan their families or protect themselves against unwanted or ill timed pregnancy? In tackling this question, we first look at the status of family planning knowledge and use in developed and developing countries. Next we discuss the antecedents of family planning knowledge and the mechanism, motivation, that links knowledge to use. Through their influence on birth control knowledge and reproductive motivation, a number of factors are discussed which determine whether and how effectively a woman will use family planning—education, age at marriage, labor force participation, age, and parity. We also consider the merits of the argument that men's dominance over women and lack of conjugal communication are obstacles to effective family planning.

1 Knowledge and Practice of Family Planning in Developed Countries

Knowledge and practice of family planning is far from being a recent phenomenon (Himes, 1963). If we include as contraceptive techniques withdrawal (*coitus interruptus*) and abstinence (*coitus reservatus*), there is no doubt that contraception has been known and practiced for centuries. Historical studies indicate that when incentives and needs were high to control family size or delay childbearing, contraceptive knowledge was applied quite effectively. In the seventeenth century, some segments of the French and British populations, particularly the upper classes, successfully delayed or prevented conception in response to periods of economic hardship. Not until the middle of the eighteenth century, however, did practice of contraception become widespread enough to exert a noticeable demographic effect (Hawthorn, 1970; Zito, 1979). Later marriage and a smaller proportion marrying were important in reducing fertility in the demographic transition, but fertility control within marriage was also essential (Hajnal, 1965).

Fertility declines in Ireland and Great Britain illustrate these points. The Irish birth rate fell in response to a pattern where most women began to marry at a later age or remained single. In England and Wales, the birth rate fell more rapidly and to lower levels than in Ireland during the same period because the institutional environment was more conducive to introducing birth control methods in marriage (Hawthorn, 1970, p. 29).

During the twentieth century, adoption of contraceptives has been widespread and rapid. For instance, in Great Britain, 40% of the women from the 1910–1919 marriage cohort used birth control at some point in marriage; for the 1920–1929 cohort, the percentage was never below 55 (Lewis-Faning, 1949); and in the 1950–1959 cohort, 70% used birth control (Rowntree and Pierce, 1961–1962). In 1976, 77% of currently married, fecund women in England and Wales were practicing contraception (Lightbourne and Singh, 1982).

Only for the last few decades do we have reliable data on contraceptive practice in the United States. Findings from four national sample surveys of United States fertility (the 1965 and 1970 National Fertility Studies and the 1973 and 1976 National Survey of Family Growth) indicate percentages of married couples with wives aged 15–44 currently using any method of contraception were 64, 65, 70, and 68, respectively, for each of the 4 survey years. A third cycle of the National Survey of Family Growth conducted between August 1982 and February 1983 showed 68% of currently married women aged 15–44 were using contraceptive methods (Bachrach, 1984). Fifty-four percent of previously wed and 35% of never-married women in this age group were also practicing contraception.

Whereas current contraceptive use by married women increased only modestly from 1965 to 1983, the distribution of methods used changed substantially. From 1965 to 1976, reliance on sterilization, the pill, or IUD doubled (Pratt *et al.*, 1980). Between 1976 and 1983, the percentage of married women relying on sterilization again nearly doubled—from 14 to 25.6%, while the pill dropped in popularity from 33.2 to 19.8% (Bachrach, 1984).

The nearly 70% level of current use United States wives reported is similar to that found today in most of Europe. A few European countries—Spain, Yugoslavia, and Romania—fall below 60%; others—Finland, Belgium, and Czechoslovakia—report current use above 80%. In the remaining countries, between 60 and 80% of currently married, fecund women are practicing contraception (Lightbourne and Singh, 1982; United Nations, 1984).

In general, developed countries reporting the lowest overall contraceptive use tend to report the highest use of less effective methods such as rhythm or withdrawal. For example, of Romanian couples using contraception. 91% rely on insufficient methods; the percentages for Yugoslavia and Spain are 78 and 58. In some countries with high use levels, the less effective methods are popular as well. Roughly one-third of Belgian and Czechoslovakian couples rely on withdrawal to control their fertility. Couples in Scandinavia, Great Britain, the Netherlands, and the United States use more effective methods such as the pill, IUD, diaphragm, or condom (Lightbourne and Singh, 1982). At the time of the World Fertility Surveys, 1976–1979, use of contraceptive sterilization by men or women in developed countries was pronounced only in Great Britain and the United States. We should add that fertility control through induced abortion has also been substantial in a number of developed countries, particularly in Eastern Europe and the United States (Tietze, 1983).

2 Knowledge and Practice of Family Planning in Developing Countries

There is no credence to the belief that couples in developing countries have been ignorant of ways to limit fertility. For millennia, numerous folk methods have been known and practiced in these countries. As was the case for most developed nations, however, not until the 1970s was systematic and reliable empirical information published on the extent of contraceptive awareness. David and Bhas (1973), studying family planning knowledge among rural Indian women, reported that 40% claimed to know at least one contraceptive method, and 20% could identify more than one. In Thailand, Knodel and Prachuabmoh (1973) and Knodel and Pitaktepsombati (1973) found 75% of urban women, compared to 50% of rural women, knew of a birth control method.

World Fertility Survey (WFS) results suggest that these figures have increased (Jones, 1984; United Nations, 1981; Vaessen, 1980). Awareness is high in almost all developing countries, particularly of modern contraceptive methods. WFS data show that, except for women in relatively isolated countries (e.g., Nepal), most are aware of at least one efficient method of contraception (Mamlouk, 1982; Vaessen, 1980). Of efficient methods known, the pill is the most popular method actually used, followed by sterilization and IUDs (Jones, 1984; Lightbourne and Singh, 1982).

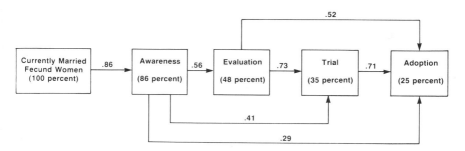

Fig. 1. Progression probabilities across stages of modern contraceptive knowledge and use among currently married fecund women in 28 developing countries—the World Fertility Survey, ca. 1977. Adapted from Tsui (1985).

Although knowledge is high in developing countries, contraceptive practice is considerably below levels observed in developed countries. According to WFS data, current use among married women of childbearing age ranges from an average low of 5% in Africa to a high of 34% in Latin America and the Caribbean (Tsui, 1985). Overall, approximately 30% of currently married, fecund women in developing countries are using contraception, compared to an average of 72% reported for the United States and Europe (Lightbourne and Singh, 1982).

Tsui (1985) analyzed WFS data on currently married, fecund women in 28 developing countries to document rates of slippage between contraceptive knowledge and contraceptive use. She employed a progression model including four stages: (1) *awareness* (whether the person has ever heard of a contraceptive method; (2) *evaluation* (whether the person has ever intended to use a modern or other contraceptive method; (3) *trial* (whether a person has ever used a modern method); and (4) *adoption* (whether a person is currently using a modern method). Tsui's results, summarized in Fig. 1, show that, on average, 86% of currently married, fecund women in the 28 nations were aware of at least one method, yet only 25% were currently practicing contraception. The greatest rate of slippage occurred between the awareness and evaluation stages, with nearly half of those who were aware of at least one contraceptive method never intending to use that or another method. Of the 48% of currently married, fecund women who responded that they had intended to practice contraception, nearly three-quarters actually tried a modern method, and of those who tried a modern method, 71% were currently practicing contraception. Since the progression probabilities are compounded, however, only 25% of the married women sampled (based on unweighted country averages) were actually practicing contraception at the time of the survey. Perhaps even more striking, of the 86% who were aware of a modern contraceptive method, only 29% of them were currently using a modern method.

Table 1 documents the age-specific degree of slippage across the contraceptive knowledge and use stages within major regions of the developing world. These data show precipitous declines between knowledge (awareness) and use (adoption) in all four regions—falling from 82 to 21% in Asia, from 94 to 34% in Latin America, from 83 to 20% in the Middle East, and from 66 to 5% in Africa. Observe further that, despite relatively high rates of knowledge, contraceptive use figures are especially low for the youngest groups of married women in all four developing regions—ranging from 2% in Africa to 18% in Latin America. Age-specific use rates show a curvilinear pattern, peaking at 27% for those aged 35–39 in Asia, and at 41, 26, and 7% respectively, for those aged 30–34 in Latin America, the Middle East, and Africa. The low rates of contraceptive use among younger married women is an important issue to which we shall return.

In sum, contraceptive *awareness* is today almost universal; the same is not true for contraceptive *practice*. Although most women in developing countries know of ways to control their fertility, they do not apply this knowledge nearly to the same degree as women in developed countries. Thus, on average, the proportion of contraceptive users in developing regions is less than half that found in developed countries (Berent, 1982; Carrasco, 1981; Sathar and Chidambaram, 1984).

3 Factors Affecting Family Planning Knowledge and Motivation for Use

It is clear that a better understanding of the causal mechanism linking family planning knowledge with its practice is necessary to facilitate program success in reducing rapid population growth. We have seen that, even though women may know about family planning techniques, many do not use them to prevent higher order births or protect themselves from ill timed or unwanted pregnancy (Lightbourne and Singh, 1982; Mamlouk, 1982; Simmons and Culagovski, 1975; Stokes, 1977). The most plausible explanation for this knowledge-use gap is lack of *motivation*—only when women have sufficient incentive to reduce their family sizes will they effectively apply their family planning knowledge. Circumstantial evidence of this motivational component may be observed from family size limitations during economic recessions (Hajnal, 1965; Easterlin, 1980).

If motivation is the primary mechanism for translating knowledge into use, what influences motivation? The same factors that determine motivation may also affect knowledge of family planning methods. As such, the factors discussed below are viewed as causally antecedent to *knowledge* of family planning

Table 1

Percentages of Currently Married Fecund Women in Each Contraceptive Knowledge–Use Stage by LDC World Region—World Fertility Survey, ca. 1977[a]

Regional averages (percentages) for modern contraceptive knowledge–use stage	Age group							
	15–19	20–24	25–29	30–34	35–39	40–44	45–49	Total
Awareness								
Asia	74	82	85	84	83	81	77	82
Latin America	91	95	95	95	93	92	90	94
Middle East	84	87	89	89	88	86	82	83
Africa	59	67	69	70	67	63	57	66
Evaluation								
Asia	48	54	58	55	50	36	20	47
Latin America	50[b]	62	65	63	58	46	31[c]	68
Middle East	44	51	53	55	50	43	31	48
Africa	22	24	26	26	22	16	11	22
Trial								
Asia	13	26	36	39	38	29	17	31
Latin America	28[b]	46	54	54	49	41	28[c]	46
Middle East	12	28	38	43	41	38	29	34
Africa	4	7	11	13	11	9	6	9
Adoption								
Asia	8	15	21	25	27	25	22	21
Latin America	18	31	38	41	38	33	27	34
Middle East	5	17	19	26	24	24	23	20
Africa	2	3	6	7	6	5	5	5

[a]Source: Tsui (1985, Table 6.4).
[b]Not including Costa Rica and Panama.
[c]Excluding Venezuela.

and the *motivation* that determines how effectively a woman applies her knowledge.

Our working thesis is that, while female status may rise as a result of successful family planning efforts, rising female status may itself help expand and sustain family planning efforts (see, e.g., Bhatnagar, 1972; Oppong and Haavio-Mannila, 1979). In previous chapters, we identified three variables closely associated with female status: education, age at marriage, and labor force participation. We look at each as it relates to family planning knowledge and motivation for use and at other instrumental factors—including age and parity, wife's role in decision making, and husband–wife communication.

Education

Empirical analyses of the relationship between education and family planning have focused primarily on contraceptive use. The most general finding in developed and developing countries alike is that education is positively related to use (Berent, 1982; Dandekar, 1965; Freedman *et al.*, 1959; Husain, 1970; Lightbourne and Singh, 1982; Miró and Rath, 1965; Sathar and Chidambaram, 1984; Sen and Sen, 1967; Yaukey, 1961). As Table 2 indicates, even a minimal improvement in overall educational attainment can result in a substantial increase in contraceptive use. For instance, when standardized for age, women in Bangladesh, the Philippines, Mexico, and Peru with only a few years of schooling are more than twice as likely to be contraceptive users than those women with no education. In these same countries, women with 7 or more years of schooling are four times more likely to be contraceptive users than those with no education.

Closely related to formal education is literacy. The role of literacy in affecting contraceptive practice has been repeatedly documented as in the Kripalani *et al.* (1971) study of Calcutta showing that, among couples where both spouses were illiterate, family planning acceptance was only 23%, compared to rates of 66% when husband or wife was literate and 70% when both were literate.

Several explanations may be offered for the positive relationship between education and contraceptive use. More educated women probably have more knowledge of contraceptives because they can read printed materials on birth control (Cernada and Lu, 1972; Freedman, 1976). As one Egyptian study showed, educated women depend less on relatives, friends, or acquaintances as their sole source of information. The more education a woman has, the more likely she is to mention public guidance, physicians, and nurses as her sources of contraceptive knowledge (Thavarajah and Farag, 1971). Generally, educated women are more likely to have contact with family planners, and they become more knowledgeable of what methods are available, how they work, and where they can be obtained.

Education also facilitates the acceptance of contraception by removing barriers created by myths and misinformation (Chi and Harris, 1978–1979; Dow, 1971; Newland, 1977). As Newland states,

> Literacy facilitates the distribution of birth control information—not only information about obtaining services, but also the more basic understanding of how and why different methods work, and of the advantages and disadvantages of different methods. Information is a great antidote to the fears and misapprehensions that surround this sensitive subject (Newland, 1977, p. 10).

A further advantage of education is in providing a better perception of the utility and cost of children. Educated women better understand the influence of children on the family's overall economic position. As cost sensitivity rises, the percentage using contraceptives increases when family resources are limited (Mueller, 1972a,b). There is support for the notion that concern for children's educational prospects—itself a function of parental education—motivates use of modern contraceptives. Ware (1976b) found 9% of the Nigerian women she interviewed said they used modern contraceptive methods because only if they kept their families small could they provide higher education for all their children.

Educated women, then, are more apt to use contraceptives because education provides the environment and resources to learn about contraception and the incentive to use it by promoting a better understanding of the benefits to be gained by limiting family size and by correcting false stereotypes or myths regarding contraceptive practice. It therefore simultaneously serves to increase knowledge, desire, *and* ability to practice effective family planning. Thus, even in cases where fertility preferences were found not to vary much by education, differential fertility patterns result from education's influence on successful contraceptive implementation. As one striking example, Lightbourne (1985, p. 194) reports that, among Philippine women desiring no more children, 82% of the most educated were contraceptive users, compared to only 33% of the least educated. Lightbourne further reports that this large educational differential in contraceptive use persisted, regardless of the number of additional variables introduced as controls.

Age at Marriage

Women who marry young are less likely to practice contraception than older brides (Presser, 1971; Westoff and Ryder, 1977). Many may marry young because they want children immediately or desire larger family sizes and, therefore, do not practice contraception. Early marriage age also increases the possibility of contraceptive failure (Jones *et al.*, 1980; Westoff, 1980). Differential knowledge of contraception may partially account for this relationship, since women marrying young are less aware of contraceptive methods and their effective use than those marrying later. Young brides may well be less motivated to practice contraception if they have had limited life experiences and have not become familiar with nonfamilial roles and options. Young brides may also lack the emotional security to challenge their husband's or relatives' pressures on them not to practice birth control.

Table 2[a]

Percentage of Exposed Women Currently Using Contraception (Including Sterilization) by Education of Respondent—Selected World Fertility Survey Countries, ca. 1977[b]

	Education			Rates standardized for age[c]			Rates standardized for number of living children[c]		
	None	Primary	Secondary	No education	Primary	Secondary	No education	Primary	Secondary
Aisa and Pacific									
Bangladesh	7.4 (3534)	14.2 (883)	27.2 (218)	8.3	18.0	35.6	8.6	17.6	37.6
Fiji	59.2 (682)	55.2 (2197)	56.1 (435)	—d	—d	—d	52.6	57.6	66.2
Indonesia	31.0 (2309)	39.2 (2976)	57.0 (319)	30.3	42.5	59.9	34.5	46.0	68.0
Jordan	27.8 (1530)	47.9 (484)	66.4 (323)	25.3	54.9	69.7	21.4	50.0	71.0
Korea, Republic of	44.7 (640)	43.4 (2002)	50.1 (1199)	36.6	39.0	47.3	37.7	41.0	56.6
Malaysia	31.3 (1403)	44.8 (2319)	56.9 (541)	—d	—d	—d	—d	—d	—d
Philippines	16.0 (299)	34.2 (1512)	53.8 (4872)	12.1	32.5	52.5	15.8	31.2	53.1
Sri Lanka	28.6 (880)	38.0 (1822)	50.0 (2008)	25.9	36.2	49.4	26.3	38.2	56.2
Thailand	27.0 (577)	38.4 (2303)	45.8 (240)	33.8	40.0	48.0	27.5	38.3	49.5

192

Latin America and Caribbean

Colombia	27 (451)	52 (1378)	74 (489)	27	53	75	25	52	75
Costa Rica	68.5[e] (445)	79.2 (1192)	82.0 (585)	68.9	79.8	82.6	64.8	77.6	85.7
Dominican Republic	17.0 (112)	37.7 (1242)	62.6 (139)	23.7	39.3	64.2	17.0	38.9	64.3
Guyana	38.0[e] (442)	38.1 (1262)	38.3 (933)	35.1	34.9	42.6	32.6	35.9	45.4
Jamaica	36.5[e] (239)	44.3 (1219)	53.1 (471)	40.1	45.4	55.7	36.4	45.6	58.9
Mexico	19.3 (809)	39.9 (2545)	71.0 (753)	18.6	40.4	70.6	17.3	39.4	73.6
Panama	47.3[f] (501)	65.8 (875)	74.5 (881)	47.2	65.5	74.6	48.4	65.6	73.0
Peru[g]	16.2 (3417)	40.0 (6940)	68.3 (3484)	15.2	39.7	68.3	19.5	39.1	69.5

[a] Source: Mamlouk (1982, Table 4) as compiled from World Fertility Survey First Country Reports.

[b] Nepal excluded because 95% of women had no education. Pakistan's first country report contained insufficient information on use rates by education.

[c] Mexico's sample of exposed women used as standard. In most cases age groups are <25, 25–34, 35–44, 45–49, and number of living children is categorized as 0, 1, 2, . . . , 5, 6+.

[d] Fiji: data not available by age; Malaysia: data not available by age and number of living children.

[e] No education includes none and less than 3 years of primary.

[f] No education includes less than 4 years of primary; no respondents had no education.

[g] Peru's percentages based on weighted data; weighted frequencies given.

193

Labor Force Participation

Employment has long been suggested as a stimulus for women to be consistent, effective, and purposeful contraceptive users (Blake, 1965; Davis, 1967; Freedman and Coombs, 1966b; Pratt and Whelpton, 1958; Ridley, 1959). In the United States, for example, working women are slightly more likely to use contraception than nonworking women (United Nations, DIESA, 1979). This general finding for developed countries is explained by the notion that employment not only exposes women to ideas and factual information about contraception, but also gives them strong incentives to adopt family planning methods.

In developing countries, however, this relationship does not seem to hold (see, e.g., Bamberger *et al.,* 1976). Location and type of employment and child care arrangements influence whether an occupational role competes with motherhood and, consequently, whether employment leads to effective contraception. If it is more convenient to combine employment with motherhood (such as having relatives readily available for babysitting), children may be less perceived as burdens or costs and less effort may be made to limit family size. Moreover, if a wife works to meet immediate economic needs rather than being committed to a career, then her work is often temporary and may not precipitate effective contraceptive use. Thus, in developing countries, employment, per se, may not stimulate contraceptive use. In fact, analyses of the World Fertility Surveys (WFS) reveal that education accounts for much of the observed differences in contraceptive use by employment status (United Nations, 1980).

Age and Parity

The relationship between a women's age and her contraceptive practice tends to be positive, at least in developing countries. The younger the woman, the less likely she is to practice contraception and do so effectively. Worldwide, many young women still lack the knowledge for effective contraceptive practice, and even if knowledgeable, they may lack the incentive to use it, since they may lack awareness of nonfamilial roles or may be more committed to launching families.

WFS data shown in Table 3 indicate that in developed countries, where the overall level of contraception is high, the relationship between age and contraceptive use is relatively weak. For instance, in the United Kingdom, 73% of married women aged 15–19 report using contraception, compared to 75% of married women in the 15- to 49-year-old range. In most developing countries, however, much lower levels of use occur among young married women, with the

Table 3[a]

Percentage of Currently Married Women Aged 15 to 19 and 15 to 49 Using Contraception—Selected World Fertility Survey Countries

Region/country	Survey year	Percentage using contraception	
		Aged 15–19	Aged 15–49
Developed countries			
Belgium[b]	1975–1976	76.5	81.0
Denmark[c]	1975	79.8	75.0
Hungary[d]	1977	52.9	73.0
Portugal	1980	76.8	76.3
United Kingdom[e]	1976	72.6	75.0
United States[f]	1982	53.1	68.0
Developing countries			
Africa			
Cameroon	1978	2.0	3.1
Egypt	1980	5.3	31.9
Ghana	1979–1980	6.5	12.4
Ivory Coast	1980–1981	(·)[g]	3.0
Kenya	1978	3.4	6.9
Lesotho	1977	(·)	7.0
Nigeria	1981–1982	4.3	5.7
Senegal	1978	5.7	5.2
Sudan (North)	1979	5.8	6.4
Tunisia	1980	11.4	43.1
Asia			
Bangladesh	1979	4.9	12.1
Indonesia	1976	13.0	26.0
Jordan	1976	9.0	26.0
Korea, South	1979	10.8	50.2
Malaysia	1974	15.0	34.0
Nepal	1981	3.9	7.0
Pakistan	1975	(·)	6.0
Philippines	1978	16.0	36.0
Sri Lanka	1981–1982	27.7	54.9
Syria	1978	12.5	29.5
Thailand	1981	29.0	56.5
Latin America			
Colombia	1980	24.7	48.5
Dominican Republic	1980	18.0	42.0
Ecuador	1979	20.7	33.5
El Salvador	1978	8.3	34.0
Guyana	1975	18.0	34.0
Honduras	1981	8.3	26.9
Jamaica	1979	—	54.9
Mexico	1980	20.4	38.7
Panama	1979	28.9	61.0

[a]Source: Senderowitz and Paxman (1985, Table 6).
[b]Ages 16–44 only. [c]Ages 18–44 only.
[d]Ages 15–39 only. [e]Ages 16–49 only.
[f]Ages 15–44 only. [g](·) = less than 1%

proportions of older women practicing contraception frequently two to three times as great (Larson, 1981; Mamlouk, 1982). These data are consistent with the age-specific contraceptive use rates shown for Africa, Asia, Latin America, and the Middle East in Table 1.

The low incidence of use among young women in developing countries likely reflects the tendency to use contraception only after several children have been born. In many developing countries, initial acceptors of family planning have been mainly women who have achieved their desired family size. The cultural preference has been to reach desired family size early in marriage. Since the prevalence and effectiveness of contraceptive use are highly correlated with motivation to limit family size, women no doubt become more effective users after desired family size has been reached (Lightbourne and Singh, 1982; Westoff *et al.*, 1963). Conversely, in developed countries it is not unusual for a woman to postpone the birth of her first child while continuing higher education or engaging in nonfamilial activities and to space subsequent births. Thus, present evidence suggests women in developing countries use family planning methods somewhat more to *maintain* a desired family size, while women in developed nations use contraception at least as much to *space* children as to *limit* family size.

Women's Role in Decision Making

The extent to which women are involved in marital decisions depends on their status within home and community, frequently determined by such factors as their education and employment status (Rosen and Simmons, 1971). Power gained through knowledge, skills, and earnings gives women greater independence from their husbands' authority and more influence in familial decision making. Miller and Inkeles (1974) further argue that women's experience in schools, factories, and other modern institutions helps them develop subjective feelings of efficacy and autonomy in the face of traditional kinship pressures and obligations.

Greater egalitarianism in husband–wife relationships, in turn, has been hypothesized to influence contraceptive use via a number of interrelated mechanisms. First, egalitarianism increases the probability that the woman's fertility desires are honored. As Mason (1984) notes, this causal link to increased contraceptive use presumes that the woman's fertility desires are lower than her husband's. Empirical evidence on this point is mixed (Hollerbach, 1983). Second, egalitarianism weakens the sexual double standard whereby the woman is prohibited from using birth control because her husband fears that consequently she will be more likely to engage in extramarital sex. Third, egalitarianism may weaken the husband's machismo image, whereby frequent pregnancies and births demonstrate his sexual potency (Mason, 1984). Fourth, the wife's greater equality in the marital relationship may increase the likelihood that health issues enter into fertility decisions.

> Egalitarian couples are likely to worry about the health consequences for the wife having an additional child, whereas men in male-dominated families are likely to decide about additional children in terms of their own needs and interests (Mason, 1984, p. 72).

Finally, egalitarianism has been posited to promote couple communication, itself linked to more effective contraceptive use. This issue will be addressed in the next section.

Despite the seemingly straightforward identification of the causal mechanisms linking female decision making to contraceptive use, there is, at best, only weak to moderate support for the hypothesis that egalitarianism positively affects birth control. Beckman (1983) and Hollerbach (1983) provide excellent reviews of this research and discuss methodological and substantive issues that may account for the lack of consistent support for the hypothesis.

Husband–Wife Communication

A variety of studies have shown that effective communication between husband and wife is important for successful practice of family planning. Frequent partner discussions of birth control are positively related to contraceptive use and use effectiveness (see, e.g., Economic and Social Commission for Asia and the Pacific, 1974; Hill et al., 1959; Kar and Talbot, 1980; Shah, 1974) as are discussions of more general matters (see, e.g., Hollerbach, 1980; Jolly, 1976; Mitchell, 1972). As Beckman (1983) notes, however, some studies (see, e.g., Brody et al., 1976; Hartford, 1971; Shedlin and Hollerbach, 1981) have suggested husband–wife communication about birth control may be a consequence of contraceptive use rather than the reverse. The extent of husband and wife communication, especially about family size preferences, appears to be a function of their education, with those with schooling beyond minimal levels better able to express their feelings about the often sensitive issues of contraception and family size (Carleton, 1967; Olusanya, 1971).

The argument that husband–wife communications result in better contraceptive practice and smaller families rests on the assumption that the number of children either spouse desires is smaller than the number perceived to be desired by the other spouse. The outcome of the communication is important in that it might well determine whether family planning is adopted. Using CELADE data, Simmons and Culagovski (1975) found discussions between spouses about desired family size did not lead to effective contraception unless they agreed on the use of birth control. Brody *et al.* (1976) reached a smiilar conclusion. In their study of family planning in Jamaica, partner agreement about contraceptive use was more highly correlated with contraceptive behavior than the report of having simply discussed contraception with the partner. If a husband and wife differ in their attitudes toward family limitation, the man's preferences often predominate which, in developing countries at least, are usually for a larger family (Cain, 1984; Chaudhury, 1982; Mitchell, 1972).

Summary Models

Figure 2 presents a synopsis of factors affecting family planning knowledge and motivation in a series of theoretical models specifying the causal mechanism(s) by which each variable affects birth control use. Model 1, the most basic, relates family planning knowledge to fertility with motivation serving to translate knowledge into use. Models 2–7 elaborate model 1 by specifying each factor previously discussed as causally antecedent to (1) family planning knowledge and (2) the motivation that determines how effectively this knowledge is applied.

Model 2 diagrams the effects of education. In brief summary, education increases a woman's exposure to and understanding of printed media that provide family planning information and improves her ability to exchange information directly with family planning practitioners. The educated woman is more motivated to apply her knowledge because of her opportunity to engage in roles other than wife and mother and her better understanding of the economic benefits of limiting her family size. Education serves as well to remove myths and fears regarding modern contraceptive practices.

Model 3 specifies the effect of age at marriage. Women who marry and/or bear children at a very early age are frequently cut off from additional formal and informal education that would broaden their exposure to contraceptive knowledge and effective means of birth control. Postponing marriage to a later age further leads to greater emotional (and sometimes financial) security, giving women additional incentive to control their destiny. Moreover, later marriage provides women with longer exposure to nonfamilial roles and alternatives that may encourage their practice of contraception.

Labor force participation (model 4) also provides exposure to new ideas and information and is an incentive for practicing birth control use, both because of anticipated or experienced role incompatibilities and alternative rewards to child-

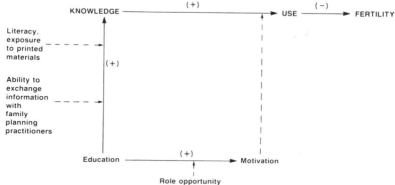

Fig. 2. Theoretical models elaborating variables influencing family planning knowledge and motivation for use.

bearing that employment may bring. However, in developing countries, the context of work need not create role incompatibilities, and employment may not motivate women to practice family planning. The somewhat higher incidence of contraceptive use among working women sometimes reported may be because of differences in educational attainment between working and nonworking women.

For reasons closely related to age at marriage effects, age and parity also influence family planning knowledge and use (model 5). Women in their late 20s and 30s tend to be more effective users than women at other ages. Younger

Model 4.

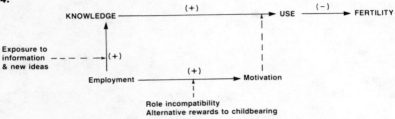

Model 5.

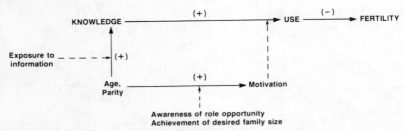

Model 6.

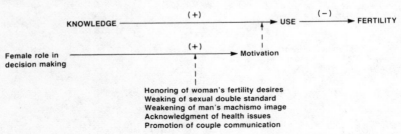

Model 7.

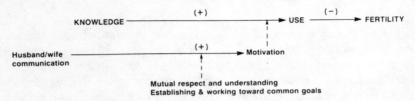

women know less about contraception and alternative roles and older women may not have been exposed to attitudes and information promoting family planning and smaller ideal family size. As to parity, women become far more effective contraceptive users once they have reached their desired family size.

Model 6 specifies the effect of the woman's role in decision making. Greater equality in the conjugal relationship may (1) increase the likelihood that the woman's fertility desires will be honored; (2) weaken the sexual double standard; (3) weaken the husband's machismo image; (4) increase the likelihood that health issues enter into fertility decisions; and (5) promote couple communication. Although all of these mechanisms have been used as reasons for predicting a positive effect of the wife's role in decision making on the couple's motivation to practice birth control, we reiterate that only weak support for this hypothesis has been found.

Finally, model 7 diagrams the effect of husband–wife communication in motivating couples to translate contraceptive knowledge into practice. The ability of husband and wife to communicate about family planning issues and other more general issues influences the extent to which they adopt family planning. The primary mechanisms by which this effect obtains involve developing mutual respect and understanding between spouses and establishing and working toward common goals.

Of all the factors in Fig. 2, we regard women's education as the pivotal variable affecting family planning knowledge and motivation for use. As discussed in this and previous chapters, education has significant consequences for a woman's understanding of her reproductive organs, her age at marriage, exposure to modern institutions and new ideas, economic independence, ability to communicate effectively with her spouse, and power in the family-size decision-making process. It is for this reason that educating women may be considered as the primary status enhancement variable influencing contraceptive knowledge and, more importantly, the underlying motivations that translate this knowledge into practice.

Chapter 12 | General Conclusions and Policy Issues

Most concur that developing nations will not experience sustained fertility declines if policies focus on family planning programs alone. Along with providing the means for effective contraceptive practices, policymakers must help create conditions that encourage men and women to want small families and thereby translate contraceptive knowledge into practice. Our working thesis is that this achievement will require concerted governmental efforts that simultaneously foster economic development and greater participation of women in the social, economic, and political mainstreams of their countries.

Expanding women's options by giving them opportunities to acquire marketable skills and achieve greater social and economic independence offers substantially more promise for successful family planning because such opportunities directly affect the motivational framework underlying reproductive choices. Where women are limited primarily to homemaking, being sexual partners, and breeding children, they (and their husbands) will have few incentives to restrict their family sizes (Oppong, 1983; United Nations, ESC, 1973).

1 Education and Status Attainment

We have argued that women will develop more modern sex role orientations and the means to pursue extrafamilial alternatives chiefly via improved formal education. In many developing countries, the uneducated woman relies almost entirely on her husband or father for status and her children for long-term economic security. As a woman becomes educated, she gains the motivation and talent to forge ahead on her own. Her enlightenment about all avenues of life increases and she obtains the skills to pursue meaningful employment and become a discriminating consumer of the mass media. She becomes aware of the biology of reproduction and what she may do to prevent or postpone conception as well as preserve her children's health.

Education, in essence, opens the vista of choice in roles women may occupy and in their reproductive behavior. If the only role model of an uneducated woman is her mother and other mothers, whose lives have centered primarily on housework and child care, she also will likely see her prime mission in life as that of wife and mother. In fact, she may well perceive that marrying young and having many children is her singular route toward gaining status, demonstrating personal accomplishment, and acquiring long-term security. Educated women will discover other routes to status, self-fulfillment, and economic security. The implications for reproductive behavior of these divergent paths to status attainment are immense.

2   Social Mobility and Fertility

In our assessment of the largely male-oriented research on social mobility and fertility, we found little statistical evidence suggesting that fertility is affected by mobility per se (i.e., the unsettling process of the move itself). We should be careful not to throw the baby out with the bath water, however. Consistent support has been provided for the acculturation hypothesis (upwardly mobile women, as measured by their fathers' and/or husbands' occupations, exhibited fertility rates between those at their origin and destination statuses). This observation is particularly pertinent for macrolevel fertility outcomes. Although status of origin may continue to affect an individual's reproductive behavior, those who rise in status will partially adopt the lower reproductive norms of their higher status destination group. And if more upward than downward mobility occurs, fertility rates of the population will decrease.

The male-dependent basis of most research on social mobility and fertility has also limited its utility for contemporary policy. As we approach the twenty-first century, more women are gaining status independent of the men in their family. For this reason alone, we urge that new research agenda be oriented to assessing the mobility of women in their own right and its consequences for reproductive behavior. We believe it highly plausible that research findings on women's self-derived social mobility and their fertility will be more impressive and more consistent than those findings based on status indicators of their male relatives.

Throughout the second half of this book, we specified and elaborated the mechanisms through which female status enhancement influences reproductive behavior, stressing education as the chief means by which women gain independent status. We specified the causal operators linking education to key intervening variables associated with female status which, in turn, bear on fertility: Educated women busy with school or career are more likely to postpone getting married or having babies. Educated women know more about the economic, physical, financial, and emotional costs of raising large families and the economic utility of children. Education affects infant and child mortality when women learn about modern medicine, good health practices, nutrition, and sanitation. Educated women know more about effective contraception and use it. In the remainder of this chapter, we summarize how these key variables which mediate the effects of education on fertility may be of special interest to policymakers.

3   Labor Force Participation as a Policy Variable

Policymakers concerned with rapid population growth have been enthusiastic about the idea that providing employment for women might dampen fertility. However, research indicated that merely being in the labor force is not enough. Women working in agriculture and domestic service where work and child care can be combined easily, wages are low, and opportunities for advancement slim, continue to have high fertility.

The key to female labor force participation as a tool for fertility reduction is that the work must be psychologically, economically, and socially satisfying and rewarding. Sufficient employment opportunities must be provided that offer a clear separation between motherhood and job and yield financial benefits to the household so that the woman worker senses that her status is rising through her work. The woman who feels that she is making an important contribution to herself and to her family through her job is more likely to limit her family so that motherhood obligations impinge less on her career plans. Clearly an educated woman is more apt to obtain a job that enhances her status in such a way.

4   The Value of Children as a Policy Variable

Implicit to the policy relevance of the value of children concept are assumptions that couples can control their reproductive behavior and that family size decisions are based on benefits of children and costs they entail. Regarding the latter, it is important to recognize that the *perceived* value of children is of as much, if not more, relevance than their *actual* value.

The economic benefits of children basically accrue from their labor value and their function as security investments (Arnold *at al.,* 1975; Bulatao and Lee, 1983; Germain, 1975), although the magnitude of such contributions has been questioned (Mueller, 1976). What we do know is that, for many people in developing countries, children are the best long-term insurance available in their world of high insecurity. Thus, as long as children contribute significantly to family income and are perceived as protection against old age, illness, or misfortune, the incentive to reduce fertility will be low. Large families will prevail until institutionalized alternatives to children offer such protection and until child labor loses some of its value (Ryder, 1983).

Since the value of children is greatest where agriculture is the main source of livelihood—where the labor contract is with the household and the workplace is the home—development policies targeted to facilitating industrial transformation may be essential. Children's costs rise and their value as labor diminishes when wage labor markets overtake family production as the chief means to subsistence (Caldwell, 1982; Chaudhury, 1982).

Introducing compulsory mass education along with changing labor market conditions should further alter the cost–benefit balance of large families. Children are unavailable for full-time work while attending school and, with structural change, parents may develop different kinds of expectations for children (Nag, 1983a), particularly rising educational aspirations (Michael, 1974; Mueller, 1972a). Expressed in Caldwell's (1982) wealth flow hypothesis, once the institutional structure changes so that the net flow of goods and services is no longer perceived to be from children to parents, but the reverse, fertility will eventually decline.

Altering the institutional structure through development policies and programs aimed at limiting economic contributions of children would decrease (though not completely diminish) the value of children. This is because children are valued emotionally as well as economically, and such emotional values are not easily manipulated. As Mueller (1972b) points out:

> It is difficult to influence deep seated attitudes by simple injunction or propaganda. For example, the noneconomic satisfaction which people expect from bringing up a large family or several sons may not be readily amenable to change. Mere abstract admonitions to have small families may have very little impact. Such advice comes closer to home when it is linked to problems which matter to the family such as education of children, achievement of a better standard of living, or support in old age (Mueller, 1972b, p. 383).

We might add to the above that, if women are provided greater opportunities to engage in rewarding economic activities outside the home that make them less dependent on their husbands' resources, children would likely lose some of their previous status value to women. Under such circumstances, women may no longer consider large families necessary for their social recognition and may, in fact, view them as competition to such recognition.

In sum, when economic factors entering into reproductive decision-making processes are known, policymakers can try to alter the cost–benefit ratio of children and encourage quality vs quantity family size tradeoffs. Our assessment of pertinent research to date indicates that to be successful, policymakers must help create meaningful employment opportunities for women, design social security systems for the aged, introduce compulsory education for the young, reduce child labor exploitation, and make health care insurance readily available. To raise aspirations, these macrolevel programs may be accompanied by government efforts to broaden the availability of modern consumer goods and services, as well as expanding media and communication networks that might facilitate the cultural transmission of newer ideas and lifestyles from more developed nations. Focus must be on such macrocontexts because microlevel decision making apropos the utility of children is largely conditioned by these contexts.

5   Infant and Child Mortality as Policy Variables

It has been generally held that only when parents could be assured that the children they bore had a strong chance of living to maturity, were they likely to consider limiting family size (R. C. Freedman, 1963; Taylor *et al.*, 1976). With advances in medical technology and vaccinations to protect youngsters from many previously fatal childhood diseases, there was hope that a resulting decrease in infant and child mortality would have a profound effect on fertility.

Researchers, however, have vacillated on the demographic impact of this variable with some arguing that reducing mortality among babies and young children may actually increase population growth. Nearly three decades ago, Coale and Hoover (1958) cautioned that the political appeal of manipulating this variable probably distorts policymaker's notions about its potential. They warned that if mortality reduction is not integrated into a carefully planned modernization policy, the population situation may even worsen.

In reviewing empirical and theoretical studies of the relationship, we found complex biological and behavioral responses to mortality reductions. The biological responses may not always lead to a desirable outcome regarding population growth. When overall health conditions are improved, there is less fertility, fewer miscarriages, and more who are born survive. On the other hand, where breast feeding is common, higher survival probabilities imply longer duration of lactation amenorrhea and thus longer periods of suppressed ovulation (Chowdhury *et al.*, 1976; Heer and Wu, 1975; Knodel, 1975).

We concur with those who argue that if population growth is to be slowed, mortality reduction policies must be integrated into a larger socioeconomic development scheme. In this regard, education is perhaps the most important socioeconomic variable for policymakers to consider because of its specific linkages to fertility as well as to mortality. We described how education can make a significant difference in the demand for children and thereby fertility.

Education must also be recognized as a primary facilitator of improved health conditions and reduced infant and child mortality by promoting better personal hygiene, increased knowledge about proper sanitation and preventive medical care, raised awareness of signs of illness at an early stage, and ability to seek out modern, rather than folk, medical assistance, and improved knowledge about nutrition and child care, especially in allocating proper food and uncontaminated water to infants and children in the family.

Whereas improved health conditions, however much desirable, may not result in an immediate slowdown in population growth, this outcome should be achieved in the longer run (Heer, 1983). Once parents become aware that health conditions do not necessitate hoarding children against future losses, their family size desires are likely to change. Education, again, can play an important role in developing this behavioral response in transforming public health contexts (Ware, 1984).

6   Age at Marriage and First Birth as Policy Variables

Since labor force participation among mothers and the value of children to parents reflect the demand for children, it is not difficult to see how they are interrelated. Age at marriage and first birth affects the supply of children. Legislating minimum age at marriage in itself cannot be expected to have a profound influence on fertility because of its complex links with possible premarital sex or alternatives to legal marriage. Again education is crucial in any policy expectations surrounding this variable. Educated women are more likely to have alternatives to early marriage and to be aware of the advantages of delaying the first birth, limiting family size, and spacing children for maximum health benefits. Age at first birth becomes the important element in situations where contraceptive technology is available and marriage is no longer automatically followed by pregnancy.

Policymakers concerned with rapid population growth find the negative relationship between age at marriage and fertility of particular interest. If later age at marriage implies lower fertility (Knodel and van de Walle, 1979), then a policy to raise the marriage age seems an easy way to curtail rapid population growth. The solution is not quite so simple. Increasing the legal age for marriage may precipitate more premarital sexual activity and undesired illegitimate births; only marital fertility would be affected. If the cultural norm is to marry young, raising the legal minimum marriage age might accomplish nothing. The law could be circumvented by failing to register marriages or through cohabitations or similar arrangements. The age established as the minimum might also make a difference. Fecundity is relatively low at the beginning of the reproductive years

(Bumpass and Mburugu, 1977), so raising the legal age at marriage from 12 to 16 might have little effect compared to raising it from 18 to 22.

It is difficult to assume that the political act of raising the legal age at marriage will lower fertility—the case of China is a notable exception (Huang, 1982; Chen, 1985). Policymakers must look on age at marriage as an essential component in social and economic development and less as a policy-manipulable variable in itself. Family planning is, however, a policy-manipulable variable crucial in shaping the nature of the relationship between nuptial age and fertility. Indeed, without use of contraception, any fertility reductions achieved by legislating against young brides might be wiped out by increases in out-of-wedlock births. Policymakers must, therefore, provide information about family planning, especially to young women; more importantly, they must provide the incentives which transmit contraceptive awareness and knowledge into contraceptive use.

We have argued that incentives to postpone marriage and delay births through contraceptive practice are predicated in large part on providing women with meaningful and rewarding nonfamilial alternatives. Policymakers must help create an environment where women can define their position in their household and community in terms other than those of wife and mother. Increasing opportunities for education and gainful employment outside the home, again, offer the greatest promise. In countries where these steps have been followed, significant fertility reductions have ensued (Henry and Piotrow, 1979).

Finally, policymakers should not lose interest in age at marriage or first birth as policy variables, but they must recognize the complexity in which these variables operate. The ultimate goal may not be delaying marriage but delaying childbearing. Catch-up effects aside, most evidence suggests that the longer the first birth is postponed, the fewer children in the completed family and the slower the rate of population growth.

7   Family Planning Knowledge and Practice as Policy Variables

Policy issues apropos family planning are so extensive that our discussion will be restricted to five factors influencing contraceptive adoption that are germane to basic issues in this book. These are socioeconomic development, nonformal education, the roles of men in family planning, availability of contraceptives, and the effects of religion.

Family Planning and Socioeconomic Development

Increasing family planning program effectiveness is often considered a sure way to lower a country's fertility. For example, Weller and Bouvier (1981, p.

285) view high fertility as "a social malady that will disappear if enough contraceptive supplies, services, and information are made available to all segments of the population." Advocates of the family planning approach stress that many women want fewer children than they are producing and eliminating these unwanted births through family planning services will substantially reduce birth rates (Kendall, 1979). They argue that family planning programs are politically and ethically acceptable to most people and can be implemented quickly and relatively cheaply.

Consistent with the above perspectives, much family planning program effort has traditionally emphasized distributing contraceptive supplies and spreading knowledge of their use under the assumption that women have more children than they want and that providing supplies and knowledge would be sufficient to lower fertility initially and to maintain it over time. These assumptions have often turned out to be invalid; the actual number of children born is frequently the desired number. Moreover, as we have repeatedly argued, unless structural conditions motivate couples to limit their family sizes, they have little incentive to adopt family planning goals or become effective users of modern birth control methods. These realizations have led to designing family planning programs that take into account broader societal contexts. Contemporary programs also focus more on making it easier for couples to have the number of children they want when they want them and providing information and guidance about individual and social benefits of smaller families. Simultaneously, modern programs encourage governmental socioeconomic development efforts, especially those that might contribute to institutional changes that will improve extrafamilial opportunities for women (World Bank, 1984).

While recognizing that the family planning and structural change approaches for reducing fertility are not alternatives but rather reinforce and complement each other, researchers and policymakers continue to be interested in the impact of family planning programs net of the effects of socioeconomic development. Decomposing the precise effect of family planning programs on fertility in developing countries is difficult [see Hermalin (1983) and Mauldin (1983) for examples and sources of estimation techniques]. This difficulty has resulted in much debate on the subject over the past two decades (Berelson, 1963; Bogue, 1967; Davis, 1967; Freedman and Takeshita, 1969; Mauldin and Berelson, 1978). For example, Mauldin and Berelson estimate 10 to 15% of the explained variance in birth rate declines in developing countries between 1965 and 1975 can be attributed to family planning programs, independent of development. Hernandez (1981), however, estimates family planning programs independently account for only 5% of that variance.

In a more recent analysis of WFS data, Entwisle and Mason (1985) show that complex interactions occur between family planning availability, level of country development, and socioeconomic–fertility differentials, making statements about the relative importance of each factor less straightforward. They report negative socioeconomic–fertility differentials in countries with a moderately high level of development and no family planning program; weaker negative socioeconomic effects in moderately developed countries with family planning programs; and positive socioeconomic–fertility differentials in countries with low levels of development and no family planning program.

The positive socioeconomic–fertility differentials in countries with low levels of development and no family planning programs likely reflect shortened breast-feeding and sexual abstinence periods following birth among higher status women that are not compensated for by alternative contraceptive practices (see Chapter 6). In such contexts, successful policies to raise the status of women could accelerate population growth unless women are persuaded to substitute more modern contraceptive practices for weakening traditional fertility restraints. If alternative family planning practices are unacceptable for religious or cultural reasons, programs may be introduced to convince more educated women of the health benefits of breast-fed children (Gille, 1985). Similarly, as nations develop and women participate more in the economic mainstream, provisions must be made for paid maternity leaves and nursery facilities at the workplace, enabling mothers to breast-feed their infants while at work.

Population Education and Targeted Nontraditional Programs

An approach emphasizing societal context issues—increasingly receiving the attention of policymakers seeking fertility reductions in developing countries—is population education. Population education is not synonymous with sex education. Rather, its objective is demonstrating the relationship between reproductive behavior and the general well-being of the individual, family, country, and world (Sherris, 1982; Viederman, 1972, 1974).

Specifically, population education aims to motivate couples to limit their family size by making them aware of:

- Basic principles of demography
- Causes of rapid population growth
- The impact of rapid population growth
- The close relationship between a country's socioeconomic development and its well-being
- The meaning and significance of environmental harmony
- The availability of methods to control family size
- Advantages of the small family for improving the quality of life

- The far-reaching consequences of population density and rapid growth for one's self, one's environment, and one's future
- The responsibility individuals share for the welfare of their nation and the world (adapted from Edlefsen, 1972, pp. 5–6).

Existing educational institutions have been used for communicating population knowledge and awareness. Many countries have focused on elementary school students because of high dropout rates before the secondary levels are reached (Edlefsen, 1972). Population education has also been incorporated into rural or village development programs, agricultural extension services, and public health organizations as well as disseminated via radio and other media campaigns (Simmons, 1970). Through population education in schools and communities, efforts are made to encourage positive attitudes toward population policies, including those promoting later marriage and increasing the role of women in development, as well as providing fundamental information about family planning (Sherris, 1982).

The effects of formal education (including population education components) on fertility typically do not become manifest until years in the future. Fertility reduction in the shorter run may be achieved by generating, through policy action, some of the longer term effects of female education. This may include nonformal education and training programs that provide specialized information and skills to illiterate or poorly educated women already of childbearing age.

There are other good reasons to consider targeted nonformal education programs. National costs incurred from compulsory mass education of young men and women through at least the seventh grade, while a recognizably valuable long-term investment in human capital, may simply be too great a fiscal burden for many governments to bear. Moreover, the current economic, institutional, and physical environments of some of the least developed areas of the world make compulsory mass education unfeasible. Under such circumstances, targeted nontraditional forms of education may be the only possible means to achieving family planning objectives. Costs of these programs would not only likely be much smaller than mass education, but, predicated on content and audience, they could have more immediate payoff in reduced fertility (compared to the approximately 15-year lag in the benefits of formal schooling for reproductive behavior). Assessment of the relative costs and benefits of traditional and nontraditional education programs in these contexts is badly needed.

Men and Family Planning

Traditionally, family planning programs have regarded women as the acceptors of contraception. Policymakers have begun to recognize that the logical focus of organized family planning efforts is on couples, not just women. A sizeable number of women cannot practice family planning because of the objections of their husbands (see, e.g., Brody, 1974; Card, 1978). In many developing countries, men deny their wives access to contraception because they fear it will encourage her promiscuity, diminish his position in the family, or reduce his machismo image (Stokes, 1980).

Men can certainly assume an important role in family planning by supporting their sexual partners' choice of birth control methods, taking the responsibility themselves, or becoming more informed about contraception. If men are ignorant or misinformed about contraception, they may retard women's acceptance and use of birth control (Hall, 1971; Kubat and Mourao, 1970). It should also be remembered that until the 1970s, most couples in developed countries still relied primarily on the man to practice contraception, and many still use a male method such as the condom or withdrawal (Lightbourne and Singh, 1982). Greater success in reducing fertility levels no doubt would be gained by involving men in family planning programs, increasing their knowledge of contraceptive methods, and encouraging further research on the development of simple, acceptable, and effective male contraceptives. Once more, the roles of formal and nonformal education in accomplishing these objectives are substantial.

Availability of Contraceptives

Successful practice of contraception, of course, rests not only on knowing about and accepting the idea, but also on availability of contraceptives. Studies have shown a positive association between the availability of birth control methods and their use (Entwisle et al., 1984; Tsui et al., 1981). If there is limited access, use will be low. For example, in Nepal, most women have to make a long and difficult journey to reach family planning clinics, and only 20% of knowledgeable women are reported ever to have used contraception (Rodríguez, 1978). Perception of the availability of birth control methods is equally important. Substantial differences in contraceptive use have been found between women who do and do not believe contraceptives are available in their community (Tsui et al., 1981). In developing countries, the monetary costs of contraceptives are also related to use (Schearer, 1983).

Although motivation appears to be a stronger determinant of contraceptive use than availability of services (Rodríguez, 1978), there is also some evidence that the two may interact (Entwisle et al., 1984). Moreover, like motivation, education is strongly associated with knowledge of contraceptive availability. Jones' (1984) analysis of the availability of contraceptive services in 15 developing

WFS countries showed that number of years of schooling distinguished currently married women's awareness of sources of family planning assistance more consistently than any other indicator. She found that in most of the countries analyzed, women with 7 or more years of schooling were more than twice as likely to know of sources of contraceptive supplies than women with no schooling. The most dramatic education gradient was in Nepal, where nearly half of the married women (under age 45) with 7 or more years of schooling knew of a source of contraceptive supplies compared to only 5% of married women (under age 45) with no education. Residence of better educated women in urban areas likely accounts for part of the strong relationship between education and knowledge of family planning sources. Nevertheless, Rodríguez's (1978) covariance analysis of WFS data shows that education's effect remains strong even after controls for type of residence, parity, and duration of marriage are introduced.

Religion

Religion, particularly Catholicism, has often been considered a major obstacle in the adoption of family planning. However, several studies indicate that for years this has not been the case. One study conducted in Colombia, the United States, and the Netherlands shows that parish priests tend to accept the use of contraception (Burch and Shea, 1971). Parish priests were selected for study because they were considered the key link in the chain of communication and influence running from Rome to laypersons. Most of the priests interviewed considered it necessary to limit family size (92% in the Netherlands, 80% in Colombia, and 78% in the United States). Moreover, a majority favored easy access to free information on family planning (98% in the Netherlands, 96% in Colombia, and 63% in the United States).

Gomez (1965) studied the importance of religion in controlling family size in Latin America by examining the impact of religion (degree of religiosity) and education on contraceptive use. Surprisingly, the proportion of women using artificial methods of contraception was higher among the more devout women than among the less devout. This finding suggests that religiosity is not necessarily an obstacle to family planning. Regardless of religious intensity, highly educated women were more likely to practice contraception than those with less education. Overall, education was more important in determining use of family planning than religion. In Brazil, Catholicism had little direct impact on family planning acceptance and contraceptive use when other factors were taken into account.

In the United States, the difference between Catholic and non-Catholic contraceptive use and fertility has become a topic of recent debate. Westoff and Jones (1979) report that in 1975 the difference between the two populations in prevalence of contraceptive use was only 3.5% and the proportion of women in each population using the pill was virtually identical. This discovery suggests that although the Roman Catholic Church officially forbids the use of contraceptives, it has lost its influence on attitudes and behavior related to family planning. More recent analyses, however, have shown some differentials in fertility (Mosher and Hendershot, 1984) and contraceptive use (Mosher and Goldscheider, 1984) between Catholics and other women in the United States. Regardless of these discrepant findings, it appears that Catholic religious beliefs hinder fertility regulation far less than is commonly thought (Bogue, 1983).

The Islamic religion has also been considered a major obstacle to the adoption of family planning. There are signs that this opposition, too, is subsiding (Battelle Institute, 1982). At a major 1982 conference in Dakar, Senegal, many Islamic religious leaders posited that if the Koran is interpreted correctly, use of contraception is approved (Lightbourne and Singh, 1982). These leaders view family planning as enhancing the family's well-being, especially as it protects potential offspring from problems of poverty, malnutrition, and ignorance (Battelle Human Affairs Research Center, 1983).

Many Muslims, however, continue to view family planning with suspicion. Discussing the African case, Omran (1985) points to findings from scientific surveys indicating the following beliefs:

- Family planning conflicts with the desire of Islam for Muslims to reproduce and populate the earth (numbers being equated with power). They also share the view of other Africans that the continent needs extensive manpower to develop its vast resources
- Family planning is equated with genocide
- Family planning is an interference with the will of God and represents a disbelief in providence and in the divine responsibility to take care of each child born on earth
- Family planning would distort the familial system of organization and inheritance, especially if it yields few or no sons
- Family planning may encourage promiscuity among the youth
- Family planning will increase the number of barren women, or women with very few children. (Barren women lose their social prestige in African society and are often social outcasts)
- Family planning is an imperialist plot by colonial powers against Islam and African growth (Omran, 1985, p. 119).

The list above illustrates once more the substantial influence culture (seen here as an interwoven complex of religious, normative, and familial beliefs) may have on attitudes toward contraceptive practice. It also illustrates the rich potential that education (both formal and informal) has as a policy instrument for correcting certain misconceptions that affect reproductive behavior. Until these erroneous notions are dealt with in places such as Muslim Africa, the success of family planning programs will remain limited.

8 The Context of Reproductive Choice

Family planning advocates and policymakers now recognize more explicitly the important role culture, as well as development, plays in shaping fertility levels. Few today would question the contention that only in *combination* with ideational changes regarding family formation and institutional changes that improve the status of women should we expect to see substantial, and lasting, reductions in fertility following the introduction of family planning programs. Acceptance of family planning and birth rate declines will be greatest in those transforming social contexts where (1) new attitudes and aspirations regarding the dignity and worth of women are adopted and (2) expanded educational and employment opportunities provide young women with a means to independent social achievement and economic gain and, thereby, rewarding alternatives to early marriage and childbearing.

What we are arguing, then, is that broader social, political, and economic measures which enhance the status of women will create an environment in which they (and their husbands) will want to limit their fertility. In this regard, policymakers in developing countries should take particular cognizance of a number of European nations where policies toward female status enhancement are progressive—where the public sector has absorbed much of women's child-bearing costs by guaranteeing medical coverage, child care, employment, and so on—and fertility has dropped to below replacement. The contemporary European experience, while certainly not directly translatable to developing countries, provides further testimony of the powerful influence context has on individual reproductive decision making. It is this macro–micro interaction that poses some of the most important and intriguing questions that future research on fertility determinants must address.

References

Adamchak, D. J. (1979). Emerging trends in the relationship between infant mortality and socioeconomic status. *Social Biology 26*, 16–29.

Adamchak, D. J., and Stockwell, E. G. (1978). Trends in the relationship between infant mortality and socioeconomic status: 1950 and 1970. *Sociological Focus 11*, 47–52.

Afzal, M., Kahn, Z., and Chaudhry, N. A. (1976). Age at marriage, fertility and infant–child mortality in a Lahore suburb (part 1). *Pakistan Development Review (Islamabad) 15*(1), 90–109.

Agarwala, S. N. (1965). Effect of a rise in female marriage age on birth rate in India. In *United Nations World Population Conference, 2nd, Belgrade, Yugoslavia, August 30–September 10, 1965 (Collected Papers)*, Vol. 2, pp. 114–118 (B.1/V/ E/18). United Nations, New York.

Aiken, M., and Goldberg, D. (1969). Social mobility and kinship: A reexamination of the hypothesis. *American Anthropologist 71*, 261–270.

Ainsworth, M. (1984). Population policy: Country experience. *Finance and Development 21*(3), 18–20.

Alam, I., and Casterline, J. B. (1984). Socio-economic differentials in recent fertility. *World Fertility Survey Comparative Studies, Cross-National Summaries*, No. 33. International Statistical Institute, Voorburg, Netherlands.

Alexander, K. L., and Reilly, T. W. (1981). Estimating the effects of marriage timing on educational attainment: Some procedural issues and substantive clarifications. *American Journal of Sociology 87*, 143–156.

Alexander, K. L., Reilly, T. W., and Fennessey, J. (1981). Issues in instrumental variables analysis: (Comment on Cramer, *ASR*, April 1980). *American Sociological Review 46*, 937–941.

Anderson, K. H. (1981). Age at marriage in Malaysia. Paper presented at the annual meeting of the Population Association of America, Washington, D.C., March 26–28.

Anker, R. B. (1982). Demographic change and the role of women: A research programme in developing countries. In *Women's Roles and Population Trends in the Third World* (R. B. Anker, M. Buvinić, and N. H. Youssef, eds.), pp. 29–51. Johns Hopkins Studies in Development. Croom Helm, London.

Arnold, F., and Fawcett, J. T. (1975). *The Value of Children: A Cross-National Study*, Vol. 3: *Hawaii*. East–West Population Institute, Honolulu.

Arnold, F., Bulatao, R. A., Buripakdi, C., Chung, B. J., Fawcett, J. T., Iritani, T., Lee, S. J., and Wu, T.-S. (1975). *The Value of Children. A Cross-National Study,* Vol. 1: *Introduction and Comparative Analysis.* East–West Population Institute, East–West Center, Honolulu.

Arriaga, E. E. (1970). *Mortality Decline and Its Demographic Effects in Latin America,* Population Monograph Series No. 6. Institute of International Studies, Univ. of California, Berkeley.

Arriaga, E. E. (1980). Direct estimates of infant mortality differentials from birth histories. In *World Fertility Survey Conference, 1980, Record of Proceedings,* Vol. 2, pp. 429–466. International Statistical Institute, Voorburg, Netherlands.

Bachrach, C. A. (1984). Contraceptive practice among American women, 1973–1982. *Family Planning Perspectives* **16,** 253–259.

Bagozzi, R. P., and Van Loo, M. F. (1978). Fertility as consumption: Theories from the behavioral sciences. *Journal of Consumer Research* **4,** 199–228.

Bagozzi, R. P., and Van Loo, M. F. (1980). Decision-making and fertility: A theory of exchange in the family. In *Demographic Behavior: Interdisciplinary Perspectives on Decision-Making* (T. K. Burch, ed.), pp. 91–124. Westview Press, Boulder, Colorado.

Bailey, J. E., and Correa, J. (1975). Evaluation of the Profamilia Rural Family Planning Program. *Studies in Family Planning* **6,** 148–155.

Baldwin, W. H., and Nord, C. W. (1984). Delayed childbearing in the U.S.: Facts and fictions. *Population Bulletin* **39**(4).

Baltzell, E. D. (1953). Social mobility and fertility within an elite group. *Milbank Memorial Fund Quarterly* **31,** 411–420.

Bamberger, M., del Negro, M., and Gamble, G. (1976). Employment and contraceptive practice in selected barrios of Caracas. In *Recent Empirical Findings on Fertility: Korea, Nigeria, Tunisia, Venezuela, Philippines,* pp. 115–144. Occasional Monograph Series No. 7, ICP Work Agreement Reports. Interdisciplinary Communications Program, Smithsonian Institution, Washington, D.C.

Banerjee, S. N. (1973). Effect of change in age-patterns of marriage on fertility rates in Bihar, 1961–1986. *Man in India* **53,** 262–278.

Barber, B. (1957). *Social Stratification: A Comparative Analysis of Structure and Process.* Harcourt, Brace & World, New York.

Bartz, K. W., and Nye, F. I. (1970). Early marriage: A proportional formulation. *Journal of Marriage and the Family* **32,** 258–268.

Basavarajappa, K. G., and Belvalgidad, M. J. (1968). Changes in age at marriage in females and their effect on the birth rate in India. *Eugenics Quarterly* **14,** 14–26.

Battelle Human Affairs Research Center. Population and Development Policy Program (1983). Summary presentation. In *Proceedings of the Seminar on Islam and Family Planning, organized by the National Population Commission of Senegal, April 1982.* Battelle Human Affairs Research Center, Washington, D.C.

Battelle Institute (1982). Islam seen as compatible with family planning. *Intercom* **10**(5/6), 4.

Bean, F. D., and Aiken, L. H. (1976). Intermarriage and unwanted fertility in the United States. *Journal of Marriage and the Family* **38,** 61–72.

Bean, F. D., and Swicegood, C. G. (1979). Intergenerational occupational mobility and fertility: A reassessment. *American Sociological Review* **44,** 608–619.

Becker, G. S. (1960). An economic analysis of fertility. In *Demographic and Economic Change in Developed Countries,* pp. 209–240. A Conference of the Universities-National Bureau Committee for Economic Research No. 11. Princeton Univ. Press, Princeton, New Jersey.

Becker, G. S. (1965). A theory of the allocation of time. *Economic Journal* **75,** 493–517.

Becker, G. S. (1981). *A Treatise on the Family.* Harvard Univ. Press, Cambridge, Massachusetts.

Beckman, L. J. (1978). The relative rewards and cost of parenthood and employment for employed women. *Psychology of Women Quarterly* **2**, 215–234.

Beckman, L. J. (1983). Communication, power, and the influence of social networks in couple decisions on fertility. In *Determinants of Fertility in Developing Countries*, Vol. 2: *Fertility Regulation and Institutional Influences* (R. A. Bulatao and R. D. Lee with P. E. Hollerbach and J. Bongaarts, eds.), pp. 415–443. Studies in Population. Academic Press, New York.

Beckman, L. J., and Houser, B. B. (1979). Perceived satisfactions and costs of motherhood and employment among married women. *Journal of Population: Behavioral, Social, and Environmental Issues* **2**, 306–327.

Beneria, L., ed. (1982). *Women and Development; The Sexual Division of Labor in Rural Societies*. Praeger Special Studies. Praeger, New York.

Ben-Porath, Y. (1974). Economic analysis of fertility in Israel. In *Economics of the Family: Marriage, Children and Human Capital* (T. W. Schultz, ed.), pp. 189–220. Univ. of Chicago Press, Chicago, Illinois.

Ben-Porath, Y. (1978). Fertility response to child mortality: Microdata from Israel. In *The Effects of Infant and Child Mortality on Fertility* (S. H. Preston, ed.), pp. 161–180. Academic Press, New York.

Berelson, B. (1963). Communication, communication research, and family planning. In *Emerging Techniques in Population Research: Proceedings of a Round Table at the 39th Annual Conference of the Milbank Memorial Fund, September 18–19, 1962*, pp. 159–171. Milbank Memorial Fund, New York.

Berelson, B., and Freedman, R. C. (1964). A study in fertility control. *Scientific American* **210**(5), 29–37.

Berent, J. (1952). Fertility and social mobility. *Population Studies* **5**, 244–260.

Berent, J. (1982). Family planning in Europe and USA in the 1970s. *World Fertility Survey Comparative Studies, ECE Analyses of WFS Surveys in Europe and USA*, No. 20. International Statistical Institute, Voorburg, Netherlands.

Berent, J. (1983). Family size preference in Europe and USA: Ultimate expected number of children. *World Fertility Survey Comparative Studies, Cross-National Summaries*, No. 6 International Statistical Institute, Voorburg, Netherlands.

Bernhardt, E. M. (1972). Fertility and economic status—Some recent findings on differentials in Sweden. *Population Studies* **26**, 176–184.

Berry, B. J. L., and Kasarda, J. D. (1977). *Contemporary Urban Ecology*. Macmillan, New York.

Berry, E. H. (1983). Migration, fertility and social mobility: An analysis of the fertility of Ecuadorian women. Paper presented at the annual meeting of the Population Association of America, Pittsburgh, April 14–16.

Bertoli, F., Rent, C. S., and Rent, G. S. (1984). Infant mortality by socio-economic status for blacks, Indians and whites: A longitudinal analysis of North Carolina, 1968–1977. *Sociology and Social Research* **68**, 364–377.

Bhatnagar, S. N. K. (1972). Status of women and family planning in India. *Journal of Family Welfare* **18**(3), 21–29.

Bibby, J. (1975). Methods of measuring mobility. *Quality and Quantity* **9**, 107–136.

Birdsall, N. (1974). The "woman issue" and fertility. *Concerned Demography* **4**(1), 11–14.

Blake, J. (1965). Demographic science and the redirection of population policy. *Journal of Chronic Diseases* **18**, 1181–1200.

Blake, J. (1966). The Americanization of Catholic reproductive ideals. *Population Studies* **20**, 27–43.

Blake, J. (1967). Reproductive ideals and educational attainment among white Americans, 1943-1960. *Population Studies* **21**, 159–174.

Blake, J. (1968). Are babies consumer durables? A critique of the economic theory of reproductive motivation. *Population Studies* **22**, 5–25.

Blake, J. (1969). Population policy for Americans: Is the government being misled? *Science (Washington, D.C.)* **164**(May 2), 522–529.

Blake, J. (1974). Can we believe recent data on birth expectations in the United States? *Demography* **11**, 25–44.

Blake, J. (1984). Catholocism and fertility: On attitudes of young Americans. *Population and Development Review* **10**, 329–340.

Blake, J., and del Pinal, J. H. (1981). The childlessness option: Recent American views of non-parenthood. In *Predicting Fertility: Demographic Studies of Birth Expectations* (G. E. Hendershot and P. J. Placek, eds.), pp. 235–264. Heath, Lexington, Massachusetts.

Blau, P. M. (1956). Social mobility and interpersonal relations. *American Sociological Review* **21**, 290–295.

Blau, P. M., and Duncan, O. D., with Tyree, A. (1967). *The American Occupational Structure.* Wiley, New York.

Blood, R. O., and Wolfe, D. M. (1960). *Husbands and Wives: The Dynamics of Married Living.* Free Press, New York.

Bloom, D. E. (1982). What's happening to the age at first birth in the United States? A study of recent cohorts. *Demography* **19**, 351–370.

Bloom, D. E. (1984). *Delayed Childbearing in the United States,* Discussion Paper No. 84-3. Center for Population Studies, Harvard Univ., Cambridge, Massachusetts.

Bloom, D. E., and Trussell, J. (1983). What are the determinants of delayed childbearing and pernament childlessness in the United States? Paper presented at the annual meeting of the Population Association of America, Pittsburgh, April 14–16.

Boggs, S. T. (1957). Family size and social mobility in a California suburb. *Eugenics Quarterly* **4**, 208–213.

Bogue, D. J. (1967). The end of the population explosion. *Public Interest* **7**(Spring), 11–20.

Bogue, D. J. (1969). *Principles of Demography.* Wiley, New York.

Bogue, D. J. (1971). *Codebook and Variable Definitions for the Urban Fertility Surveys of CELADE.* Community and Family Study Center, Univ. of Chicago, Chicago, Illinois.

Bogue, D. J. (1983). Normative and psychic costs of contraception. In *Determinants of Fertility in Developing Countries,* Vol. 2: *Fertility Regulation and Institutional Influences* (R. A. Bulatao and R. D. Lee with P. E. Hollerbach and J. Bongaarts, eds.), pp. 151–192. Studies in Population. Academic Press, New York.

Bongaarts, J. P. (1978). A framework for analyzing the proximate determinants of fertility. *Population and Development Review* **4**, 105–132.

Bongaarts, J. P. (1980). Does malnutrition affect fecundity? A summary of the evidence. *Science (Washington, D.C.)* **208**(May 9), 564–569.

Bongaarts, J. P., and Menken, J. A. (1983). The supply of children: A critical essay. In *Determinants of Fertility in Developing Countries,* Vol. 1: *Supply and Demand for Children* (R. A. Bulatao and R. D. Lee with P. E. Hollerbach and J. P. Bongaarts, eds.), pp. 27–60. Studies in Population. Academic Press, New York.

Bowen, W. G., and Finegan, T. A. (1969). *The Economics of Labor Force Participation.* Princeton Univ. Press, Princeton, New Jersey.

Boyd, M. (1971). Occupational mobility and fertility in urban Latin America. Ph.D. Thesis, Duke Univ., Durham, North Carolina.

Boyd, M. (1973). Occupational mobility and fertility in metropolitan Latin America. *Demography* **10**, 1–17.

Brackett, J. W. (1981). The role of family planning availability and accessibility in family planning use in developing countries. In *World Fertility Survey Conference, 1980, Record of Proceedings,* Vol. 2, pp. 13–65. International Statistical Institute, Voorburg, Netherlands.

Brass, W. I. (1973). Mortality estimation by indirect means. *Population Bulletin of the United Nations Economic and Social Office in Beirut* No. 4, 9–19.

Brass, W. I. (1979). Screening procedures for detecting errors in maternity history data. In *Regional Workshop on Techniques of Analysis of World Fertility Survey Data: Reports and Selected Papers,* Asian Population Study Series No. 44, ST/ESCAP/89. United Nations Economic and Social Commission for Asia and the Pacific, Bangkok.

Breiger, R. L. (1981). The social class structure of occupational mobility. *American Journal of Sociology* **87,** 578–611.

Bresard, M. (1950). Mobilité sociale et dimension de la famille. *Population* **5,** 533–566.

Brody, E. B. (1974). Psychocultural aspects of contraceptive behavior in Jamaica: Individual fertility control in a developing country. *Journal of Nervous and Mental Disease* **159,** 108–119.

Brody, E. B., Ottey, F., and LaGranade, J. (1976). Fertility-related behavior in Jamaica. In *Cultural Factors and Population in Developing Countries,* pp. 15–30. Occasional Monograph Series No. 6, ICP Work Agreement Reports. Interdisciplinary Communications Program, Smithsonian Institution, Washington, D.C.

Brooks, H. E., and Henry, F. J. (1958). An empirical study of the relationships of Catholic practice and occupational mobility to fertility. *Milbank Memorial Fund Quarterly* **36,** 222–281.

Brown, L. (1976). *World Population Trends: Signs of Hope, Signs of Stress,* Worldwatch Paper No. 8. Worldwatch Institute, Washington, D.C.

Bulatao, R. (1979a). On the nature of the transition in the value of children. *Current Studies on the Value of Children,* Papers of the East–West Population Institute No. 60-A. East–West Population Institute, Honolulu.

Bulatao, R. (1979b). Further evidence of the transition in the value of children. *Current Studies on the Value of Children,* Papers of the East–West Population Institute No. 60-B. East–West Population Institute, Honolulu.

Bulatao, R. (1982). The transition in the value of children and the fertility transition. In *Determinants of Fertility Trends: Theories Re-Examined* (C. Hohn and R. Mackenson, eds.), pp. 95–122. Ordina Editions, Liège.

Bulatao, R. A., and Fawcett, J. T. (1983). Influences on childbearing intentions across the fertility career: Demographic and socioeconomic factors and the value of children. *Current Studies on the Value of Children,* Papers of the East–West Population Institute No. 60-F. East–West Population Institute, Honolulu.

Bulatao, R. A., and Lee, R. D., with Hollerbach, P. E., and Bongaarts, J. P., eds. (1983). *Determinants of Fertility in Developing Countries,* 2 vols. Studies in Population. Academic Press, New York.

Bumpass, L. L. (1969). Age at marriage as a variable in socio-economic differentials in fertility. *Demography* **6,** 45–54.

Bumpass, L. L. (1982). The changing linkage of nuptiality and fertility in the United States. In *Nuptiality and Fertility* (L. T. Ruzicka, ed.), pp. 195–209. Ordina Editions, Liège.

Bumpass, L. L., and Mburugu, E. K. (1977). Age at marriage and completed family size. *Social Biology* **24,** 31–37.

Bumpass, L. L., and Westoff, C. F. (1970). *The Later Years of Childbearing.* Princeton Univ. Press, Princeton, New Jersey.

Burch, T. K., and Shea, G. A. (1971). Catholic parish priests and birth control: A comparative study of opinion in Colombia, the United States, and the Netherlands. *Studies in Family Planning* **2,** 121–136.

Burks, B. S. (1941). Social promotion in relation to differential fecundity. *Human Biology* **13,** 103–113.

Busfield, N. J. (1972). Age at marriage and family size: Social causation and social selection hypothesis. *Journal of Biosocial Science* **4,** 117–134.

Butz, W. P., and Ward, M. P. (1979). The emergence of countercyclical U.S. fertility. *American Economic Review* **69,** 318–328.

Byrne, J. J. (1975). Occupational mobility, geographic mobility, and secondary migrants. Paper presented at the annual meeting of the Population Association of America, Seattle, April 17–19.

Cain, G. G. (1966). *Married Women in the Labor Force: An Economic Analysis,* Studies in Economics of the Economic Research Center of the Univ. of Chicago. Univ. of Chicago Press, Chicago, Illinois.

Cain, G. G., and Weininger, A. (1973). Economic determinants of fertility: Results from cross-sectional aggregate data. *Demography* **10,** 205–223.

Cain, M. T. (1977). The economic activities of children in a village in Bangladesh. *Population and Development Review* **3,** 201–227.

Cain, M. T. (1980). Risk, fertility, and family planning in a Bangladesh village. *Studies in Family Planning* **11,** 219–223.

Cain, M. T. (1982). Perspectives on family and fertility in developing countries. *Population Studies* **36,** 159–175.

Cain, M. T. (1984). *Women's Status and Fertility in Developing Countries: Son Preference and Economic Security,* Working Paper No. 110. Population Council, New York.

Cain, M. T., Khanam, S. R., and Nahar, S. (1979). Class, patriarchy, and women's work in Bangladesh. *Population and Development Review* **5,** 405–438.

Cain, P. S. (1979). The determinants of marital labor supply, fertility, and sex role attitudes. Paper presented at the annual meeting of the Population Association of America, Philadelphia, April 26–28.

Caldwell, J. C. (1968a). The demographic implications of the extension of education in a developing country: Ghana. Paper presented at the annual meeting of the Population Association of America, Boston, April 18–20.

Caldwell, J. C. (1968b). *Population Growth and Family Change in Africa: The New Urban Elite in Ghana.* Humanities Press, New York.

Caldwell, J. C. (1976). Toward a restatement of demographic transition theory. *Population and Development Review* **2,** 321–336.

Caldwell, J. C. (1977). Measuring wealth flows and the rationality of fertility: Thoughts and plans based in the first place on African work. In *The Economic and Social Supports for High Fertility* (L. T. Ruzicka, ed.), pp. 439–454. Australian National Univ., Canberra.

Caldwell, J. C. (1978). A theory of fertility: From high plateau to destabilization. *Population and Development Review* **4,** 553–577.

Caldwell, J. C. (1979). Education as a factor in mortality decline: An examination of Nigerian data. *Population Studies* **33,** 395–413.

Caldwell, J. C. (1980). Mass education as a determinant of the timing of fertility decline. *Population and Development Review* **6,** 225–255.

Caldwell, J. C. (1982). *Theory of Fertility Decline,* Population and Social Structure: Advances in Historical Demography. Academic Press, London.

Caldwell, J. C. (1983). Direct economic costs and benefits of children. In *Determinants of Fertility in Developing Countries,* Vol. 1: *Supply and Demand for Children* (R. A. Bulatao and R. D. Lee with P. E. Hollerbach and J. P. Bongaarts, eds.), pp. 458–493. Studies in Population. Academic Press, New York.

Caldwell, J. C., and McDonald, P. (1982). Influence of maternal education on infant and child mortality: Levels and causes. In *International Population Conference, Manila, 1981, Solicited Papers*, Vol. 2, pp. 79–96. International Union for the Scientific Study of Population, Liège.

Call, V. R. A., and Otto, L. B. (1977). Age at marriage as a mobility contingency: Estimates for the Nye-Berardo model. *Journal of Marriage and the Family* **39**, 67–79.

Cantrelle, P., Ferry, B., and Mondot, J. (1975). The relationships between fertility and mortality in tropical Africa. In *The Effects of Infant and Child Mortality on Fertility* (S. H. Preston, ed.), pp. 181–205. Academic Press, New York.

Card, J. J. (1978). The correspondence of data gathered from husband and wife: Implications for family planning studies. *Social Biology* **25**, 196–204.

Carleton, R. O. (1967). The effect of educational improvement on fertility trends in Latin America. In *Proceedings of the World Population Conference, Belgrade, 1965*, Vol. 4, pp. 141–145. United Nations, New York.

Carlson, E. (1979). Family background, school and early marriage. *Journal of Marriage and the Family* **41**, 341–353.

Carrasco, E. (1981). Contraceptive practice. *World Fertility Survey Comparative Studies: Cross-National Summaries*, No. 9. International Statistical Institute, Voorburg, Netherlands.

Cassen, R. H. (1976). Population and development: A survey. *World Development* **4**, 785–830.

Casterline, J. B., Singh, S., Cleland, S., and Ashurst, H. (1984). The proximate determinants of fertility. *World Fertility Survey Comparative Studies: Cross-National Summaries*, No. 39. International Statistical Institute, Voorburg, Netherlands.

CELADE and Community and Family Study Center, eds. (1972). *Fertility and Family Planning in Metropolitan Latin America*. Community and Family Study Center, Univ. of Chicago, Chicago, Illinois.

Centro Latinoamericano de Demografia (1974). *Alphabetical List of Variables by Subject in the Comparative Fertility Studies Pecfal-Rural*, Document Pecfal-Rural No. 38. Centro Latinoamericano de Demografia.

Centro Latinoamericano de Demografia (1976). *Manual para Usarios de las Encuestas Comparativas de Fecundidad Pecfal-Rural*, Document Pecfal-Rural No. 39. Centro Latinoamericano de Demografia.

Cernada, G. P., and Lu, L. P. (1972). The Daoshiung study. *Studies in Family Planning* **3**, 198–203.

Chandrasekhar, S. (1972). *Infant Mortality, Population Growth and Family Planning in India*. Allen & Unwin, London.

Chang, C.-T. (1979). Female employment and fertility behavior. In *Public Policy and Population Change in Singapore* (P. S. J. Chen and J. T. Fawcett, eds.), pp. 167–186. Population Council, New York.

Chaudhury, R. H. (1977). Education and fertility in Bangladesh. *Bangladesh Development Studies* **5**,(1), 81–110.

Chaudhury, R. H. (1982). *Social Aspects of Fertility, with Special Reference to Developing Countries*. Vikas, New Delhi.

Chen, L. C. (1983). Child survival: Levels, trend, and determinants. In *Determinants of Fertility in Developing Countries*, Vol. 1: *Supply and Demand for Children* (R. A. Bulatao and R. D. Lee with P. E. Hollerbach and J. P. Bongaarts, eds.), pp. 199–231. Studies in Population. Academic Press, New York.

Chen, X. (1985). The one-child population policy, modernization, and the extended Chinese family. *Journal of Marriage and the Family* **47**, 193–202.

Cherlin, A. (1981). *Marriage, Divorce, Remarriage*. Harvard Univ. Press, Cambridge, Massachusetts.

Chi, P. S. K., and Harris, R. J. (1978–1979). Interaction between action programs and social structural variables: A study of family planning and fertility differentials in four Colombian cities. *Population Review* **22/23**, 42–55.

Cho, L.-J., and Retherford, R. D. (1974). Comparative analysis of recent fertility trends in East Asia. In *International Population Conference, Liège, Belgium, Aug. 27–Sept. 1, 1973, Proceedings,* Vol. 2, pp. 163–181. International Union for the Scientific Study of Population, Liège.

Chowdhury, A. K. M. A., Khan, A. R., and Chen, L. C. (1976). The effect of child mortality experience on subsequent fertility: In Pakistan and Bangladesh. *Population Studies* **30**, 249–261.

Chung, B. M., Palmore, J. A., Lee, S. J., and Lee, S. J. (1972). *Psychological Perspectives: Family Planning in Korea.* Korean Institute for Research in the Behavioral Sciences, Seoul.

Committee for International Cooperation in National Research in Demography. (1983). *Infant and Child Mortality in the Third World,* Inter-Centre Cooperative Research Programme, Project No. 1: Final Report. CICRED, WHO/OMS, Paris.

Cleland, J. G., and Sathar, Z. A. (1983). The effect of birth spacing on childhood mortality in Pakistan. *Population Studies* **38**, 401–418.

Cleland, J. G., Verall, J., and Vaessen, M. (1983). Preferences for the sex of children and their influence on reproductive behavior. *World Fertility Survey Comparative Studies,* No. 27. International Statistical Institute, Voorburg, Netherlands.

Coale, A. J. (1973). The demographic transition. In *International Population Conference, Liège, August 27–September 1, 1973, Proceedings,* Vol. 1, pp. 53–71. International Union for the Scientific Study of Population, Liège.

Coale, A. J., and Hoover, E. M. (1958). *Population Growth and Economic Development in Low-Income Countries: A Case Study of India's Prospects.* Princeton Univ. Press, Princeton, New Jersey.

Coale, A. J., and Tye, C.-Y. (1961). The significance of age-patterns of fertility in high fertility populations. *Milbank Memorial Fund Quarterly* **39**, 631–646.

Coale, A. J., Anderson, B. A., and Härm, E. (1979). *Human Fertility in Russia since the Nineteenth Century.* Princeton Univ. Press, Princeton, New Jersey.

Cochrane, S. H. (1979). Fertility and education: What do we really know? *World Bank Staff Occasional Papers,* No. 26. Johns Hopkins Univ. Press, Baltimore, Maryland.

Cochrane, S. H. (1983). Effects of education and urbanization on fertility. In *Determinants of Fertility in Developing Countries,* Vol. 2: *Fertility Regulation and Institutional Influences* (R. A. Bulatao and R. D. Lee with P. E. Hollerbach and J. P. Bongaarts, eds.), pp. 587–626. Studies in Population. Academic Press, New York.

Cochrane, S. H., and Zachariah, K. C. (1983). Infant and child mortality as a determinant of fertility: The policy implications. *World Bank Staff Working Paper,* No. 556. World Bank, Washington, D.C.

Cochrane, S. H., O'Hare, D. J., and Leslie, J. (1980). The effects of education on health. *World Bank Staff Working Paper,* No. 405. World Bank, Washington, D.C.

Cohen, J., and Cohen, P. (1975). *Applied Multiple Regression/Correlation Analysis for the Behavioral Sciences.* Lawrence Earlbaum, Hillsdale, New Jersey.

Cohen, S. B., and Sweet, J. A. (1974). The impact of marital disruption and remarriage on fertility. *Journal of Marriage and the Family* **36**, 87–96.

Collver, O. A. (1968). Women's work participation and fertility in metropolitan areas. *Demography* **5**, 55–60.

Collver, O. A., and Langlois, E. (1962). The female labor force in metropolitan areas: An international comparison. *Economic Development and Cultural Change* **10**, 367–385.

Commission on Population Growth and the American Future (1972). *Population and the American*

Future: The Report of the Commission on Population Growth and the American Future. New American Library, New York.

Concepción, M. B. (1981). Family formation and contraception in selected developing countries: Policy implications of WFS findings. In *World Fertility Survey Conference, 1980, Record of Proceedings,* pp. 191–276. International Statistical Institute, Voorburg, Netherlands.

Cramer, J. C. (1980). Fertility and female employment: Problems of causal direction. *American Sociological Review* **45**, 167–190.

Cramer, J. C. (1981). Instrumental variables analysis. (Reply to Alexander *et al.*) *American Sociological Review* **46**, 942.

Cunningham, I. C. M. and Green, R. T. (1979). Working wives in the United States and Venezuela: A cross-national study of decision making. *Journal of Comparative Studies* **10**, 67–80.

Curtin, L. B. (1982). *Status of Women: A Comparative Analysis of Twenty Developing Countries,* Reports on the World Fertility Survey No. 5. Population Reference Bureau, Washington, D.C.

Dandekar, K. (1965). Effects of education on fertility. In *United Nations World Population Conference, 2nd, Belgrade, Yugoslavia, Aug. 30–Sept. 10, 1965 (Collected Papers),* Vol. 7, pp. 22–25 (A.6/I/E/46). United Nations, New York.

Das, N. C. (1965). A note on the effect of postponement of marriage on fertility. In *United Nations World Population Conference, 2nd, Belgrade, Yugoslavia, Aug. 30–Sept. 10, 1965 (Collected Papers),* Vol. 2, pp. 186–189 (B.1/I/E/391). United Nations, New York.

Da Vanzo, J. S. (1972). *Determinants of Family Formation in Chile, 1960: An Econometric Study of Female Labor Force Participation, Marriage, and Fertility Decisions* (R-830-AID). Rand Corp., Santa Monica, California.

Da Vanzo, J. S., and Lee, D. L. P. (1983). The compatibility of child care with market and nonmarket activities: Preliminary evidence from Malaysia. In *Women and Poverty in the Third World* (M. Buviníc, M. A. Lycette, and W. P. McGreevey, eds.), pp. 62–91. Johns Hopkins Studies in Development. Johns Hopkins Univ. Press, Baltimore, Maryland.

David, L. H., and Bhas, M. (1973). Knowledge of contraceptive methods in a rural area. *Journal of Family Welfare* **20**(2), 3–9.

Davidson, M. (1973). A comparative study of fertility in Mexico City and Caracas. *Social Biology* **20**, 460–472.

Davidson, M. (1977). Female work status and fertility in Latin America. In *The Fertility of Working Women: A Synthesis of International Research* (S. Kupinsky, ed.), pp. 342–354. Praeger Special Studies. Praeger, New York.

Davis, K. (1945). The world demographic transition. *Annals of the American Academy of Political and Social Science* **237**, 1–11.

Davis, K. (1955). Institutional patterns favoring high fertility in underdeveloped areas. *Eugenics Quarterly* **2**, 33–39.

Davis, K. (1967). Population policy: Will current programs succeed? *Science (Washington, D.C.)* **158**(Nov. 10), 730–739.

Davis, K., and Blake, J. (1956). Social structure and fertility: An analytic framework. *Economic Development and Cultural Change* **4**, 211–235.

Davis, N. J., and Bumpass, L. L. (1976). The continuation of education after marriage among women in the United States: 1970. *Demography* **13**, 161–174.

Dean, D. G. (1961). Alienation: Its meaning and measurement. *American Sociological Review* **26**, 753–758.

de Guzman, E. A. (1975). *Occupational Mobility in the Philippines: 1973 Data,* Research Note No. 38. Population Institute, Univ. of the Philippines System, Manila.

Deming, M. B. (1974. The influence of marriage and childbearing on occupational mobility in the

Philippines. Paper presented at the annual meeting of the Population Association of America, New York, April 18–20.

De Tray, D. N. (1973). Child quality and the demand for children. *Journal of Political Economics* **81**(2), Part 2, 70S–95S.

De Tray, D. N.(1977). Age of marriage and fertility: A policy review. *Pakistan Development Review* **16**, 89–100.

Dixon, R. B. (1971). Explaining cross-cultural variations in age at marriage and proportions never marrying. *Population Studies* **25**, 215–233.

Dixon, R. B. (1975a). Education and employment—Keys to smaller families. *Journal of Family Welfare* **22**(2), 38–49.

Dixon, R. B. (1975b). Women's rights and fertility. *Reports on Population/Family Planning* No. 17, 1–20.

Dixon, R. B. (1976). The roles of rural women: Female seclusion, economic production, and reproductive choice. In *Population and Development: The Search for Selective Interventions* (R. G. Ridker, ed.), pp. 290–321. Johns Hopkins Univ. Press, Baltimore, Maryland.

Dow, T. E., Jr. (1971). Family planning patterns in Sierra Leone. *Studies in Family Planning* **2**, 211–222.

Dube, L. (1980). *Studies on Women in South East Asia: A Status Report*. UNESCO Regional Office for Education in Asia and Oceania, Bangkok.

Dumont, A. (1890). *Dépopulation et civilisation: Étude démographique*. Bibliothèque Anthropologique. Lecrosnier & Babé, Paris.

Dumont, A. (1901). *La morale basée sur la démographie*. Schliecher Frères, Paris.

Duncan, O. D. (1966). Methodological issues in the analysis of social mobility. In *Social Structure and Mobility in Economic Development* (N. J. Smelser and S. M. Lipset, eds.), pp. 51–97. Aldine, Chicago, Illinois.

Duncan, O. D. (1968). Social stratification and mobility: Problems in the measurement of trend. In *Indicators of Social Change: Concepts and Measurements* (E. B. Sheldon and W. E. Moore, eds.), pp. 675–719. Russell Sage Foundation, New York.

Dyson, T. P., and Moore, M. (1983). On kinship structure, female autonomy, and demographic behavior in India. *Population and Development Review* **9**, 35–60.

Easterlin, R. A. (1966). On the relation of economic factors to recent and projected fertility changes. *Demography* **3**, 131–153.

Easterlin, R. A. (1969). Towards a socioeconomic theory of fertility: A survey of recent research on economic factors in American fertility. In *Fertility and Family Planning: A World View* (S. J. Behrman, L. Corsa, Jr., and R. Freedman, eds.), pp. 127–156. Univ. of Michigan Press, Ann Arbor.

Easterlin, R. A. (1973). Relative economic status and the American fertility swing. In *Family Economic Behavior: Problems and Prospects* (E. B. Sheldon, ed.), pp. 170–223. Lippincott, Philadelphia, Pennsylvania.

Easterlin, R. A. (1975). An economic framework for fertility analysis. *Studies in Family Planning* **6**, 54–63.

Easterlin, R. A. (1978). What will 1984 be like? Socioeconomic implications of recent twists in age structure. *Demography* **15**, 397–432.

Easterlin, R. A. (1980). *Birth and Fortune: The Impact of Numbers on Personal Welfare*. Basic Books, New York.

Edlefsen, J. B. (1972). Population education—A vital concern. In *Asian Population Conference, 2nd, Tokyo, Japan, Nov. 1–13, 1972, Papers*, Vol. 4, pp. 106–115 (POP/APC.2/1P/20). Economic Commission for Asia and the Far East, Bangkok.

Elder, G. H., Jr., and Rockwell, R. C. (1976). Marital timing in women's life patterns. *Journal of Family History* **1**, 34–53.

El-Guindy, M. H. (1971). Age at marriage in relation to fertility in Egypt. In *Fertility Trends and Differentials in Arab Countries*, pp. 107–115. Research Monograph Series No. 2. Cairo Demographic Center, Cairo.

Elizaga, J. C. (1975). The participation of women in the labor force of Latin America: Fertility and other factors. *Ekistics* **40,** 40–45.

Ellis, R. A., and Lane, W. C. (1966). Social mobility and career orientation. *Sociology and Social Research* **50,** 280–296.

El-Rafie, M. (1973). Determinants of family planning acceptance in a low socioeconomic group of women. *Egyptian Population and Family Planning Review* **6,** 15–24.

Entwisle, B., and Mason, W. M. (1985). The multilevel effects of socioeconomic development and family planning on children ever born. *American Journal of Sociology* **91,** 616–649.

Entwisle, B., and Winegarden, C. R. (1984). Fertility and pension programs in LDCs: A model of mutual reinforcement. *Economic Development and Cultural Change* **32,** 331–354.

Entwisle, B., Hermalin, A. E., and Mason, W. M. (1982). *Socioeconomic Determinants of Fertility Behavior in Developing Nations: Theory and Initial Results,* National Academy of Sciences Committee on Population and Demography Report No. 17. National Academy Press, Washington, D.C.

Entwisle, B., Hermalin, A. I., Kamnuasilpa, P., and Chamratrithirong, A. (1984). A multilevel model of family planning availability and contraceptive use in rural Thailand. *Demography* **21,** 559–574.

Ermisch, J. F. (1980). Changes in the socio-economic environment and the emergence of below-replacement fertility. In *International Population Conference, Manila, 1980, Solicited Papers,* Vol. 1, pp. 181–197. International Union for the Scientific Study of Population, Liège.

Espenshade, T. J. (1973). *The Cost of Children in Urban United States,* Population Monograph Series No. 14. Institute for International Studies, Univ. of California, Berkeley.

Espenshade, T. J. (1980). Raising a child can now cost $85.000. *Intercom* **8**(9), 1+.

Espenshade, T. W. (1984). *Investing in Children: New Estimates of Parental Expenditures.* Urban Institute Press, Baltimore, Maryland.

Fawcett, J. T., ed. (1972). *The Satisfactions and Costs of Children: Theories, Concepts, Methods.* East–West Population Institute, Honolulu.

Fawcett, J. T. (1984). Perceptions of the value of children: Satisfactions and costs. In *Determinants of Fertility in Developing Countries*, Vol. 1: *Supply and Demand for Children* (R. A. Bulatao and R. D. Lee with P. E. Hollerbach and J. Bongaarts, eds.), pp. 428–457. Studies in Population. Academic Press, New York.

Fawcett, J. T., and Bornstein, M. H. (1973). Modernization, individual modernity, and fertility. In *Psychological Perspectives on Population* (J. T. Fawcett, ed.), pp. 106–131. Basic Books, New York.

Featherman, D. L. (1970). Marital fertility and the process of socioeconomic achievement: An examination of the mobility hypothesis. In *The Later Years of Childbearing* (L. L. Bumpass and C. F. Westoff, eds.), pp. 104–131. Princeton Univ. Press, Princeton, New Jersey.

Featherman, D. L., and Hauser, R. M. (1973). On the measurement of occupation in social surveys. *Sociological Methods and Research* **2,** 239–251.

Featherman, D. L., Hauser, R. M., and Sewell, W. H. (1974). Toward comparable data on inequality and stratification: Perspectives on the second generation of national mobility studies. *American Sociologist* **9,** 18–25.

Featherman, D. L., Jones, F. L., and Hauser, R. M. (1975). Assumptions of social mobility research in the U.S.: The case of occupational status. *Social Science Research* **4,** 329–360.

Ferry, B., and Smith, D. P. (1983). Breastfeeding differentials. *World Fertility Survey Comparative Studies, Cross-National Summaries,* No. 23. International Statistical Institute, Voorburg, Netherlands.

Figa-Talamanca, E. (1972). Inconsistencies of attitude and behavior in family-planning studies. *Journal of Marriage and the Family* **34**, 336–344.

Fisher, R. A. (1930). *The Genetical Theory of Natural Selection.* Clarendon Press, Oxford, England.

Fong, M. S. (1976). Female labor force participation and fertility: Some methodological and theoretical considerations. *Social Biology* **23**, 45–54.

Ford, K. (1981). Socioeconomic differentials and trends in the timing of births. *Vital and Health Statistics Series 23: Data from the National Survey of Family Growth* No. 6.

Fox, G. L. (1973). Some determinants of modernism among women in Ankara, Turkey. *Journal of Marriage and the Family* **35**, 520–529.

Freedman, D. S. (1963). The relation of economic status to fertility. *American Economic Review* **53**, 414–426.

Freedman, D. S. (1976). Mass media and modern consumer goods: Their suitability for policy interventions to decrease fertility. In *Population and Development: The Search for Selective Interventions* (R. G. Ridker, ed.), pp. 356–386. Johns Hopkins Univ. Press, Baltimore, Maryland.

Freedman, R. C. (1961–1962). The sociology of human fertility: A trend report and bibliography. *Current Sociology* **10/11**(2), 35–121.

Freedman, R. C. (1962). American studies of family planning and fertility: A review of major trends and issues. In *Conference on Research in Family Planning, Carnegie International Center, New York, October 13–19, 1960* (C. V. Kiser, ed.), pp. 211–227. Princeton Univ. Press, Princeton, New Jersey.

Freedman, R. C. (1963). Norms for family size in underdeveloped areas. *Proceedings of the Royal Society of London, Series B* **159**, 220–245.

Freedman, R. C., and Coombs, L. C. (1966a). Childspacing and family economic position. *American Sociological Review* **31**, 631–648.

Freedman, R. C., and Coombs, L. C. (1966b). Economic considerations in family growth decisions. *Population Studies* **20**, 197–222.

Freedman, R. C., and Hawley, A. H. (1949). Migration and occupational mobility in the Depression. *American Journal of Sociology* **55**, 171–177.

Freedman, R. C., and Takeshita, J. Y. (1969). *Family Planning in Taiwan: An Experiment in Social Change.* Princeton Univ. Press, Princeton, New Jersey.

Freedman, R. C., Whelpton, P. L., and Campbell, A. A. (1959). *Family Planning, Sterility and Population Growth.* McGraw-Hill, New York.

Freedman, R. C., Coombs, L. C., and Bumpass, L. L. (1965). Stability and change in expectations about family size: A longitudinal study. *Demography* **2**, 250–275.

Freeman, D. H., Jr., Freeman, J. L., and Koch, G. G., (1977). An application of log-linear models to the study of occupational mobility and migration. Paper presented at the annual meeting of the Population Association of America, Montreal, April 29–May 1.

Fried, E. S., and Udry, J. R. (1979). Wives' and husbands' expected costs and benefits of childbearing as predictors of pregnancy. *Social Biology* **26**, 265–274.

Fried, E. S., and Udry, J. R. (1980). Normative pressures on fertility planning. *Population and Environment: Behavioral and Social Issues* **3**, 199–209.

Friedlander, S. L., and Silver, M. (1967). A quantitative study of the determinants of fertility behavior. *Demography* **4**, 30–70.

Galton, Sir F. (1900). *Hereditary Genius: An Inquiry into Its Laws and Consequences,* New and rev. ed. Appleton, New York.

Garcia y Garma, I. O. (1983). Determinants of infant and child mortality in Mexico. In *Infant and Child Mortality in the Third World,* Inter-Centre Cooperative Research Programme, Project No. 1: Final Report, pp. 91–128. CICRED, WHO/OMS, Paris.

Gelbald, A. H. (1978). Catholicism and family planning attitudes in Brazil. Paper presented at the annual meeting of the Population Association of America, Atlanta, April 13–15.

Gendell, M. (1965). The influence of family-building activities on women's rate of economic activity. *World Population Conference, Belgrade, Yugoslavia, Aug. 30–Sept. 10, 1965 (Collected Papers)*, Vol. 6, pp. 20–24 (A.5/I/E/32). United Nations, New York.

Gendell, M., Maraviela, M. N., and Kreitner, P. C. (1970). Fertility and economic activity of women in Guatemala City, 1964. *Demography* **7**, 273–278.

Germain, A. (1975). Status and roles of women as factors in fertility behavior: A policy analysis. *Studies in Family Planning* **6**, 192–200.

Gille, H. (1985). Policy implications. In *Reproductive Change in Developing Countries* (J. Cleland and J. Hobcraft, in collaboration with B. Dinesen, eds.), pp. 115–138. Oxford University Press, London and New York.

Girard, A. (1951). Mobilité sociale et dimension de la famille. Deuxième partie. Enquête dans les lycées et les facultés. *Population* **6**, 103–124.

Glass, D. V., and Grebenik, E. (1954). *The Trend and Pattern of Fertility in Great Britain. A Report on the Family Census of 1946 (in Two Parts)*, 2 vols. Papers of the Royal Commission on Population. Her Majesty's Stationery Office, London.

Glick, P. C. (1967). Permanence of marriage. *Population Index* **33**, 517–526.

Goldberg, D. (1959). The fertility of two-generation urbanites. *Population Studies* **12**, 214–222.

Goldberg, D. (1976). Residential location and fertility. In *Population and Development: The Search for Selective Interventions* (R. G. Ridker, ed.), pp. 387–428. Johns Hopkins Univ. Press, Baltimore, Maryland.

Goldstein, S. (1955). Migration and occupational mobility in Norristown, Pennsylvania. *American Sociological Review* **20**, 402–408.

Goldstein, S. (1972). Influence of labour force participation and education on fertility in Thailand. *Population Studies* **26**, 419–436.

Goldthorpe, J. H., and Hope, K. (1972). Occupational grading and occupational prestige. In *The Analysis of Social Mobility: Methods and Approaches* (K. Hope, ed.), pp. 19–79. Oxford Univ. Press (Clarendon), London and New York.

Gomez, C. J. (1965). Religion, education, and fertility control in Latin American societies. In *United Nations World Population Conference, 2nd, Belgrade, Yugoslavia, Aug. 30–Sept. 10, 1965 (Collected Papers)*, Vol. 2, pp. 251–255 (B.1/V/E/471). United Nations, New York.

Goode, W. J. (1963). *World Revolution and Family Patterns*. Free Press, New York.

Goodman, L. A. (1969). On the measurement of social mobility: An index of status persistence. *American Sociological Review* **34**, 831–850.

Grabill, W. H. (1958). *The Fertility of American Women*, Census Monograph Series. Wiley, New York.

Graff, H. J. (1969). Literacy, education, and fertility, past and present: A critical review. *Population and Development Review* **5**, 105–140.

Gray, R. H. (1983). The impact of health and nutrition on natural fertility. In *Determinants of Fertility in Developing Countries*, Vol. 1: *Supply and Demand for Children* (R. A. Bulatao and R. D. Lee with P. E. Hollerbach and J. P. Bongaarts, eds.), pp. 139–162. Studies in Population. Academic Press, New York.

Grossman, A. S. (1978). Children of working mothers, March 1977. *Monthly Labor Review* **101**(1), 30–33.

Grossman, A. S. (1983). *Children of Working Mothers*. Bureau of Labor Statistics, U.S. Department of Labor, Washington, D.C.

Gurak, D., and Kritz, M. M. (1982). Female employment and fertility in the Dominican Republic: A dynamic perspective. *American Sociological Review* **47**, 810–818.

Haer, J. L. (1957). Predictive utility of five indices of social stratification. *American Sociological Review* **22,** 541–546.

Haines, M. R., Avery, R. C., and Strong, M. A. (1983). Differentials in infant and child mortality and their change over time: Guatemala, 1959–1973. *Demography* **20,** 607–621.

Hajnal, J. (1965). European marriage patterns in perspectives. In *Population in History: Essays in Historical Demography* (D. V. Glass and D. E. C. Eversley, eds.), pp. 101–143. Arnold, London.

Hall, M.-F. (1971). Family planning in Santiago, Chile: The male viewpoint. *Studies in Family Planning* **2,** 143–147.

Hargens, L. L., McCann, J. C., and Reskin, B. F. (1978). Productivity and reproductivity: Fertility and professional achievement among research scientists. *Social Forces* **57,** 154–163.

Harman, A. J. (1970). *Fertility and Economic Behavior of Families in the Philippines* (RM-6385-AID). Rand Corp., Santa Monica, California.

Hartford, R. B. (1971). Attitudes, information, and fertility in Medellín, Colombia. In *Ideology, Faith and Family Planning in Latin Studies in Public and Private Opinion on Fertility Control* (J. M. Stycos, ed.), pp. 206–317. Population Council Book, America. McGraw-Hill, New York.

Hass, P. H. (1972). Maternal role incompatibility and fertility in urban Latin America. *Journal of Social Issues* **28,** 111–127.

Hassan, S. S., Sallam, A. G., and Ahmed, A. M. (1971). Factors affecting fertility in rural areas of lower Egypt. In *Fertility Trends and Differentials in Arab Countries*. Cairo Demographic Centre, Cairo.

Hatt, P. K. (1950). Occupation and social stratification. *American Journal of Sociology* **55,** 533–543.

Hauser, P. M. (1967). Family planning and population programs: A book review article. *Demography* **4,** 397–414.

Hauser, R. M. (1972). The mobility table as an imcomplete multiway array: An analysis of mobility to first jobs among American men. Paper presented to the annual meeting of the Population Association of America, St. Louis, April 21–23.

Hawthorn, G. P. (1970). *The Sociology of Fertility.* Collier, MacMillan, London.

Hazelrigg, L. E. (1974). Cross-national comparisons of father-to-son occupational mobility. In *Social Stratification: A Reader* (J. Lopreato and L. S. Lewis, eds.), pp. 469–493. Harper & Row, New York.

Hazelrigg, L. E., and Garnier, M. A. (1976). Occupational mobility in industrial societies: A comparative analysis of differential access to rank in seventeen countries. *American Sociological Review* **41,** 498–511.

Heckman, J. J., and Macurdy, T. E. (1980). A life cycle model of female labour supply. *Review of Economic Studies* **47,** 47–74.

Heckman, J. J., and Willis, R. J. (1977). A beta-logistic model for the analysis of sequential force participation by married women. *Journal of Political Economy* **85,** 27–58.

Heer, D. M. (1971). Educational advance and fertility change. In *International Population Conference, London, 1969,* Vol. 3, pp. 1903–1915. International Union for the Scientific Study of Population, Liège.

Heer, D. M. (1983). Infant and child mortality and the demand for children. In *Determinants of Fertility in Developing Countries,* Vol. 1: *Supply and Demand for Children* (R. A. Bulatao and R. D. Lee with P. E. Hollerbach and J. P. Bongaarts, eds.), pp. 369–387. Studies in Population. Academic Press, New York.

Heer, D. M., and Wu, H.-Y. (1975). The separate effects of individual child loss, perception of child survival and community mortality level upon fertility and family-planning in rural Taiwan with comparison data from urban Morocco. In *Seminar on Infant Mortality in Relation to the Level of Fertility, May 6–12, 1975, Bangkok (Thailand)*, pp. 203–224. CICRED, [Paris].

Heer, D. M., and Wu, H.-Y. (1978). Effects in rural Taiwan and urban Morocco: Combining individual and aggregate data. In *The Effects of Infant and Child Mortality on Fertility* (S. H. Preston, ed.), pp. 135–159. Academic Press, New York.

Heller, P. S. (1976). *Interactions of Childhood Mortality and Fertility in W. Malaysia: 1947–1970*, Discussion Paper No. 57. Center for Research on Economic Development, Univ. of Michigan, Ann Arbor.

Hendershot, G. E., and Bauman, K. E. (1982). Use of services for family planning and infertility: United States. *Vital and Health Statistics Series 23: Data from the National Survey of Family Growth* No. 8.

Henry, A., and Piotrow, P. T. (1979). Age at marriage and fertility. *Population Reports, Series M: Special Topic Monographs* No. 4.

Henry, L. (1961). Some data on natural fertility. *Eugenics Quarterly* **8**, 81–91.

Hermalin, A. I. (1983). Fertility regulation and its costs: A critical essay. In *Determinants of Fertility in Developing Countries*, Vol. 2: *Fertility Regulation and Institutional Influences* (R. A. Bulatao and R. D. Lee with P. E. Hollerbach and J. Bongaarts, eds.), pp. 1–53. Studies in Population. Academic Press, New York.

Hermalin, A. I., and Mason, W. M. (1980). A strategy for the comparative analysis of WFS data, with illustrating examples. In *The United Nations Programme for Comparative Analysis of World Fertility Survey Data*, pp. 90–168. United Nations, New York.

Hernandez, D. J. (1981). A note on measuring the independent impact of family planning programs on fertility decline. *Demography* **18**, 627–634.

Hiday, V. A. (1978). Migration, urbanization, and fertility in the Philippines. *International Migration Review* **12**, 370–385.

Hill, R., Stycos, J. M., and Back, K. W. (1959). *The Family and Population Control: A Puerto Rican Experiment in Social Change*. Univ. of North Carolina Press, Chapel Hill.

Himes, N. E. (1963). *Medical History of Contraception*. Gamut, New York.

Hirschman, C. (1982). Premarital socioeconomic roles and the timing of family formation: A comparative study of five Asian societies. Paper presented at the annual meeting of the Population Association of America, San Diego, April 29–May 1.

Hirschman, C., and Rindfuss, R. F. (1980). Social, cultural, and economic determinants of age at birth of first child in peninsular Malaysia. *Population Studies* **34**, 507–518.

Hobcraft, J., and Casterline, J. B. (1983). Speed of reproduction. *World Fertility Survey Comparative Studies*, No. 25. International Statistical Institute, Voorburg, Netherlands.

Hobcraft, J. N., McDonald, J., and Rutstein, S. (1983). *Socio-Economic Factors in Infant and Child Mortality: A Cross National Comparison* (WFS/TECH:2132). International Statistical Institute, Voorburg, Netherlands.

Hodge, R. W. (1981). The measurement of occupational status. *Social Science Research* **10**, 396–415.

Hodge, R. W., and Siegel, P. M. (1968). The measurement of social class. In *International Encyclopedia of the Social Sciences* (D. L. Sills, ed.), Vol. 15, pp. 316–325. Macmillan and Free Press, New York.

Hodgson, M., and Gibbs, J. (1980). Children ever born. *World Fertility Survey Comparative Studies, Cross-National Summaries*, No. 12. International Statistical Institute, Voorburg, Netherlands.

Hofferth, S. L. (1984). Long-term economic consequences for women of delayed childbearing and reduced family size. *Demography* **21**, 141–155.

Hofferth, S. L., and Udry, J. R. (1976). The contribution of marital outcomes to explaining the reproductive behavior of couples. Paper presented at the annual meeting of the American Sociological Association, New York, August 30–September 3.

Hoffman, L. W., and Hoffman, M. L. (1973). The value of children to parents. In *Psychological Perspectives on Population* (J. T. Fawcett, ed.), pp. 19–76. Basic Books, New York.

Hoffman, L. W., Thornton, A. D., and Manis, J. D. (1978). The value of children to parents in the United States. *Journal of Population: Behavioral, Social and Environmental Issues* **1**, 91–131.

Hohm, C. F. (1975). Social security and fertility: An international perspective. *Demography* **12**, 629–644.

Holland, B. K. (1983). Breast-feeding and infant mortality: A hazards model analysis of the case of Malaysia. Ph.D. Thesis, Princeton Univ., Princeton, New Jersey.

Hollerbach, P. E. (1980). Power in families, communication, and fertility decision-making. *Population and Environment: Behavioral and Social Issues* **3**, 146–173.

Hollerbach, P. E. (1983). Fertility decision-making processes: A critical essay. In *Determinants of Fertility in Developing Countries*, Vol. 2: *Fertility Regulation and Institutional Influences* (R. A. Bulatao and R. D. Lee with P. E. Hollerbach and J. Bongaarts, eds.), pp. 340–380. Studies in Population. Academic Press, New York.

Hollingsworth, T. H. (1957). A demographic study of British ducal families. *Population Studies* **11**, 4–26.

Holsinger, D. B. (1974). The elementary school as a modernizer: A Brazilian study. In *Education and Individual Modernity in Developing Countries* (A. Inkeles and D. B. Holsinger, eds.), pp. 24–46. International Studies in Sociology and Social Anthropology, Vol. 14. Brill, Leiden.

Holsinger, D. B., and Kasarda, J. D. (1976). Education and human fertility: Sociological perspectives. In *Population and Development: The Search for Selective Interventions* (R. G. Ridker, ed.), pp. 154–181. Johns Hopkins Univ. Press, Baltimore, Maryland.

Hope, K. (1971). Social mobility and fertility. *American Sociological Review* **36**, 1019–1032.

Hope, K. (1975). Models of status inconsistency and social mobility effects. *American Sociological Review* **40**, 322–343.

Hope, K. (1981). Vertical mobility in Britain: A structured analysis. *Sociology* **15**, 19–55.

House, J. S. (1978). Facets and flaws of Hope's diamond model. *American Sociological Review* **43**, 439–442.

Hout, M. (1976). The determinants of marital fertility in the United States, 1960–1970. Ph.D. Thesis, Indiana Univ., Bloomington.

Hout, M. (1978). The determinants of marital fertility in the United States, 1968–1970: Influences from a dynamic model. *Demography* **15**, 139–160.

Hout, M. (1983). *Mobility Tables*. Sage, Beverly Hills, California.

Hout, M. (1984). Status, autonomy, and training in occupational mobility. *American Journal of Sociology* **89**, 1379–1409.

Huang, L. J. (1982). Planned fertility of one-couple/one-child policy in the People's Republic of China. *Journal of Marriage and the Family* **44**, 775–784.

Huffman, S. L. (1984). Determinants of breastfeeding in developing countries: Overview and policy implications. *Studies in Family Planning* **15**, 170–183.

Hull, T. H., and Hull, V. J. (1977a). Indonesia. In *The Persistence of High Fertility: Population Prospects in the Third World* (J. C. Caldwell, ed.), pp. 827–896. Department of Demography, Australian National Univ., Canberra.

Hull, T. H., and Hull, V. J. (1977b). The relation of economic class and fertility: An analysis of some Indonesian data. *Population Studies* **31**, 43–57.

Hull, V. J. (1977). Fertility, women's work and economic class: A case study for Southeast Asia. In *The Fertility of Working Women* (S. Kupinsky, ed.), pp. 35–80. Synthesis of International Research–Praeger Special Studies. Praeger, New York.

Huntington, E., and Whitney, L. F. (1927). *Builders of America*. Morrow, New York.

Husain, I. Z. (1970). *An Urban Fertility Field: A Report on City of Lucknow*. Demographic Research Center, Lucknow Univ., Lucknow, India.

Husain, I. Z. (1972). Educational status and differential fertility in India. In *Population Analysis and Studies: Radhakamal Mukerjee Commemoration Volume* (I. Z. Husain, ed.), pp. 261–270. Somaiya Publications, Bombay.

Hutchinson, B. (1958). Structural and exchange mobility in the assimilation of immigrants to Brazil. *Population Studies* **12,** 111–120.

Hutchinson, B. (1961). Fertility, social mobility and urban migration in Brazil. *Population Studies* **14,** 182–189.

Inglehart, A. P. (1979). *Married Women and Work: Nineteen Fifty-Seven and Nineteen Seventy-Six*. Lexington Books, Lexington, Massachusetts.

Inkeles, A. (1974). The school as a context for modernization. In *Education and Individual Modernity in Developing Countries* (A. Inkeles and D. B. Holsinger, eds.), pp. 7–23. International Studies in Sociology and Social Anthropology, Vol. 14. Brill, Leiden.

Inkeles, A., and Rossi, P. H. (1956). National comparisons of occupational prestige. *American Journal of Sociology* **61,** 329–339.

International Conference on Family Planning in the 1980's (1981). Family planning in the 1980's: Challenges and opportunities. *Studies in Family Planning* **12,** 251–256.

Jaffe, A. J. (1959). *People, Jobs, and Economic Development: A Case History of Puerto Rico Supplemented by Recent Mexican Experiences*. Free Press, Glencoe, Illinois.

Jaffe, A. J., and Azumi, K. (1960). The birth rate and cottage industries in underdeveloped countries. *Economic Development and Cultural Change* **9,** 52–63.

Jain, A. K. (1969). Socio-economic correlates of fecundability in a sample of Taiwanese women. *Demography* **6,** 75–90.

Jain, A. K. (1981). The effect of female education on fertility. A simple explanation. *Demography* **18,** 577–595.

Jain, A. K., and Bongaarts, J. P. (1981). Breastfeeding: Patterns, correlates, and fertility effects. *Studies in Family Planning* **12,** 79–99.

Jain, S. P. (1964). Indian fertility: Our knowledge and gaps (part 2). *Journal of Family Welfare* **11**(1), 6–19.

Janowitz, B. S. (1976). An analysis of the impact of education on family size. *Demography* **13,** 189–198.

Jolly, S. K. G. (1976). Impact of inter-spouse communication on family planning adoption. *Journal of Family Welfare* **23,** 38–44.

Jones, E. F. (1981). The impact of women's employment on marital fertility in the U.S. 1970–1975. *Population Studies* **35,** 161–173.

Jones, E. F. (1982). Socio-economic differentials in achieved fertility. *World Fertility Survey Comparative Studies, ECE Analyses of WFS Surveys in Europe and USA,* No. 21. International Statistical Institute, Voorburg, Netherlands.

Jones, E. F. (1984). The availability of contraceptive services. *World Fertility Survey Comparative Studies,* No. 38. International Statistical Institute, Voorburg, Netherlands.

Jones, E. F., Paul, L., and Westoff, C. F. (1980). Contraceptive efficacy: The significance of method and motivation. *Studies in Family Planning* **11,** 39–50.

Kagitcibasi, C. (1979). Effects of employment and children on women's status and fertility decision. Paper prepared for the International Development Research Centre Workshop on Women's Roles and Fertility, Ottawa.

Kagitcibasi, C., and Esmer, Y. (1980). *Development, Value of Children, and Fertility: A Multiple Indicator Approach*. Report prepared for the Middle East Awards Program. Bogazici Univ., Istanbul.

Kahl, J. A. (1957). *The American Class Structure*. Rinehart, New York.

Kahl, J. A., and Davis, J. A. (1955). A comparison of indexes of socio-economic status. *American Sociological Review* **20**, 317–325.

Kantner, J. F., and Kiser, C. V. (1954). The interrelation of fertility, fertility planning, and intergenerational mobility. *Milbank Memorial Fund Quarterly* **32**, 69–103.

Kar, S. B., and Talbot, J. M. (1980). Attitudinal and nonattitudinal determinants of contraception: A cross-cultural study. *Studies in Family Planning* **11**, 51–64.

Kasarda, J. D. (1971). Economic structure and fertility: A comparative analysis. *Demography* **8**, 307–317.

Kendall, M. G. (1979). The world fertility survey: Current status and findings. *Population Reports, Series M: Special Topic Monographs* No. 3.

Kerlinger, F. N., and Pedhazur, E. J. (1973). *Multiple Regression in Behavioral Research*. Holt, Rinehart & Winston, New York.

Khan, M. A., and Sirageldin, I. (1977). Son preference and the demand for additional children in Pakistan. *Demography* **14**, 481–495.

Kim, M., Rider, R. V., Harper, P. A., and Yang, J.-M. (1974). Age at marriage, family planning practices and other variables as correlates of fertility in Korea. *Demography* **11**, 641–656.

Kirk, D. (1957). The fertility of a gifted group: A study of the number of children of men in "Who's Who." In *The Nature and Transmission of the Genetic and Cultural Characteristics of Human Populations*. Papers presented at the 1956 annual conference of the Milbank Memorial Fund, pp. 78–98. Milbank Memorial Fund, New York.

Knodel, J. E. (1974). *The Decline of Fertility in Germany, 1871–1939*. Princeton Univ. Press, Princeton, New Jersey.

Knodel, J. E. (1975). The influence of child mortality on fertility in European populations in the past: Results from individual data. In *Seminar on Infant Mortality in Relation to the Level of Fertility, May 6–12, 1975, Bangkok (Thailand)*, pp. 103–118. CICRED, [Paris].

Knodel, J. E. (1982a). Breastfeeding. In *International Encyclopedia of Population* (J. A. Ross, ed.), Vol. 1, pp. 71–76. Free Press, New York.

Knodel, J. E. (1982b). Child mortality and reproductive behavior in German village populations in the past: A micro-level analysis of the replacement effect. *Population Studies* **36**, 177–200.

Knodel, J., and Pitaktepsombati, P. (1973). Thailand: Fertility and family planning among rural and urban women. *Studies in Family Planning* **4**, 229–255.

Knodel, J., and Prachuabmoh, V. (1973). Desired family size in Thailand: Are the responses meaningful? *Demography* **10**, 619–637.

Knodel, J., and van de Walle, E. (1979). Lessons from the past: Policy implications of historical fertility studies. *Population and Development Review* **5**, 217–245.

Kocher, J. E. (1977). Socioeconomic development and fertility change in rural Africa. *Food Research Institute Studies* **16**(2), 63–75.

Koh, K.-S., and Smith, D. P. (1970). *The Koran 1968 Fertility and Family Planning Survey*. National Family Planning Center, Seoul.

Kreps, J. M., ed. (1976). *Women and the American Economy: A Look to the 1980s*. A Spectrum Book. Prentice-Hall, Englewood Cliffs, New Jersey.

Kripalani, G. B., Maitra, P., and Bose, T. (1971). Education and its relation to family planning. *Journal of Family Welfare* **18**(2), 3–8.

Kritzer, H. M. (1976). Problems in the use of two stage least squares: Standardization of coefficients and multicolinearity. *Political Methodology* **3**, 71–93.

Kubat, D., and Mourao, F. A. A. (1970). Family planning among the Sao Paulo industrial workers: Attitudes, practices and results. Paper presented at the annual meeting of the Population Association of America, Atlanta, April 16–18.

Kupinsky, S. (1971). Non-familial activity and socio-economic differentials in fertility. *Demography* **8,** 353–367.

Kupinsky, S. (1977). *The Fertility of Working Women. A Synthesis of International Research.* Praeger Special Studies. Praeger, New York.

Larson, A. (1981). *Patterns of Contraceptive Use around the World.* Population Reference Bureau, Washington, D.C.

Laslett, P. (1980). Introduction: Comparing illegitimacy over time and between cultures. In *Bastardy and Its Comparative History* (P. Laslett, K. Oosterveen, and R. M. Smith, eds.), pp. 1–68. Studies in Social and Demographic History. Harvard Univ. Press, Cambridge, Massachusetts.

Lawson, E. D., and Boek, W. E. (1960). Correlations of indexes of families' socio-economic status. *Social Forces* **39,** 149–152.

Leasure, J. W. (1963). Malthus, marriage and multiplication. *Milbank Memorial Fund Quarterly* **41,** 419–435.

Lee, H.-C., and Cho, H. (1976). Fertility and women's labor force participation in Korea. In *Recent Empirical Findings on Fertility: Korea, Nigeria, Tunisia, Venezuela, Philippines,* Occasional Monograph Series No. 7. Interdisciplinary Communications Program, Smithsonian Institution, Washington, D.C.

Lee, R. D., and Bulatao, R. A. (1983). The demand for children: A critical essay. In *The Determinants of Fertility in Developing Countries,* Vol. 1: *Supply and Demand for Children* (R. A. Bulatao and R. D. Lee with P. E. Hollerbach and J. Bongaarts, eds.), pp. 233–282. Studies in Population. Academic Press, New York.

Lee, S. J., and Kim, J.-O. (1977). *The Value of Children: A Cross-National Study,* Vol. 7: *Korea.* East–Wast Population Institute, Honolulu.

Lehner, A. (1954). Mobilité social par rapport a la dimension de la famille. In *World Population Conference, Rome, Italy, Aug. 31–Sept. 10, 1954, Proceedings,* Vol. 6, pp. 911–931 (E/CONF.13/418). United Nations, New York.

Lehrer, E. (1984). The impact of child mortality on spacing by parity: A Cox-regression analysis. *Demography* **21,** 323–337.

Lehrer, E., and Nerlove, M. (1979). *Female Labor Supply Behavior over the Life Cycle: An Econometric Study.* Discussion Paper No. 382. Northwestern Univ., Evanston, Illinois.

Lehrer, E., and Nerlove, M. (1982). An econometric analysis of the fertility and labor supply of unmarried women. In *Research in Population Economics. A Research Annual* (J. L. Simon and P. H. Lindert, eds.), Vol. 4, pp. 217–235. Jai Press, Greenwich, Connecticut.

Leibenstein, H. (1957). *Economic Backwardness and Economic Growth. Studies in the Theory of Economic Development.* Wiley, New York.

Leibenstein, H. (1974). An interpretation of the economic theory of fertility: Promising path or blind alley? *Journal of Economic Literature* **12,** 457–479.

LeMasters, E. E. (1954). Social class mobility and family integration. *Marriage and Family Living* **16,** 226–232.

Lesthaeghe, R. J. (1975). Infant mortality and marital fertility decline in Belgium, 1880–1910—A short research note. In *Seminar on Infant Mortality in Relation to the Level of Fertility, May 6–12, 1974, Bangkok (Thailand),* pp. 343–350. CICRED, [Paris].

Lesthaeghe, R. J. (1982). Lactation and lactation related variables, contraception and fertility: An overview of data problems and world trends. Paper presented at the National Academy of Sciences Seminar on Breastfeeding and Fertility Regulation, Geneva.

Lesthaeghe, R. J., Shah, I. H., and Page, H. J. (ca. 1982). Compensating changes in intermediate variables and the onset of marital fertility transition. In *International Population Conference, Manila, 1981, Solicited Paper,* Vol. 1, pp. 71–94. International Union for the Scientific Study of Population, Liège.

Lewis-Faning, E. (1949). *Report on an Enquiry into Family Limitation and Its Influence on Human*

Fertility during the Past Fifty Years, Papers of the Royal Commission on Population, Vol. 1. His Majesty's Stationery Office, London.

Lightbourne, R. E., Jr. (1985). Individual preferences and fertility behavior. In *Reproductive Change in Developing Countries* (J. Cleland and J. Hobcraft, in collaboration with B. Dinesen, eds.), pp. 165–198. Oxford University Press, London and New York.

Lightbourne, R. E., Jr., and Singh, S., with Green, C. P. (1982). The world fertility survey: Charting global childbearing. *Population Bulletin* **37**(1).

Lindenbaum, S. (1981). Implications for women of changing marriage transactions in Bangladesh. *Studies in Family Planning* **12**, 394–401.

Lindert, P. H. (1978). *Fertility and Scarcity in America.* Princeton Univ. Press, Princeton, New Jersey.

Lindert, P. H. (1980). Child costs and economic development. In *Population and Economic Change in Developing Countries* (R. A. Easterlin, ed.), pp. 5–79. Univ. of Chicago Press, Chicago, Illinois.

Lindert, P. H. (1983). The changing economic costs and benefits of having children. In *Determinants of Fertility in Developing Countries,* Vol. 1: *Supply and Demand for Children* (R. A. Bulatao and R. D. Lee with P. E. Hollerbach and J. Bongaarts, eds.), pp. 494–516. Studies in Population. Academic Press, New York.

Lipset, S. M., and Zetterberg, H. L. (1956). A theory of social mobility. In *Transactions of the Third World Congress of Sociology,* Koninklijk Instituut voor de Tropen, Amsterdam, August 22–29, 1956. Problems of Social Change in the 20th Century, Vol. 3: *Changes in Class Structure,* pp. 155–177. International Sociological Association, London.

Lopreato, J., Bean, F. D., and Lopreato, S. C. (1976). Occupational mobility and political behavior: Some unresolved issues. *Journal of Political and Military Sociology* **4**, 1–15.

McCabe, J. L., and Rosenzweig, M. R. (1976). Female labor-force participation, occupational choice, and fertility in developing countries. *Journal of Development Economics* **3**, 141–160.

McCarthy, J. F. (1982). Differentials in age at first marriage. *World Fertility Survey Comparative Studies, Cross-National Summaries,* No. 19. International Statistical Institute, Voorburg, Netherlands.

MacDonald, M. M., and Rindfuss, R. R. (1978). Relative economic status and fertility: Evidence from a cross-section. In *Research in Population Economics* (J. L. Simon, ed.), Vol. 1, pp. 291–307. Jai Press, Greenwich, Connecticut.

McGreevey, W. P. (1973). Fertility variables, population policy in El Salvador. *Population Dynamics Quarterly* **1**(3), 2–3.

McGuire, C. (1950). Social stratification and mobility patterns. *American Sociological Review* **15**, 195–204.

Macisco, J. J., Bouvier, L. F., and Renzi, M. J. (1969). Migration status, education and fertility in Puerto Rico, 1960. *Milbank Memorial Fund Quarterly* **47**, 167–187.

McLaughlin, S. D. (1982). Differential patterns of female labor-force participation surrounding the first birth. *Journal of Marriage and the Family* **44**, 407–420.

Mamlouk, M. (1982). *Knowledge and Use of Contraception in Twenty Developing Countries,* Reports on the World Fertility Survey No. 3. Population Reference Bureau, Washington, D.C.

Mandelbaum, D. G. (1974). *Human Fertility in India: Social Components and Policy Perspectives.* Univ. of California Press, Berkeley.

Marini, M. M. (1978). The transition to adulthood: Sex differences in educational attainment and age at marriage. *American Sociological Review* **43**, 483–501.

Marini, M. M. (1984). Women's educational attainment and timing of entry into parenthood. *American Sociological Review* **49**, 491–511.

Marsden, P. V. and Lin, N. (1982). *Social Structure and Network Analysis.* Sage, Beverly Hills, California.

Martine, G. R. (1972). Migrant fertility adjustment and urban growth in Latin America. In *International Population Conference, Liège, August 27–September 1, 1973, Proceedings*, pp. 293–304. International Union for the Scientific Study of Population, Liège.

Mason, K. O. (1984). *The Status of Women. A Review of Its Relationships to Fertility and Mortality*. Population Sciences Division, Rockefeller Foundation, New York.

Mason, K. O., and Palan, V. T. (1981). Female employment and fertility in peninsular Malaysia: The maternal role incompatibility hypothesis reconsidered. *Demography* **18**, 549–575.

Mason, K. O., and Schultz, B. S. (1972). Fertility, Work Experience, Potential Earnings and Occupation of American Women Ages 30–44: Evidence from Survey Data. Research Triangle Institute, Research Triangle Park, North Carolina.

Mason, K. O., David, A. S., Gerstel, E. K., Lindsey, Q. W., and Rulison, M. V. E. (1971). *Social and Economic Correlates of Family Fertility: A Survey of the Evidence*. Research Triangle Institute, Research Triangle Park, North Carolina.

Massialas, B. G. (1972). Population education as exploration of alternatives. *Social Education* **36**, 346–356.

Matthiessen, P. C., and McCann, J. C. (1978). The role of mortality in the European fertility transition: Aggregate-level relations. In *The Effects of Infant and Child Mortality on Fertility* (S. H. Preston, ed.), pp. 47–68. Academic Press, New York.

Mauldin, W. P. (1983). Population programs and fertility regulation. In *Determinants of Fertility in Developing Countries*, Vol. 2: *Fertility Regulation and Institutional Influences* (R. A. Bulatao and R. D. Lee with P. E. Hollerbach and J. Bongaarts, eds.), pp. 267–294. Studies in Population. Academic Press, New York.

Mauldin. W. P., and Berelson, B. (1978). Conditions of fertility decline in developing countries, 1965–1975. *Studies in Family Planning* **9**, 89–147.

Meeks, T. J., and Lee, B. S. (1979). The Relationship of Fertility to Income and Wealth in Rural Development. Research Triangle Institute and South East Consortium for International Development, Research Triangle Park, North Carolina.

Mernissi, F. (1975). Obstacles to family planning practice in urban Morocco. *Studies in Family Planning* **6**, 418–425.

Merrick, T. W., and Schmink, M. (1983). Households headed by women and urban poverty in Brazil. In *Women and Poverty in the Third World* (M. Buviníc, M. A. Lycette, and W. P. McGreevey, eds.), pp. 244–271. Johns Hopkins Series in Development. Johns Hopkins Univ. Press, Baltimore, Maryland.

Michael, R. T. (1973). Education and the derived demand for children. *Journal of Political Economy* **81**(2), Part 2, S128–S164.

Michael, R. T. (1974). Education and the derived demand for children. In *Economics of the Family: Marriage, Children and Human Capital* (T. W. Schultz, ed.), A Conference Report of the National Bureau of Economic Research, pp. 120–156. Univ. of Chicago Press, Chicago, Illinois.

Miller, K. A., and Inkeles, A. (1974). Modernity and acceptance of family limitation in four developing countries. *Journal of Social Issues* **30**, 167–188.

Miller, S. M. (1961). Comparative social mobility. A trend report and bibliography. *Current Sociology* **9**, 1–89.

Millman, S. R., and Hendershot, G. E. (1980). Early fertility and lifetime fertility. *Family Planning Perspectives* **12**, 139–149.

Millman, S. R., and Palloni, A. (1984). *Breastfeeding and Infant Mortality: Methodological Issues and a Research Strategy*, CDE Working Paper No. 84–10. Center for Demography and Ecology, Univ. of Wisconsin, Madison.

Mincer, J. (1962). Labor force participation of married women. In *Aspects of Labor Economics*, A Conference of the Universities-National Bureau Committee for Economic Research, National

Bureau of Economic Research Special Conference Series, Vol. 14, pp. 63–105. Princeton Univ. Press, Princeton, New Jersey.

Mincer, J., and Ofek, H. (1982). Interrupted work careers: Depreciation and restoration of human capital. *Journal of Human Resources* **17**, 3–24.

Minkler, M. (1970). Fertility and female labour force participation in India: A survey of workers in Old Delhi area. *Journal of Family Welfare* **17**(1), 31–43.

Miró, C. A. (1966). Some misconceptions disproved: A program of comparative fertility surveys in Latin America. In *Family Planning and Population Programs: A Review of World Developments* (B. Berelson, R. K. Anderson, O. Harkavy, J. Maier, W. P. Mauldin, and S. T. Segal, eds.), pp. 615–634. Univ. of Chicago Press, Chicago, Illinois.

Miró, C. A., and Mertens, W. (1968). Influences affecting fertility in urban and rural Latin America. *Milbank Memorial Fund Quarterly* **46**(3), Part 2, 89–120.

Miró, C. A., and Rath, F. (1965). Preliminary findings of comparative fertility surveys in three Latin American cities. *Milbank Memorial Fund Quarterly* **43**(4), Part 2, 36–68.

Mitchell, R. E. (1972). Husband–wife relations and family-planning practices in urban Hong-Kong. *Journal of Marriage and the Family* **34**, 139–146.

Mitra, A. (1972). Benefit cost approaches to family planning programmes: A review. *Demography India* **1**(1), 63–77.

Mitra, S. (1966). Occupation and fertility in the United States. *Eugenics Quarterly* **13**, 141–146.

Modell, J., Furstenberg, F. F., Jr., and Strong, D. (1978). The timing of marriage in the transition to adulthood: Continuity and change, 1860–1975. In *Turning Points: Historical and Sociological Essays on the Family* (J. Demos and S. S. Boocock, eds.), pp. 120–150. Univ. of Chicago Press, Chicago, Illinois.

Momeni, D. A. (1972). The difficulties of changing the age of marriage in Iran. *Journal of Marriage and the Family* **34**, 545–551.

Morgan, R. W. (1975). Fertility levels and fertility change. In *Population Growth and Socioeconomic Change in West Africa* (J. C. Caldwell, N. O. Addo, S. K. Gaisie, A. A. Ogun, and P. O. Olusanya, eds.), pp. 187–235. Columbia Univ. Press, New York.

Morgan, S. P. (1982). Parity-specific fertility intentions and uncertainty: The United States, 1970 to 1976. *Demography* **19**, 315–334.

Morgan, S. P., and R. R. Rindfuss (1984). Household structures and the tempo of family formation in comparative perspective. *Population Studies* **38**, 129–139.

Morris, R. T., and Murphy, R. J. (1959). The situs dimension in occupational structure. *American Sociological Review* **24**, 231–239.

Mosher, W. D., and Goldscheider, C. (1984). Contraceptive patterns of religious and racial groups in the United States, 1955–76: Convergence and distinctiveness. *Studies in Family Planning* **15**, 101–111.

Mosher, W. D., and Hendershot, G. E. (1984). Religion and fertility: A replication. *Demography* **21**, 185–191.

Mott, F. L. (1972). Fertility, life cycle stage and female labor force participation in Rhode Island: A retrospective overview. *Demography* **9**, 173–185.

Mott, F. L., and Shapiro, D. (1983). Complementarity of work and fertility among young American mothers. *Population Studies* **37**, 239–252.

Mount, H. S. (1968). Employed wives: Their fertility experience and selected socio-demographic characteristics. Paper presented at the annual meeting of the Population Association of America, Boston, April 18–20.

Mueller, E. (1972a). Economic cost and value of children: Conceptualization and measurement. In *The Satisfactions and Costs of Children: Theories, Concepts, Methods* (J. T. Fawcett, ed.), pp. 174–205. East–West Population Institute, Honolulu.

Mueller, E. (1972b). Economic motives for family limitation: A study conducted in Taiwan. *Population Studies* **26**, 383–403.

Mueller, E. (1976). The economic value of children in peasant agriculture. In *Population and Development: The Search for Selective Interventions* (R. G. Ridker, ed.), pp. 98–153. Johns Hopkins Univ. Press, Baltimore, Maryland.

Mueller, E. (1982). The allocation of women's time and its relation to fertility. In *Women's Roles and Population Trends in the Third World* (R. B. Anker, M. Buviníc, and N. H. Youssef, eds.), pp. 55–86. Johns Hopkins Studies in Development. Croom Helm, London.

Mueller, E., Chon, R., and Reineck, S. (1971). Female labor force participation and fertility in Taiwan. Unpublished manuscript, Department of Economics, Univ. of Michigan, Ann Arbor.

Mukherjee, B. N. (1975). Status of women as related to family planning. *Journal of Population Research* **2**(1), 5–33.

Nag, M. (1973). Cultural factors affecting family planning. *Journal of Family Welfare* **19**(3), 3–7.

Nag, M. (1983a). *The Equity–Fertility Hypothesis as an Explanation of the Fertility Differential between Kerala and West Bengal,* Center for Policy Studies Working Paper No. 96. Population Council Center for Policy Studies, New York.

Nag, M. (1983b). The impact of sociocultural factors on breastfeeding and sexual behavior. In *Determinants of Fertility in Developing Countries,* Vol. 1: *Supply and Demand for Children* (R. A. Bulatao and R. D. Lee with P. E. Hollerbach and J. P. Bongaarts, eds.), pp. 163–198. Studies in Population. Academic Press, New York.

Nag, M. (1983c). Modernization affects fertility. *Populi* **10**(1), 56–77.

Nag, M., White, B. N. F., and Peet, R. C. (1980). An anthropological approach to the study of the economic value of children in Java and Nepal. In *Rural Household Studies in Asia* (H. P. Binswanger, R. E. Evenson, C. A. Florencio, and B. N. F. White, eds.), pp. 248–288. Singapore Univ. Press, Singapore.

Nam, C. B., and Folger, J. K. (1965). Factors related to school retention. *Demography* **2**, 456–462.

Namboodiri, N. (1964). The wife's work experience and child spacing. *Milbank Memorial Fund Quarterly* **42**(3), Part 2, 65–77.

Namboodiri, N. K. (1972a). Abstract experimental models for analyzing mobility–fertility data. *Demography India* **1**(1), 92–107.

Namboodiri, N. K. (1972b). Integrative potential of a fertility model: An analytical test. *Population Studies* **26**, 465–485.

Namboodiri, N. K. (1972c). Some observations on the economic framework for fertility analysis. *Population Studies* **26**, 185–206.

Namboodiri, N. K. (1974). Which couples at given parities expect to have additional births? An exercise in discriminant analysis. *Demography* **11**, 45–56.

Namboodiri, N. K. (1975). Review symposium. Theodore W. Schultz, Economics of the family: Marriage, children, and human capital. *Demography* **12**, 561–569.

Namboodiri, N. K. (1983). Sequential fertility decision making and the life course. In *Determinants of Fertility in Developing Countries,* Vol. 2: *Fertility Regulation and Institutional Influences* (R. A. Bulatao and R. D. Lee with P. E. Hollerbach and J. Bongaarts, eds.), pp. 444–472. Studies in Population. Academic Press, New York.

Natsis, M. (1966). Social mobility and differential fertility among American Baptist ministers. Master's Thesis, Purdue Univ., Lafayette, Indiana.

Nerlove, M., and Schultz, T. P. (1970). *Love and Life between the Censuses: A Model of Family Decision Making in Puerto Rico, 1950–1960.* Rand Corp., Santa Monica, California.

Newland, K. (1977). *Women and Population Growth: Choices beyond Childbearing,* Worldwatch Paper No. 16. Worldwatch Institute, Washington, D.C.

New South Wales Royal Commission (1904). *Decline of the Birth Rate and the Mortality of Infants in New South Wales,* Vol. 1. [Sydney].

Niphuis-Nell, M., ed. (1978). *Demographic Aspects of the Changing Status of Women in Europe: Proceedings of the Second European Population Seminar, The Hague/Brussels, December 13– 17, 1976,* Publications of the Netherlands Interuniversity Demographic Institute and the Population and Family Study Center, Vol. 7. Martinus Nijhoff Social Sciences Division, Boston, Massachusetts.

Notestein, F. W. (1945). Population—The long view. In *Food for the World* (T. W. Schultz, ed.), pp. 36–57. Univ. of Chicago Press, Chicago, Illinois.

Nugent, J. B. (1985). The old-age security motive for fertility. *Population and Development Review* **11,** 75–97.

O'Connell, M., and Rogers, C. C. (1984). Out-of-wedlock births, premarital pregnancies and their effect on family formation and dissolution. *Family Planning Perspectives* **16,** 157–162.

Olneck, M. R., and Wolfe, B. L. (1978). A note on some evidence on the Easterlin hypothesis. *Journal of Political Economy* **86,** 953–958.

Olsen, R. J. (1980). Estimating the effect of child mortality on the number of births. *Demography* **17,** 429–443.

Olson, L. (1983). *Costs of Children.* Lexington Books, Lexington, Massachusetts.

Olusanya, P. O. (1971). Status differentials in the fertility attitudes of married women in two communities in western Nigeria. *Economic Development and Cultural Change* **19,** 641–651.

Omran, A. R. (1971). *The Health Theme in Family Planning,* Monograph No. 16. Carolina Population Center, Univ. of North Carolina at Chapel Hill.

Omran, A. R., ed., with Johnston, A. G. (1985). *Family Planning for Health in Africa.* Carolina Population Center, Univ. of North Carolina at Chapel Hill.

Oppong, C. (1983). Women's roles, opportunity costs and fertility. In *The Determinants of Fertility in Developing Countries,* Vol. 1: *Supply and Demand for Children* (R. A. Bulatao and R. D. Lee with P. E. Hollerbach and J. Bongaarts, eds.), pp. 547–589. Studies in Population. Academic Press, New York.

Oppong, C., and Haavio-Mannila, E. (1979). Women, population and development. In *World Population and Development: Challenges and Prospects* (P. M. Hauser, ed.), pp. 440–485. Syracuse Univ. Press, Syracuse, New York.

Osborn, R. W., and Thomas, B. S. (1979). Male–female variations in value of children. Paper presented at the annual meeting of the Population Association of America, Philadelphia, April 26–28.

Otto, L. B. (1979). Antecedents and consequences of marital timing. In *Contemporary theories about the Family; Research-Based Theories* (W. R. Burr, R. Hill, F. I. Nye, and I. L. Reiss, eds.), Vol. 1, pp. 101–126. Free Press, New York.

Palloni, A. (1981). Mortality in Latin America: Emerging patterns. *Population and Development Review* **7,** 623–649.

Palloni, A., and Tienda, M. (1983). *The Effects of Pace of Childbearing and Breastfeeding on Mortality at Early Ages: The Case of Peru,* CDE Working Paper No. 83-43. Center for Demography and Ecology, Univ. of Wisconsin, Madison.

Palloni, A., and Tienda, M. (1986). The effects of breastfeeding and pace of childbearing on mortality at early ages. *Demography* **23,** 31–52.

Palmore, J. A. (1974). Social and psychological aspects of fertility in the United States. In *Social and Psychological Aspects of Fertility in Asia: Proceedings of the Technical Seminar, Choonchun, Korea, Nov. 7–9, 1973* (H. P. David and S. J. Lee, eds.), pp. 69–101. Transnational Family Research Institute, Washington, D.C.

Parnell, A. M. (1985). Marriage and motherhood: Changing social relationships in the United States. Ph.D. Thesis prospectus. Univ. of North Carolina at Chapel Hill.

Pearson, L. B. (1969). *Partners in Development: Report of the Commission on International Development.* Praeger, New York.

Pebley, A. R., Delgado, H., and Brinemann, E. (1979). Fertility desires and child mortality experience among Guatemalan women. *Studies in Family Planning* **10,** 129–136.

Pebley, A. R., Casterline, J. B., and Trussell, J. (1982). Age at first birth in 19 countries. *International Family Planning Perspectives* **8,** 2–7.

Peek, P. (1975). Female employment and fertility, a study based on Chilean data. *International Labour Review* **112,** 207–216.

Peel, J. H., and Potts, M. (1969). *Textbook of Contraceptive Practice.* Cambridge Univ. Press, London and New York.

Peipmeier, K. B., and Adkins, T. S. (1973). The status of women and fertility. *Journal of Biosocial Sciences* **5,** 507–520.

Perrucci, C. C. (1967). Social origins, mobility patterns and fertility. *American Sociological Review* **32,** 615–625.

Pihlblad, C. T., and Aas, D. (1960). Residential and occupational mobility in an area of rapid industrialization in Norway. *American Sociological Review* **25,** 369–375.

Pinnelli, A. (1971). Female labour and fertility in relationship to contrasting social and economic conditions. *Human Relations* **24,** 603–610.

Polgar, S., and Hiday, V. A. (1974). The effect of an additional birth on low-income urban families. *Population Studies* **28,** 463–471.

Popkin, B. M., Lasky, T., Litvin, J., Spicer, D., and Yamamoto, M. E. (1986). *The Infant-Feeding Triad: Mother, Infant, and Household.* Gordon & Breach, New York.

Population Council (1970). *A Manual for Surveys of Fertility and Family Planning: Knowledge, Attitudes, and Practice.* Population Council, New York.

Poti, S. J., and Datta, S. (1960). Pilot study on social mobility and its association with fertility in West Bengal in 1956. *Eugenics Quarterly* **7,** 235–237.

Potter, R. G., New, M. L., Wyon, J. B., and Gordon, J. E. (1965). Lactation and its effects upon birth intervals in eleven Punjab villages, India. *Journal of Chronic Diseases* **18,** 1125–1140.

Pratt, L., and Whelpton, P. K. (1958). Extra-familial participation of wives in relation to interest in and liking for children, fertility planning, and actual and desired family size. In *Social and Psychological Factors Affecting Fertility* (P. K. Whelpton and C. V. Kiser, eds.), Vol. 5, pp. 1211–1244. Milbank Memorial Fund, New York.

Pratt, W. F., Grady, W. R., Menken, J. A., and Trussell, J. (1980). An overview of experience with vaginal contraceptives in the United States. In *Vaginal Contraception—New Developments* (G. I. Zatuchni, A. J. Sobrero, J. J. Speidel, and J. J. Sciarra, Jr., eds.), pp. 82–99. Harper & Row, New York.

Prehn, J. W. (1967). Vertical mobility and community type as factors in the migration of college graduates. *Demography* **4,** 283–292.

Presser, H. B. (1971). The timing of the first birth, female roles and black fertility. *Milbank Memorial Fund Quarterly* **49,** 329–361.

Presser, H. B., and Cain, V. S. (1983). Shift work among dual-earner couples with children. *Science (Washington, D.C.)* **219**(Feb. 18), 876–879.

Preston, S. H. (1972). Interrelations between death rates and birth rates. *Theoretical Population Biology* **3,** 162–185.

Preston, S. H. (1975a). Areas de investigacion sugeridas para el futuro [Suggested areas for future research]. In *Seminar on Infant Mortality in Relation to the Level of Fertility, May 6–12, 1975, Bangkok, (Thailand),* pp. 317–324. CICRED, [Paris].

Preston, S. H. (1975b). Introduction. In *Seminar on Infant Mortality in Relation to the Level of Fertility, Bangkok, May 6–12, 1975,* pp. 10–22. CICRED, [Paris].

Preston, S. H., ed. (1978). *The Effects of Infant and Child Mortality on Fertility.* Academic Press, New York.

Pullum, T. W. (1975). *Measuring Occupational Inheritance,* Progress in Mathematical Social Sciences, Vol. 5. Elsevier, Amsterdam.

Ramu, G. N. (1972). Geographic mobility, kinship, and the family in South India. *Journal of Marriage and the Family* **34,** 147–152.

Razin, A. (1980). Number, spacing and quality of children: A microeconomic viewpoint. In *Research in Population Economics: A Research Annual* (J. L. Simon and J. Da Vanzo, eds.), Vol. 2, pp. 279–293. Jai Press, Greenwich, Connecticut.

Reed, F. W., and Udry, J. R. (1973). Female work, fertility and contraceptive use in a biracial sample. *Journal of Marriage and the Family* **35,** 597–602.

Repetto, R. G. (1976a). Direct economic costs and values of children. In *Population and Development: The Search for Selective Interventions* (R. G. Ridker, ed.), pp. 77–97. Johns Hopkins Univ. Press, Baltimore, Maryland.

Repetto, R. G. (1976b). Inequality and the Birth Rate in Puerto Rico: Evidence from Household Census Data, Research Paper No. 14. Center for Population Studies, Harvard Univ., Cambridge, Massachusetts.

Repetto, R. G. (1978). Comments on the article by Moni Nag, Benjamin N. F. White, and R. Creighton Peet, An anthropological approach to the study of the economic value of children in Java and Nepal. *Current Anthropology* **19,** 304.

Retherford, R. D. (1974). Population aspects of social development. In *Report and Selected Papers: The Regional Seminar on Population Aspects of Social Development, Bangkok, Thailand, Jan. 11–20, 1972,* pp. 23–57. Prepared under the auspices of the Economic Commission for Asia and the Far East. ECAFE, Bangkok.

Retherford, R. D. (1975). The influence of child mortality on fertility: Review of mechanisms. In *Seminar on Infant Mortality in Relation to the Level of Fertility, May 6–12, 1975, Bangkok (Thailand),* pp. 65–86. CICRED, [Paris].

Richmond, A. H. (1964). Social mobility of immigrants in Canada. *Population Studies* **18,** 53–69.

Ridley, J. C. (1959). Number of children expected in relation to non-familial activities of wife. *Milbank Memorial Fund Quarterly* **37,** 277–296.

Ridley, J. C. (1968). Demographic change and the roles and status of women. *Annals of the American Academy of Political and Social Science* **375,** 15–25.

Riemer, R., and Kiser, C. V. (1954). Social and psychological factors affecting fertility, 23. Economic tension and social mobility in relation to fertility planning and size of planned family. *Milbank Memorial Fund Quarterly* **32,** 167–231.

Rindfuss, R. R., and Bumpass, L. L. (1978). Age and the sociology of fertility: How old is too old? In *Social Demography: Studies in Population* (K. E. Taeuber, L. L. Bumpass, and J. A. Sweet, eds.), pp. 43–56. Academic Press, New York.

Rindfuss, R. R., and Morgan, S. P. (1983). Marriage, sex, and the first birth interval: The quiet revolution in Asia. *Population and Development Review* **9,** 259–278.

Rindfuss, R. R., and St. John, C. (1983). Social determinants of the age of the first birth. *Journal of Marriage and the Family* **45,** 553–565.

Rindfuss, R. R., and Sweet, J. A. (1977). *Postwar Fertility Trends and Differentials in the United States,* Studies in Population. Academic Press, New York.

Rindfuss, R. R., and Westoff, C. F. (1974). The initiation of contraception. *Demography* **11,** 75–87.

Rindfuss, R. R., Bumpass, L. L., and St. John, C. (1980). Education and fertility: Implications for the roles women occupy. *American Sociological Review* **45,** 431–447.

Rindfuss, R. R., Swicegood, C. G., and Morgan, S. P. (1984). Career paths and timing of the first birth: A longitudinal approach to delayed childbearing. Paper presented at the annual meeting of the American Sociological Association, San Antonio, August 27–31.

Rivera-Batiz, F. L. (1982). *Child Labor Patterns and Legislation in Relation to Fertility,* Project Paper No. 3. Prepared for the Fertility Determinants Group, Indiana Univ., Bloomington.

Robinson, W. C. (1971). Population growth and economic welfare. *Reports on Population–Family Planning* No. 6.

Rodman, H. (1972). Marital power and the theory of resources in cultural context. *Journal of Comparative Family Studies* **3**, 50–69.

Rodríguez, G. (1978). Family planning availability and contraceptive practice. *International Family Planning Perspectives and Digest* **4**, 100–115.

Rodríguez, G., and Cleland, J. (1981). Socio-economic determinants of marital fertility in twenty countries: A multivariate approach. In *World Fertility Survey Conference, 1980, Record of Proceedings*, Vol. 2, pp. 325–425. International Statistical Institute, Voorburg, Netherlands.

Rogers, E. M. (1979). Network analysis of the diffusion of innovations. In *Perspectives on Social Network Research* (P. W. Holland and S. Leinhardt, eds.), pp. 137–164. Academic Press, New York.

Rosen, B. C., and LaRaia, A. L. (1972). Modernity in women: An index of social change in Brazil. *Journal of Marriage and the Family* **34**, 353–360.

Rosen, B. C., and Simmons, A. B. (1971). Industrialization, family and fertility: A structural–psychological analysis of the Brazilian case. *Demography* **8**, 49–69.

Rosenfeld, R. A. (1978). Women's intergenerational occupational mobility. *American Sociological Review* **43**, 36–46.

Rosenzweig, M. R. (1976). Female work experience, employment status and birth expectations: Sequential decision-making in the Philippines. *Demography* **13**, 339–356.

Rosenzweig, M. R. (1978). The value of children's time, family size and non-household child activities in a developing country: Evidence from household data. In *Research in Population Economics* (J. L. Simon, ed.), Vol. 1, pp. 331–347. Jai Press, Greenwich, Connecticut.

Rosenzweig, M. R., and Schultz, T. P. (1983). Consumer demand and household production: The relationship between fertility and child mortality. *American Economic Review* **73**, 38–42.

Ross, S. G. (1973). The timing and spacing of births and women's labor force participation: An economic analysis. Ph.D. Thesis, Columbia Univ., New York.

Rotella, E. J. (1984). *Nuptiality and Fertility in LDCs*, Project Paper No. 6. Prepared for the Fertility Determinants Group, Indiana Univ., Bloomington.

Rothman de Biscossa, A. M. (1969). *La participación femenina en actividades económicas en su relatión con el nivel de fecundidad en Buenos Aires y Mexico*, Series C No. 108. CELADE, Santiago, Chile.

Rowntree, G., and Pierce, R. M. (1961–1962). Birth control in Britain. *Population Studies* **15**, 3–31; 121–160.

Rukanuddin, A. R. (1982). Infant–child mortality and son preference as factors influencing fertility in Pakistan. *Pakistan Development Review* **21**, 298–328.

Rutstein, S. O. (1983). Infant and child mortality: Levels, trends and demographic differentials. *World Fertility Survey Comparative Studies*, No. 24. International Statistical Institute, Voorburg, Netherlands and World Fertility Survey, London.

Rutstein, S. O. and Medica, V. (1975). The effects of infant and child mortality on fertility in Latin America. In *Seminar on Infant Mortality in Relation to the Level of Fertility, May 6–12, 1975, Bangkok (Thailand)*, pp. 225–246. CICRED, [Paris].

Ryder, N. B. (1973). The future growth of the American population. In *Towards the End of Growth: Population in America* (C. F. Westoff, ed.), pp. 85–96. A Spectrum Book. Prentice-Hall, Englewood Cliffs, New Jersey.

Ryder, N. B. (1983). Fertility and family structure. *Population Bulletin of the United Nations* No. 15, pp. 15–34.

Ryder, N. B., and Westoff, C. F. (1971a). Fertility planning status: United States, 1965. *Demography* **6**, 435–444.

Ryder, N. B., and Westoff, C. F. (1971b). *Reproduction in the United States, 1965*. Princeton Univ. Press, Princeton, New Jersey.

Safilios-Rothschild, C. (1972). The relationship between work commitment and fertility. *International Journal of Sociology of the Family* **2**, 64–71.

Safilios-Rothschild, C. (1977). The relationship between women's work and fertility: Some methodological and theoretical issues. In *The Fertility of Working Women: A Synthesis of International Research* (S. Kupinsky, ed.), pp. 355–368. Praeger, New York.

Safilios-Rothschild, C. (1982). Female power, autonomy and demographic change in the Third World. In *Women's Roles and Population Trends in the Third World* (R. Anker, M. Buvinic, and N. H. Youssef, eds.), pp. 117–132. Croom Helm, London.

Salaff, J. W., and Wong, A. K. (1977). Chinese women at work. Work commitment and fertility in the Asian setting. In *The Fertility of Working Women: A Synthesis of International Research* (S. Kupinsky, ed.), pp. 81–145. Praeger, New York.

Sathar, Z. A., and Chidambaram, V. C. (1984). Differentials in contraceptive use. *World Fertility Survey Comparative Studies, Cross-National Summaries*, No. 36. International Statistical Institute, Voorburg, Netherlands.

Scanzoni, J. H. (1975). *Sex Roles, Styles, and Childbearing: Changing Patterns in Marriage and the Family*. Free Press, New York.

Schearer, S. B. (1983). Monetary and health costs of contraception. In *Determinants of Fertility in Developing Countries*, Vol. 2: *Fertility Regulation and Institutional Influences* (R. A. Bulatao and R. D. Lee with P. E. Hollerbach and J. Bongaarts, eds.), pp. 89–150. Academic Press, New York.

Schnore, L. F. (1961). Social mobility in demographic perspective. *American Sociological Review* **26**, 407–423.

Schultz, T. (1969). An economic model of family planning and fertility. *Journal of Political Economy* **77**, 153–180.

Schultz, T. P. (1976). Interrelationships between mortality and fertility. In *Population and Development: The Search for Selective Interventions* (R. G. Ridker, ed.), pp. 239–289. Johns Hopkins Univ. Press, Baltimore, Maryland.

Schultz, T. P. (1984). Studying the impact of household economic and community variables on child mortality. *Population and Development Review* **10**, Suppl., 215–235.

Schultz, T. W., ed. (1973). *Economics of the Family: Marriage, Children, and Human Capital*. Univ. of Chicago Press, Chicago, Illinois.

Schwarz, K. (1982). Development of the labour force participation of married women and reproductive behaviour in the Federal Republic of Germany since 1900. In *Referate zum Deutsch–Franzosischen Arbeitstreffen auf dem Gebiet der Demographie vom 5 bis 9 Oktober 1981 in Colmar*, pp. 263–280. Bundesinstitut fur Bevolkerungsforschung, Wiesbaden.

Scott, W. (1958). Fertility and social mobility among teachers. *Population Studies* **11**, 251–261.

Scott, W. J., and Morgan, C. S. (1983). An analysis of factors affecting traditional family expectations and perception of ideal fertility. *Sex Roles* **9**, 901–914.

Scrimshaw, S. C. M. (1978). Infant mortality and behavior in the regulation of family size. *Population and Development Review* **4**, 383–403.

Scrimshaw, S. C. M., and Pelto, G. H. (1979). The impact of nutrition and health programs on family size and structure. In *The Practice of Impact Evaluation* (R. Klein *et al.*, eds.), pp. 183–217. Plenum Press, New York.

Sen, N., and Sen, D. K. (1967). Family planning practice of couples of reproductive age group in a selected locality in Calcutta—June, 1965. *Journal of Family Welfare* **14**(1), 13–24.

Senderowitz, J., and Paxman, J. M. (1985). Adolescent fertility: Worldwide concerns. *Population Bulletin* **40**, No. 2.

Shah, N. M.(1974). The role of interspousal communication in adoption of family planning methods: A couple approach. *Pakistan Development Review* **13**, 454–469.

Shah, N. M. (1975). Female labour force participation and fertility desires in Pakistan: An empirical investigation. *Pakistan Development Review* **14**, 185–206.

Shedlin, M. G., and Hollerbach, P. E. (1981). Modern and traditional fertility regulation in a Mexican community: The process of decision making. *Studies in Family Planning* **12**, 278–296.

Sherris, J. D., with Quillen, W. F. (1982). Population education in the schools. *Population Reports Series M: Special Topic Monographs* No. 6, 201–243.

Shin, E. H. (1975). Economic and social correlates of infant mortality: A cross-sectional and longitudinal analysis of 63 selected countries. *Social Biology* **22**, 315–325.

Simmons, A. B., and Culagovski, M. (1975). If they know, why don't they use? Selected factors influencing contraceptive adoption in rural Latin America. Paper presented at the annual meeting of the Population Association of America, Seattle, April 17–19.

Simmons, O. G. (1970). Population education: A review of the field. *Studies in Family Planning* **52**, 1–5.

Simon, J. L. (1975). The welfare effect of an additional child cannot be stated simply and unequivocally. *Demography* **12**, 89–105.

Singh, K. P. (1982). Modernity value orientations, fertility and family planning. *Journal of Family Welfare* **29**, 84–88.

Sinha, J. N. (1957). Differential fertility and family limitation in an urban community of Uttar Pradesh. *Population Studies* **11**, 157–169.

Sloan, F. (1971). *Survival of Progeny in Developing Countries: Analysis of Evidence from Costa Rica, Mexico, East Pakistan, and Puerto Rico* (R-773 AID). Rand Corp., Santa Monica, California.

Smith, D. P. (1980). Age at first marriage. *World Fertility Survey Comparative Studies, Cross-National Summaries,* No. 7. International Statistical Institute, Voorburg, Netherlands.

Smith, P. C. (1983). The impact of age at marriage and proportions marrying on fertility. In *Determinants of Fertility in Developing Countries,* Vol. 2: *Fertility Regulation and Institutional Influences* (R. A. Bulatao and R. D. Lee with P. E. Hollerbach and J. P. Bongaarts, eds.), pp. 473–531. Studies in Population. Academic Press, New York.

Smith, S. K. (1981). Women's work, fertility, and competing time use in Mexico City. In *Research in Population Economics* (J. L. Simon and P. H. Lindert, eds.), Vol. 3, pp. 167–187. Jai Press, Greenwich, Connecticut.

Smith-Lovin, L., and Tickamyer, A. R. (1978). Nonrecursive models of labor force participation, fertility behavior and sex role attitudes. *American Sociological Review* **43**, 541–557.

Snyder, D. W. (1974). Economic determinants of family size in West Africa. *Demography* **11**, 613–627.

Sobel, M. E. (1981). Diagonal mobility models: A substantively motivated class of designs for the analysis of mobility effects. *American Sociological Review* **46**, 893–906.

Sobel, M. E. (1984). Social mobility and fertility revisited: Some new models for the analysis of mobility effects hypothesis. Paper presented at the annual meeting of the American Sociological Association, San Antonio, August 27–31.

Standing, G. (1983). Women's work activity and fertility. In *Determinants of Fertility in Developing Countries,* Vol. 1: *Supply and Demand for Children* (R. A. Bulatao and R. D. Lee with P. E. Hollerbach and J. P. Bongaarts, eds.), pp. 517–545. Studies in Population. Academic Press, New York.

Stephens, P. W. (1984). *The Relationship between the Level of Household Sanitation and Child Mortality—An Examination of Ghanaian Data,* African Demography Working Paper No. 10. Population Studies Center, Univ. of Pennsylvania, Philadelphia.

Stevens, G. (1981). Social mobility and fertility: Two effects in one. *American Sociological Review* **46**, 573–585.

Stockwell, E. G., and Hutchinson, B. W. (1975). A note on mortality correlates of economic development. *Population Review* **19**, 46–50.

Stokes, B. (1977). *Filling the Family Planning Gap,* Worldwatch Paper No. 12. Worldwatch Institute, Washington, D.C.

Stokes, B. (1980). *Men and Family Planning,* Worldwatch Paper No. 41. Worldwatch Institute, Washington, D.C.

Stolnitz, G. J. (1983). Three to five main challenges to demographic research. *Demography* **20**, 415–432.

Stolzenberg, R. M., and Waite, L. J. (1976). Age and the relationship between young women's plans for childbearing and employment. Paper presented at the annual meeting of the Population Association of America, Montreal, April 29–May 1.

Stout, T. (1984). Some relations between educational attainment and fertility in the developing world: A review of the literature. Project paper prepared for the Fertility Determinants Group, Indiana Univ., Bloomington.

Stuckert, R. P. (1963). Occupational mobility and family relationships. *Social Forces* **41**, 301–307.

Stycos, J. M. (1963). Culture and differential fertility in Peru. *Population Studies* **16**, 257–270.

Stycos, J. M. (1965). Female employment and fertility in Lima, Peru. *Milbank Memorial Fund Quarterly* **43**, 42–54.

Stycos, J. M. (1967). Education and fertility in Puerto Rico. In *Proceedings of the World Population Conference, Belgrade, 1965,* Vol. 7, pp. 53–56 (A.6/I/E/236). United Nations, New York.

Stycos, J. M. (1968). *Human Fertility in Latin America: Sociological Perspectives.* Cornell Univ. Press, Ithaca, New York.

Stycos, J. M. (1979). Education, modernity and fertility in Costa Rica. *Setimo Seminario Nacional de Demografia,* pp. 101–111. Direccion General de Estadistica y Censos, San Jose, Costa Rica.

Stycos, J. M. (1982). Status of women. In *International Encyclopedia of Population* (J. A. Ross, ed.), Vol. 2, pp. 620–622. Free Press, New York.

Stycos, J. M., and Weller, R. H. (1967). Female working roles and fertility. *Demography* **4**, 210–217.

Stycos, J. M., Back, K. W., and Hill, R. (1956). Problems of communication between husband and wife on matters relating to family limitation. *Human Relations* **9**, 207–215.

Suchindran, C. M., and Adlakha, A. L. (1984). Effect of infant mortality on subsequent fertility of women in Jordan: A life table analysis. *Journal of Biosocial Science* **16**, 219–229.

Sweet, J. A. (1968). Family composition and the labor force activity of married women in the United States. Ph.D. Thesis, Univ. of Michigan, Ann Arbor.

Sweet, J. A. (1973). *Women in the Labor Force,* Studies in Population. Seminar Press, New York.

Tanfer, K., and Horn, M. C. (1985). Contraceptive use, pregnancy and fertility patterns among single American women in their 20s. *Family Planning Perspectives* **17**, 10–19.

Taylor, C. E., Newman, J. S., and Kelly, N. U. (1976). The child survival hypothesis. *Population Studies* **30**, 263–278.

Terhune, K. W. (1974). *Exploration in Fertility Values.* Calspan Corp., Buffalo, New York.

Thavarajah, A., and Farag, M. W. (1971). Demographic and socio-economic characteristics of women seeking fertility control. In *Fertility Trends and Differentials in Arab Countries,* pp. 311–344. Cairo Demographic Centre, Cairo.

Thompson, W. S., and Lewis, D. T. (1965). *Population Problems,* 5th ed. McGraw-Hill, New York.

Thomson, E. (1983). Individual and couple utility of children. *Demography* **20**, 507–518.

Thornton, A. D. (1978a). Marital dissolution, remarriage, and childbearing. *Demography* **15**, 361–380.

Thornton, A. D. (1978b). The relationship between fertility and income, relative income, and subjective well-being. In *Research in Population Economics* (J. L. Simon, ed.), Vol. 1, pp. 261–290. Jai Press, Greenwich, Connecticut.

Tickamyer, A. R. (1979). Women's roles and fertility intentions. *Pacific Sociological Review* **22**, 167–184.

Tien, H. Y. (1961). The social mobility/fertility hypothesis reconsidered: An empirical study. *American Sociological Review* **26**, 247–257.

Tien, H. Y. (1965a). *Social Mobility and Controlled Fertility: Family Origins and Structure of the Australian Academic Elite.* College and Univ. Press, New Haven, Connecticut.

Tien, H. Y. (1965b). Sterilization, oral contraception, and population control in China. *Population Studies* **18**, 215–236.

Tien, H. Y. (1967). Mobility, non-familial activity and fertility. *Demography* **4**, 218–227.

Tienda, M. (1984). Community characteristics, women's education, and fertility in Peru. *Studies in Family Planning* **15**, 162–169.

Tietze, C. (1983). *Induced Abortion: A World Review, 1983,* 5th ed. Population Council Fact Book. Population Council, New York.

Tomasson, R. F. (1966). Social mobility and family size in two high-status populations. *Eugenics Quarterly* **13**, 113–121.

Treiman, D. J. (1970). Industrialization and social stratification. In *Social Stratification: Research and Theory for the 1970s* (E. O. Laumann, ed.), pp. 207–234. Bobbs-Merrill, Indianapolis, Indiana.

Treiman, D. J. (1975). Problems of concept and measurement in the comparative study of occupational mobility. *Social Science Research* **4**, 183–230.

Treiman, D. J. (1977). *Occupational Prestige in Comparative Perspective,* Quantitative Studies in Social Relations. Academic Press, New York.

Trussell, J., and Hammerslough, C. (1983). A hazards-model analysis of the covariates of infant and child mortality in Sri Lanka. *Demography* **20**, 1–26.

Trussell, J., and Olsen, R. (1983). Evaluation of the Olsen technique for estimating the fertility response to child mortality. *Demography* **20**, 391–405.

Trussell, J., and Pebley, A. R. (1984). The potential impact of changes in fertility on infant, child and maternal mortality. *Studies in Family Planning* **15**, 267–280.

Trussell, J., Menken, J. A., and Coale, A. J.(1982). A general model for analyzing the effects of nuptiality on fertility. In *Nuptiality and Fertility* (L. T. Ruzicka, ed.), pp. 7–27. Ordina Editions, Liège.

Tsui, A. O. (1982). The family formation process among U.S. marriage cohorts. *Demography* **19**, 1–27.

Tsui, A. O. (1985). The rise of modern contraception. In *Reproductive Change in Developing Countries* (J. Cleland and J. Hobcraft, in collaboration with B. Dinesen, eds.), pp. 115–138. Oxford University Press, London and New York.

Tsui, A. O., Hogan, D. P., Teachman, J. D., and Welti-Chanes, C. (1981). Community availability of contraceptives and family limitation. *Demography* **18**, 615–625.

Tuan, C.-H. (1958–1959). Reproductive histories of Chinese women in rural Taiwan. *Population Studies* **12**, 40–50.

Tuma, N. B., and Hannan, M. T. (1984). *Social Dynamics: Models and Methods.* Academic Press, Orlando, Florida.

Tumin, M. M., and Feldman, A. S. (1957). Theory and measurement of occupational mobility. *American Sociological Review* **22**, 281–288.

Turchi, B. A. (1975). *The Demand for Children: The Economics of Fertility in the United States.* Ballinger, Cambridge, Massachusetts.

Turchi, B. A., and Bryant, E. S. (1979). *Rural Development Activities, Fertility and the Cost and Value of Children.* Research Triangle Institute and South East Consortium for International Development, Research Triangle Park, North Carolina.

Udry, J. R., and Cliquet, R. L. (1982). A cross-cultural examination of the relationship between ages at menarche, marriage, and first birth. *Demography* **19**, 53–63.

UNESCO (1983). *Bibliographic Guide to Studies on the Status of Women, Development and Population Trends.* United Nations Educational, Scientific, and Cultural Organization, Paris; Bowker, Essex, England; UNIPUB, New York.

United Nations (1953). *The Determinants and Consequences of Population Trends: New Summary of Findings on Interaction of Demographic, Economic and Social Factors,* Population Studies No. 50 (ST/SOA/Ser.A/50/Add.1). United Nations, New York.

United Nations (1980). *Report of the World Conference of the United Nations Decade for Women: Equality, Development and Peace, Copenhagen, 14 to 30 July, 1980* (A/CONF. 94/35). United Nations, New York.

United Nations, Department of Economic and Social Affairs (1961). *The Mysore Population Study: Report of a Field Survey Carried Out in Selected Areas of Mysore State India*, Population Studies No. 34 (ST/SOA/SER.A/34). United Nations, New York.

United Nations, Department of International Economic and Social Affairs (1979). *Factors Affecting the Use and Non-Use of Contraception: Findings from a Comparative Analysis of Selected KAP Surveys*, Population Studies No. 69 (ST/ESA/SER.A/69). United Nations, New York.

United Nations, Department of International Economic and Social Affairs (1981). *Variations in the Incidence of Knowledge and Use of Contraception: A Comparative Analysis of World Fertility Survey Results for Twenty Developing Countries* (ST/ESA/SER.R/40). United Nations, New York.

United Nations, Department of International Economic and Social Affairs (1983). *Marital Status and Fertility: A Comparative Analysis of World Fertility Survey Data for Twenty-One Countries* (ST/ESA/SER. R/52). United Nations, New York.

United Nations, Department of International Economic and Social Affairs (1984). *Recent Levels and Trends of Contraceptive Use as Assessed in 1983*, Population Studies No. 92 (ST/ESA/SER. A/92). United Nations, New York.

United Nations, Economic and Social Commission for Asia and the Pacific (1974). *Husband–Wife Communication and Practice of Family Planning*, Asian Population Studies Series No. 16 (E/CN.11/1212). Economic and Social Commission for Asia and the South Pacific, United Nations, Bangkok.

United Nations, Economic and Social Council (1973). Influence of change in the family cycle upon family life: Women's rights and fertility. In *World Population Conference, 1974, Symposium on Population and the Family, Honolulu, Aug. 6–15* (E/CONF.60/BP/11). Economic and Social Council, United Nations, New York.

United Nations Secretariat, Department of International Economic and Social Affairs, Population Division (1980). Some demographic characteristics of women's work in ten World Fertility Survey countries. In *Report on Monitoring of Population Trends*, pp. 405–24. Department of International Economic and Social Affairs, United Nations, New York.

Vaessen, M. (1980). Knowledge of contraceptive methods. *World Fertility Survey Comparative Studies*, No. 8. International Statistical Institute, Voorburg, Netherlands.

van de Walle, F. (1976). Education and the fertility transition in Switzerland. Paper presented to the annual meeting of the Population Association of America, Montreal, April 28–May 1.

van de Walle, F. (1980). Education and the demographic transition in Switzerland. *Population and Development Review* **6**, 463–472.

Van Esterik, P., and Greiner, T. (1981). Breastfeeding and women's work: Constraints and opportunities. *Studies in Family Planning* **12**, 184–197.

Veevers, J. E. (1971). Childlessness and age at first marriage. *Social Biology* **18**, 292–295.

Venkatacharya, K. (1968). *Postponement of Age at Marriage and Its Short-Term Impact on Fertility*, Research Paper Series No. I.I.P.S./Sim-7/1968. International Institute for Population Studies, Bombay.

Viederman, S. (1972). Population education in the United States. *Social Education* **36**, 337–346.

Viederman, S. (1974). Towards a broader definition of population education. *International Social Science Journal* **26**, 315–327.

Vig, O. P. (1977). Banishment of dowry—A means to lower birth rate. *PopCen Newsletter* **3**(3), 8–11.

Vining, D. R., Jr. (1982). Fertility differentials and the status of nations: A speculative essay on Japan and the West. *Mankind Quarterly* **22**, 311–353.

Vlassoff, M., and Vlassoff, C. (1980). Old age security and the utility of children in rural India. *Population Studies* **34**, 487–499.

von Ungern-Sternberg, R. (1931). *The Causes of the Decline in Birth-Rate within the European Sphere of Civilization* (H. H. Wullen, transl.), Eugenics Research Assoc. Monograph Series No. 4. Eugenics Research Assoc., Cold Spring Harbor, New York.

Vorwaller, D. J. (1970). Social mobility and membership in voluntary associations. *American Journal of Sociology* **75**, 481–495.

Voss, P. R. (1977). Social determinants of age at first marriage in the United States. Paper presented at the annual meeting of the Population Association of America, St. Louis, April 21–23.

Wagner-Manslau, W. (1932). Human fertility. A demonstration of its genetic base. Transl. by E. O. Lorimer. *Eugenics Review* **24**, 195–210.

Waite, L. J. (1975). Working wives and the life cycle. Ph.D. Thesis, Univ. of Michigan, Ann Arbor.

Waite, L. J. (1977). Social and economic determinants of employment of wives over the family life cycle. Unpublished manuscript, Department of Sociology, Univ. of Illinois, Urbana-Champaign.

Waite, L. J. (1981). U.S. women at work. *Population Bulletin* **36**(2).

Waite, L. J., and Spitze, G. D. (1981). Young women's transition to marriage. *Demography* **18**, 681–694.

Waite, L. J., and Stolzenberg, R. M. (1976). Intended childbearing and labor force participation of young women: Insights from nonrecursive models. *American Sociological Review* **41**, 235–251.

Ware, H. (1976a). Fertility and work-force participation: The experience of Melbourne wives. *Population Studies* **30**, 413–427.

Ware, H. (1976b). Motivations for the use of birth control: Evidence from West Africa. *Demography* **13**, 479–493.

Ware, H. (1984). Effects of maternal education, women's roles, and child care on child mortality. *Population and Development Review* **10**, Suppl., 191–214.

Watson, W. B., and Lapham, R. J., eds. (1975). Family planning programs: World review 1974. *Studies in Family Planning* **6**, 205–322.

Welch, F. R. (1974). *Sex of Children: Prior Uncertainty and Subsequent Fertility Behavior*, Rand Report R-1510-RF. Rand Corp., Santa Monica, California.

Weller, R. H. (1968). The employment of wives, role incompatibility and fertility. A study among lower- and middle-class residents of San Juan, Puerto Rico. *Milbank Memorial Fund Quarterly* **16**, 507–527.

Weller, R. H. (1977). Wife's employment and cumulative family size in the United States, 1970 and 1960. *Demography* **14**, 43–65.

Weller, R. H., and Bouvier, L. F. (1981). *Population: Demography and Policy*. St. Martin's Press, New York.

West, K. B. (1980). Sequential fertility behavior: A study of socioeconomic and demographic determinants of parity transitions. Ph.D. Thesis, Univ. of North Carolina at Chapel Hill.

Westoff, C. F. (1953). The changing focus of differential fertility research: The social mobility hypothesis. *Milbank Memorial Fund Quarterly* **31**, 24–38.

Westoff, C. F. (1980). Unwanted fertility in six developing countries. In *World Fertility Survey Conference, 1980, Record of Proceedings*, Vol. 2, pp. 701–769. International Statistical Institute, Voorburg, Netherlands.

Westoff, C. F. (1981). Another look at fertility and social mobility. *Population Studies* **35**, 132–135.

Westoff, C. F., and Jones, E. F. (1979). The end of "Catholic" fertility. *Demography* **16**, 209–217.

Westoff, C. F., and Potvin, R. H. (1967). *College Women and Fertility Values*. Princeton Univ. Press, Princeton, New Jersey.

Westoff, C. F., and Ryder, N. B. (1977). *The Contraceptive Revolution*. Princeton Univ. Press, Princeton, New Jersey.

Westoff, C. F., Bressler, M., and Sagi, P. C. (1960). The concept of social mobility. *American Sociological Review* **25**, 375–385.

Westoff, C. F., Potter, R. G., Jr., Sagi, P. C., and Mishler, E. G. (1961). *Family Growth in Metropolitan America*. Princeton Univ. Press, Princeton, New Jersey.

Westoff, C. F., Potter, R. G., Jr., and Sagi, P. C. (1963). *The Third Child: A Study in the Prediction of Fertility*. Princeton Univ. Press, Princeton, New Jersey.

Whelpton, P. K., Campbell, A. A., and Patterson, J. E. (1966). *Fertility and Family Planning in the United States*. Princeton Univ. Press, Princeton, New Jersey.

Whyte, M. K. (1978). *The Status of Women in Preindustrial Societies*. Princeton Univ. Press, Princeton, New Jersey.

Wildasin, D. E. (1982). *Old Age Security and Fertility,* Project Paper No. 4. Prepared for the Fertility Determinants Group, Indiana Univ., Bloomington.

Wilensky, H. L. (1968). Women's work: Economic growth, ideology, structure. *Industrial Relations* **7**, 235–248.

Williamson, N. E. (1976). *Sons or Daughters: A Cross-Cultural Survey of Parental Preferences,* Sage Library of Social Research, Vol. 31. Sage Publications, Beverly Hills, California.

Willis, R. J. (1973). A new approach to the economic theory of fertility behavior. *Journal of Political Economy* **82**(2), Part 2, S14–S64.

Wilson, W. J. (1985). The urban underclass in advanced industrial society. In *The New Urban Reality* (P. E. Peterson, ed.), pp. 129–160. Brookings Institution, Washington, D.C.

Winikoff, B. (1983). The effects of birth spacing on child and maternal health. *Studies in Family Planning* **14**, 231–245.

Wolf, M. (1972). *Women and the Family in Rural Taiwan*. Stanford Univ. Press, Stanford, California.

Wolfe, B. L. (1975). The effect of education on fertility and women's labor force participation. Paper presented at the annual meeting of the Population Association of America, Seattle, April 17–19.

Wolfe, B. L. (1980). Childbearing and/or labor force participation: The education connection. In *Research in Political Economics* (J. L. Simon and J. Da Vanzo, eds.), Vol. 2, pp. 365–385. Jai Press, Greenwich, Connecticut.

World Bank (1984). *World Development Report 1984*. Oxford Univ. Press for the World Bank, New York.

Wu, T.-S., with the assistance of S. E. Ward (1977). *The Value of Children: A Cross-National Study,* Vol. 5: *Taiwan*. East–West Population Institute, Honolulu.

Wyon, J. B., and Gordon, J. E. (1971). *The Khanna Study: Population Problems in the Rural Punjab*. Harvard Univ. Press, Cambridge, Massachusetts.

Yamaguchi, K. (1983). The structure of intergenerational occupational mobility: Generality and specificity in resources, channels, and barriers. *American Journal of Sociology* **88**, 718–745.

Yankelovich, D. (1981). *New Rules: Searching for Self-Fulfillment in a World Turned Upside Down*. Random House, New York.

Yaukey, D. W. (1961). *Fertility Differences in a Modernizing Country: A Survey of Lebanese Couples*. Princeton Univ. Press, Princeton, New Jersey.

Yaukey, D. W. (1973). *Marriage Reduction and Fertility*. Lexington Books, Lexington, Massachusetts.

Yaukey, D. W., and Thorsen, T. (1972). Differential female age at first marriage in six Latin American cities. *Journal of Marriage and the Family* **34**, 375–379.

Youssef, N. H. (1974). *Women and Work in Developing Societies,* Studies in Population and Urban Demography No. 15. Institute of International Studies, Univ. of California, Berkeley.

Zelinsky, W. (1971). The hypothesis of the mobility transition. *Geographical Review* **61**, 219–249.

Zelnik, M., and Kantner, J. F. (1972). Some preliminary observations on pre-adult fertility and family formation. *Studies in Family Planning* **3,** 59–65.

Zelnik, M., and Kantner, J. F. (1980). Sexual activity, contraceptive use and pregnancy among metropolitan-area teenagers: 1971–1979. *Family Planning Perspectives* **12,** 230–237.

Zimmer, B. G. (1979). *Urban Family Building Patterns: The Social Mobility–Fertility Hypothesis Re-Examined.* National Technical Information Service, Springfield, Virginia.

Zimmer, B. G. (1981a). The impact of social mobility on fertility: A reconsideration. *Population Studies* **35,** 120–131.

Zimmer, B. G. (1981b). A rejoinder. *Population Studies* **35,** 136.

Zito, G. V. (1979). *Population and Its Problems.* Human Sciences Press, New York.

Author Index

Viederman, Stephen, 210
Vig, Om Parkash, 95
Vlassoff, Carol, 137
Vlassoff, Michael, 137
von Ungern-Sternberg, Roderich, 9n
Vorwaller, Darrel J., 31n

W

Wagner-Manslau, Willy, 9, 10
Waite, Linda J., 56, 101, 108, 113, 115, 116,
    122, 126, 132, 175, 176
Ward, Michael P., 182
Ware, Helen, 101, 115, 157, 158, 162, 163,
    191, 207
Weininger, Adriana, 127
Welch, Finis R., 152
Weller, Robert H., 92, 100, 112, 113, 117,
    118, 119, 120, 122, 123, 124, 208
West, Kirsten B., 131, 144
Westoff, Charles F., 8, 9, 10, 20, 21, 22, 39,
    43, 43n, 44n, 52, 60, 61, 62, 65, 95,
    102, 104, 113, 115, 171, 191, 196, 214
Whelpton, Pascal K., 109, 113, 115, 121,
    124, 194
Whitney, Leon F., 10
Whyte, Martin K., 3
Wildasin, David E., 138
Wilensky, Harold L., 95

Williamson, Nancy E., 135
Willis, Robert J., 125, 130
Wilson, William J., 181
Winegarden, C. R., 134, 138
Winikoff, Beverly, 162, 163
Wolf, Margery, 135
Wolfe, Barbara L., 39, 88, 89
Wolfe, Donald M., 88
Wong, Aline K., 176, 179
Wu, Hsin-Ying, 150, 152, 153, 206
Wu, Tsong-Shien, 135
Wyon, John B., 15

Y

Yankelovich, Daniel, 119
Yaukey, David W., 101, 170, 190
Youssef, Nadia H., 100

Z

Zachariah, K. C., 148, 160, 163
Zelnik, Melvin, 177, 181
Zimmer, Basil G., 43, 43n, 44, 44n, 45, 63,
    64, 86
Zito, George V., 185

Subject Index